Separating Church
and State

Separating Church and State

Roger Williams and Religious Liberty

Timothy L. Hall

UNIVERSITY OF ILLINOIS PRESS

URBANA AND CHICAGO

This book is printed on acid-free paper.

Library of Congress Cataloging-in-Publication Data
Hall, Timothy, 1955–
  Separating church and state : Roger Williams and religious
liberty / Timothy L. Hall.
    p.   cm.
  Includes bibliographical references and index.
    ISBN 0-252-06664-2 (pbk. : acid-free paper). / ISBN 978-0-252-06664-1
  ISBN 0-252-02360-9 (cloth : acid-free paper) / ISBN 978-0-252-02360-6
    1. Freedom of religion—United States—History. 2. Church
and state—United States—History. 3. Williams, Roger, 1604?–
1683—Contributions in law. I. Title.
KF4783.H35   1997
342.78'0852—dc21   97-4688
CIP

For Lee

Contents

Acknowledgments

Work on this book has encumbered me with more debts of appreciation than I can easily recite. My colleagues at the University of Mississippi Law School have participated enthusiastically in one informal colloquium concerning Roger Williams and have read and commented upon both the article that commenced my research concerning Williams and other articles from which I have drawn in writing this book. George Cochran, Tom Mason, Richard Barnes, Robert Davis, Michael Hoffheimer, Ronald Rychlak, and Gary Myers offered me valuable comments on my original work concerning Williams. Michael Hoffheimer, Ronald Rychlak, and Silvia Robertshaw read and commented upon the manuscript of this book. I also benefited from comments received in connection with a presentation I made entitled "The Curious Case of the Tolerant Bigot" to the Section on Law and Religion at the 1994 American Association of Law Schools annual meeting. Edwin Gaustad and Marci Hamilton graciously provided me with copies of reviews that they did for the University of Illinois Press. I am especially grateful to the members of the Lamar Order of the University of Mississippi Law School, from which I received research support at several points over the eight years necessary to complete this project.

This book is a significant revision and expansion of "Roger Williams and the Foundations of Religious Liberty," *Boston University Law Review* 71 (1991): 455-524. Portions of chapter 6 are derived from "Religion, Equality, and Difference," *Temple Law Review* 65 (1992): 1-89, and "Sacred Solemnity: Civic Prayer, Civil Communion, and the Establishment Clause," *Iowa Law Review* 79 (1993): 35-93.

Introduction

In 1940, nearly three centuries after the publication of his chief works, Roger Williams entered the modern conversation about the meaning of the First Amendment's prohibition against laws "respecting an establishment of religion or prohibiting the free exercise thereof."[1] He did so less as a real participant in an important public dialogue than as a constitutional icon. In *Minersville School District v. Gobitis,* the Supreme Court cited Williams as a prooftext in support of its declaration that religious belief does not relieve an individual from the obligation to obey laws of general applicability that are not aimed at the promotion or restriction of religion.[2] With Williams as one of its standard-bearers, the Court concluded that a school district could force Jehovah's Witness children to recite the Pledge of Allegiance even though the children and their parents believed this recitation amounted to an act of idolatry. The law requiring recitation of the Pledge had not been intended to harry Jehovah's Witnesses on account of their faith; therefore, the Court reasoned, that the law inadvertently collided with the beliefs of Jehovah's Witnesses was of no constitutional consequence.

The use of Roger Williams to buttress its conclusion was a classic example of "law office history," the practice of picking and choosing only those historical materials supportive of a client's cause.[3] Williams, in fact, had pondered the issue of whether believers ought to be exempted from general legal requirements that conflicted with their religious tenets. His answer to that question was neither completely favorable to the claims of civil society on the one hand nor to the claims of religious conscience on the other. But with lawyerlike facility for ignoring unfavorable precedent the Court collapsed what had, in Williams's hands, been a complicated argument about the relationship between law and religious belief into a tidy, black-letter rule that trampled religious conscience.[4]

Twenty years later, when the Court determined in *Engel v. Vitale* that a state-composed prayer recited in a public school violated the establishment clause, it summoned Roger Williams again.[5] This time Justice Hugo P. Black, writing for the majority, was less interested in finding a prooftext than in securing the blessing of a pater familias. The justice quoted two excerpts from Williams's work, illustrative perhaps of the broad current of his thought but uninformative about specific concerns, and then proclaimed him to have been one of the earliest exponents of the doctrine of separation of church and state. Thereafter, in *Abington School District v. Schempp,* the Court renewed its homage to the image of Williams by declaring that his views, along with those of James Madison and Thomas Jefferson, were incorporated not only into the federal Constitution but also into the constitutions of most states.[6] The Court saw no need to support this sweeping historical assertion: Williams had attained the status of symbol, and citation was superfluous.

Legal scholars have also tended to treat Roger Williams as a metaphor for a certain element of the American experience rather than engage his views in any serious conversation. Mark DeWolfe Howe, for example, whose book *The Garden and the Wilderness* canonized Williams as a constitutional saint, devoted almost no attention to investigating Williams's arguments on behalf of religious liberty. Instead, he simply portrayed Roger Williams as a symbol of an evangelical influence on First Amendment history that he contrasted with the skeptical rationalism of Thomas Jefferson.[7] Howe argued that the First Amendment's establishment clause originated primarily in the "believing affirmations" of people such as Williams rather than in the "questioning doubts" of a Jeffersonian minority.[8] He reasoned that evangelical currents played an important role in fashioning the original commitment to disestablishment and that the continued force of these currents helps explain the prevalence in American public life of various tributes to religious belief—what Howe called a de facto establishment of religion.[9] Robert Cover similarly emphasized that contrasting constitutional worlds grew out of the radically different starting points represented by the thoughts of Williams on the one hand and Jefferson on the other.[10]

Both Howe and Cover sought to stress that the First Amendment's religion clauses had almost no genesis in hostility or skepticism toward religion. On the contrary, they suggested, the First Amendment was the product of religious enthusiasm more than anything else, and that enthusiasm has sometimes been muffled in attempts to construe the religion clauses. I emphatically agree with this general thesis. In the following discussion, which stresses the importance of Williams's "believing affirmations" to the cause of religious liberty, I argue in a similar vein that one cannot trace the genesis of the American commitment to religious freedom without reckoning the values and presuppositions of Williams and later evangelical Protestants. But the attempts of Howe and Cover to rescue the First Amendment from secular caretakers have muffled Roger Williams's distinctive voice within the American tradition. They have treated him as an exemplar of a diverse range of evangelical influences on the First Amendment's history without adequately attending to the specific contours of his thought.[11] By canonizing Williams as evangelical saint of religious liberty, scholars such as Howe and Cover left a unique voice silent. Among both judges and constitutional scholars, then, Williams tends to resemble the statue of him in Geneva, Switzerland, where he is enshrined as the American representative among the luminaries of Calvinism: a powerful but mute symbol of religious liberty in the United States.[12]

Roger Williams's thought—not simply the aura of democratic sainthood that surrounds his name—deserves a larger place in the current revival of interest in the original historical understanding of the First Amendment's religion clauses. This revival, illustrated by a growing body of scholarly commentary and by opinions of the Supreme Court, will suffer if Williams's perspective is neglected.[13] As Harold Berman has noted, "In the American legal tradition the question 'whither' cannot be divorced from the question 'whence.' "[14] And, by asking the question "whence," we are thrown back upon the thought of Roger Williams, who possesses for American history, as Perry Miller said, "one indubitable importance, that he stands at the beginning of it."[15]

Yet Williams's importance to the contemporary debate over the appropriate relation between religion and government arises not so much because his views can be traced in some specific way to the views of the framers of the First Amendment. Attempts to demonstrate that constitutional architects such as James Madison received tutelage in the principles of religious liberty from Williams are far from persuasive. In any event, the significance of Roger Williams does not hinge on any precise genealogical line between his ideas and the constitutional text. He is important rather as an intellectual resource for contemporary discussions concerning religious liberty and as a representative of a perspective critical to the development of the American tradition of religious liberty.

In the first place, Roger Williams's long argument with the Massachusetts Puritans about religious liberty and religious establishments remains one of the most comprehensive discussions of the issue articulated by a single thinker in American history and certainly by any American figure writing during the colonial and revolutionary periods. For nearly forty years he wrestled with questions still very much alive: Why is religious persecution evil? What harms does it inflict on its victims and its perpetrators? Why shouldn't government supervise religion? and, Does a stable society require some measure of religious homogeneity?

Judges and legal scholars faced with interpreting the religion clauses of the First Amendment have realized that answers to these kinds of questions may well assist constitutional interpretation and have sought them at least partially in the past. Courts and commentators have been incorrigible poachers in the preserve of American history. Nevertheless, in terms of finding a usable past to sustain a present commitment to religious liberty, the jurisprudence of the First Amendment religion clauses has been erected on a shockingly scanty historical base. A triumvirate of sources, consisting of a bare handful of printed pages, has exerted the most profound influence upon constitutional development. These include a letter from Thomas Jefferson to the Danbury Baptist Association in Connecticut, written a decade after the First Amendment was enacted; the Virginia Bill for Establishing Religious Freedom, which Jefferson drafted in 1779 and Virginia enacted as law in 1786; and James Madison's "A Memorial and Remonstrance," written in protest of an establishment scheme proposed and ultimately defeated in Virginia during the later part of the 1780s.[16]

Even if one ignores the dubiousness of gauging constitutional meaning by the thought of essentially two spokesmen—Jefferson and, to a lesser extent, Madison—an overly zealous reliance upon these sources has left First Amendment jurisprudence theoretically impoverished. For decades this narrow focus, especially its choice of Jefferson as principal mentor for the religion clauses, burdened the establishment clause with a crude form of law by metaphor, according to which the Supreme Court purported to find answers to complex issues chiefly through appeal to Jefferson's image of the "wall of separation" between church and state. In *Everson v. Board of Education,* the Court enthroned Jefferson's metaphor and announced that the establishment clause had created a wall between church and state "that must be kept high and impregnable."[17] Although the Court ultimately escaped Jeffersonian domination, its earliest theoretical encounters with the establishment clause were marred by a childlike confidence in Jefferson's metaphor to yield correct results.[18] Furthermore, the Court's enthusiastic choice of Jefferson as authoritative interpreter of the free-exercise clause left the clause severed from the arguments that gave it birth.[19] Consequently, it deprived First Amendment jurisprudence of any meaningful answer to the most simple question: Why did religion obtain a special place in the Constitution?[20]

To know what counts as a prohibited establishment of religion, one must have some sense of why establishments were prohibited in the first place. To know when the free exercise of religion has been abridged, one must ponder the reasons why religion was singled out for constitutional protection. This is so whether one is an originalist and believes that the Constitution should be construed to reflect the intent of its framers or whether one seeks to infuse the words of the First Amendment with some concept of religious liberty not necessarily coextensive with the Framers' intent. Nevertheless, the most commonly cited historical sources—Jefferson's letter to the Danbury Baptists, the Virginia Bill for Establishing Religious Freedom, and Madison's "Memorial and Remonstrance"—fail to provide anything but the most cursory answers to these inquiries. Roger Williams's writings, however, provide a framework of argument and theory more comprehensive than those set forth by any other writer either before or during the constitutional period.[21] They present elements of a theoretical foundation that would justify the constitutional protection of religion and elaborate a basis for determining the limits of that protection. Compared to Williams's treatment of the subject of religious liberty, Thomas Jefferson's often-quoted reference to the "wall of separation" between church and state is the equivalent of a constitutional sound bite.

Williams is significant also because he represents a perspective on religious toleration that played a critical role in the struggle for religious liberty. In the hurry to make Williams a democratic icon, a central aspect of his religious character has sometimes been forgotten: He was a religious Separatist of the most dogmatic persuasion. Before Thomas Jefferson ever pronounced to the Danbury Baptists his happiness over the Constitution's enactment of a wall of separation between church and state, Roger Williams had envisioned such a wall. In his mind, though, it was a wall that divided the godly and the profane, the righteous and those whose lives were polluted by spiritual error. Throughout his successive careers as Massachusetts gadfly and Rhode Island patriarch, Roger Williams championed a vision of government that would leave untroubled the consciences of its citizens, a vision more expansive—more liberal—than almost any other advanced for the next century. But he did not champion a proto-ecumenism and was not the sort of person likely to attend an interfaith community worship service. Nevertheless, although Williams's dogmatism seems inconsistent with a vigorous commitment to religious liberty, in fact, his religious separatism was the fountain of his religious tolerance.

In the discussion that follows, I attempt to make Williams's arguments for religious liberty accessible to legal analysis. Williams has received well-deserved attention from historians, but that attention has not typically demonstrated familiarity with the precise legal issues that frame current establishment and free-exercise jurisprudence.[22] Edmund S. Morgan, for example, in an overview of church and state relations in the United States, has demonstrated the broad strokes with which historians have sometimes painted those issues: "The Constitution originally made no mention either of religion or of God, and the First Amendment, adopted in 1791, took up the subject only to provide that 'Congress shall make no law respecting an establishment of religion, or prohibiting the free exercise thereof.' This provision has been pretty rigorously adhered to. Not only the federal government but the state governments too have generally followed the principle behind it, that church and state should be entirely separate."[23] Church-state affairs have never been quite so simple. In the years since Morgan wrote these lines, the situation has become if anything more complex. But the basic controversies that still dominate First Amendment jurisprudence revolve around questions as old as the Puritans who harried Williams out of Massachusetts and the colony he thereafter helped establish in Rhode Island.

One might sum up current free-exercise and establishment clause debate under three broad questions, only one of which reflects anything like a fundamental change between the twentieth century and the one Williams occupied. First, under what circumstances should believers be granted exemptions from laws serving legitimate public purposes and not aimed at the suppression of religion when those laws conflict with the claims of religious conscience? Second, does a nation need a common religious foundation and should government be able to foster such commonality? Third, to what extent should concerns for keeping religion and government separate disqualify religious believers and religious institutions from receiving benefits made generally available in the modern welfare state? Only the last question raises issues that were not debated in seventeenth-century New England, because it has its genesis in important changes that have occurred in the role of government over the last century. But the first two questions were very much alive at the time that Williams lived and debated. Historians such as Perry Miller and Edmund Morgan introduced Williams as a partner in the contemporary dialogue concerning religion and the public order, but they did not ask the right questions to elicit his responses in a form meaningful to present legal debate.

I hope to rectify the silence in which Williams's thought has been left by situating his arguments within the broad currents of constitutional tradition relating to the religion clauses. Yet even though I argue that Roger Williams deserves a place within attempts to frame a jurisprudence of the First Amendment's religion clauses, I think his importance extends beyond the narrow confines of constitutional doctrine. It is a mistake to imagine that the long American discussion about religious liberty can be reduced to an annotation of cases decided under the religion clauses. In fact, courts armed with the doctrine of judicial review have made only a relatively late entrance into the discourse concerning the appropriate relation between government and religion in the United States. Long before the Supreme Court undertook the task of interpreting the establishment clause, the states that had so long supported one denomination or another in colonial times repudiated those establishments and granted at least a basic measure of religious liberty to all their citizens.[24] When, for example, Massachusetts finally disestablished the Congregationalist Church in 1833, there were no Supreme Court precedents to be cited. There were only the rich assortment of arguments and counterarguments that colonial and revolutionary America had nourished over the previous two centuries.

Even after the Supreme Court added its voice to the American discourse concerning religious liberty, the need to sustain an ongoing deliberation concerning religious liberty and religious establishment remained. At most the Court has been an important participant in a public debate about the meaning of religious freedom in America. It has never been—nor should it be—the last voice to speak in this debate. There is evidence that discussion may continue even after the Supreme Court has made its pronouncements.[25] When the Court determined that the free-exercise clause did not protect religious believers from general laws at odds with the demands of their consciences, Congress—apparently accepting the proposition that a robust notion of religious liberty requires sensitivity to even unintended legislative burdens on religious belief and practice—enacted the Religious Freedom Restoration Act.[26] Furthermore, in the face of the Court's pronouncements concerning prayer in schools, an ongoing debate over the issue of school prayer continues to produce suggestions that the Constitution be amended to reverse at least some aspect of the Court's precedents in this area.[27] Although I staunchly agree with the Court's school prayer decisions, I nevertheless believe that the ongoing debate about them is healthy—and, in fact, critical—to the vitality of the tradition of religious liberty in the United States. It is to this larger debate about religious freedom and religious establishment that Roger Williams deserves a renewed invitation.

But although I assert Williams's importance to constitutional and political discussions about religious liberty, I by no means think that either kind of discussion can be reduced to his voice alone. The American political tradition has never embraced a single theory of religious liberty.[28] On the contrary, it has been formed out of an intersection of conflicting normative visions that cannot be encapsulated by a single broad principle. Attempts to generalize about the precise contours of this intersection have tended to overemphasize the extent to which these differing normative visions agreed about specific questions relating to religious liberty and religious establishment. In reality, the lack of any overarching principle yielded a patchwork of legal and social practices that would have pleased no one completely, least of all Roger Williams. He would have been happy to see the Constitution's silence regarding the Almighty and its renunciation of religious test oaths, for example, but profoundly consternated by the willingness of the First Congress to cloak its proceedings with the solemnity of prayer. In this alternating satisfaction and dismay Williams would not have been alone. Every holder of a specific theory or principle of church-state relations would have experienced—and must continue to experience—the same mixed reaction simply because no broad consensus of principle in matters of religious liberty and disestablishment has ever achieved dominance in the American political tradition.

Legal commentators have spent a good deal of energy in the search for some unified principle of religious liberty that has never existed and shows no signs of emerging any time soon. I suggest that a more profitable enterprise would involve exploring more closely the unruly consensus that has yielded the commitment to religious liberty in the American tradition. Instead of attempting to elaborate a single normative principle of religious liberty, it would investigate the multiple normative worlds that collectively sustain this commitment. This kind of investigation would seek to increase our proficiency in a kind of normative multilingualism according to which the holders of different normative visions might nevertheless communicate meaningfully enough to craft an ongoing consensus in favor of religious liberty. As a historical matter, the normative worlds of Protestant dissenters have been among the chief contributors to this consensus. Accordingly, by entering the world of Roger Williams—one such dissenter—both those who are attracted to this world and those who find it repelling will be better equipped to engage in an ongoing consensus-building dialogue concerning religious liberty.

The chief barrier to engaging Roger Williams in a dialogue relevant to current issues involving religious liberty lies in the foreignness of his Puritan world to the modern consciousness.[29] If Daniel Boorstin must remind us of Thomas Jefferson's "lost world," we have even more reason to acknowledge the great gulf that separates Williams's world from that of most contemporary thinkers.[30] Readers expecting to find in Roger Williams early resonances of Jeffersonian enlightenment are invariably confounded by the overwhelming religious tenor of his arguments. He erected his system of religious liberty on a foundation in which painstaking and seemingly interminable biblical exegesis commanded a preeminent position. One scholar has observed that "students have been known to open one of Roger Williams's pamphlets, under the impression that they were going to meet a familiar figure, only to shut it hastily again with the feeling that there must have been some mistake."[31] To the difficulties posed by the discontinuity between Williams's world and ours must be added the frustrations posed by his writing style. Archaic punctuation and spelling aside, Roger Williams was accomplished at hiding a sentence's subject in a tangle of subordinate clauses and at pushing allusions and metaphors to the point of obscurity.[32] He once admitted that the lines of his writing might be "thick and over-busy as the mosquitoes."[33]

This study seeks then to fulfill two broad aims. First, it endeavors to chart the main arguments Williams used to defend freedom of conscience and to explore the tension between this freedom and the demands of the social order. This tension was demonstrated both in Williams's writings and in his activities as a leader in the early colony that became Rhode Island. By surveying Williams's substantial corpus and comparing his arguments for religious liberty with those made subsequently by John Locke, Thomas Jefferson, and James Madison, I attempt to clarify the general theoretical background that culminated in the First Amendment's religion clauses. Second, this book seeks to examine current free-exercise and establishment clause jurisprudence from the perspective of Protestant dissent that Roger Williams represents. Here I am not concerned with mechanical arguments about the Framers' intent so much as I am with suggesting other interpretive possibilities for the First Amendment

that have been overlooked in the hurry to designate the Enlightenment
as its midwife.

The argument of the book proceeds in several stages. Chapter 1 contends that the soul of Roger Williams's commitment to religious toleration was his religious dogmatism. Williams was a Puritan—but more
important, a Separatist. Unlike the Massachusetts Puritans who hesitated
to fracture fellowship with the seventeenth-century Church of England,
Williams labeled that church a spiritual wreck and proceeded to abandon
it. He drew a sharp line of demarcation between the holy and unholy and
opposed establishments of religion chiefly because they were constantly
confounding the sacred with the profane. He did not advocate religious ·
liberty out of a personal lack of faith but out of an exuberance of it. The
argument of chapter 1 will be familiar to historians but seems to have escaped the notice of most legal historians, who have tended to view religious dogmatism as the implacable foe of religious toleration. But Williams
and other Protestant dissenters after him defeat this simplification. As I
argue in the final chapter, the failure to appreciate the role of Separatism
in securing religious liberty has jeopardized the contemporary task of
maintaining an overlapping consensus of believers and unbelievers in favor of religious freedom.

Before appreciating Roger Williams's argument for religious liberty
one must first understand the social premises relied upon by the Massachusetts Puritans—Williams's chief rhetorical opponents—to support religious establishment and persecution. Chapter 2 explores the details of
the axioms that banished Roger Williams and others from the colony and
caused three Quakers to be executed on the Boston Common in the
mid-seventeenth century. Chapter 3 then reconstructs the main elements
of Roger Williams's critique of the New England way of church and state.
It explores the premises of the Puritan syllogism of establishment that he
rejected and the arguments he mustered to label that syllogism the
"Bloudy Tenent of Persecution."

Chapter 4 considers Williams's position on an enduring issue concerning religious freedom: whether religious believers should be entitled to
exemptions from generally applicable laws that conflict with their religious beliefs. For example, must a government committed to religious
liberty permit human sacrifice? Should Jehovah's Witnesses be exempt
from a requirement that public school children pledge allegiance to the
flag of the United States or Native Americans be exempt from drug laws
that prevent their religiously motivated use of peyote? In Williams's century some religious believers sought to escape obligations relating to civil

defense and the payment of taxes. Williams was generally unreceptive to these claims. Nevertheless, he was also suspicious of laws ostensibly for the public good that trampled on religious conscience.

Once the general contours of Williams's thought have been explored, chapter 5 locates his perspective within the stream of ideas more directly influential upon the American tradition of religious liberty. The discussion focuses upon the ideas of John Locke, Thomas Jefferson, and James Madison, the triumvirate of Enlightenment representatives most often appealed to by judges and legal scholars seeking to interpret the First Amendment's religion clauses. Although the arguments these three figures muster to support religious liberty have much in common with each other and with Williams's, Locke and Jefferson especially embraced a stunted view of religious diversity and religious life that ultimately yielded a meager theory of religious liberty.

The book's final chapter is a discussion of the significance of Roger Williams's thought for current attempts to give content to the First Amendment's religion clauses. First, it is an attempt to illustrate how Williams's concept of religious liberty as freedom to be ruled by God— a concept mediated into the mainstream of constitutional theory by John Locke and James Madison—forms a theoretical anchor for resolving issues critical to the interpretation of the free-exercise clause. Second, it is an exploration of Williams's vision of the church and the "city" for modern establishment clause theory. In particular, I will investigate the place of Roger Williams's Separatist beliefs in his overall theory of church and state and the possible contributions of Separatism to current establishment interpretation and to the theory of religious toleration in general.

Notes

1. The primary source of Williams's writings is *The Complete Writings of Roger Williams*, 7 vols. (New York: Russell and Russell, 1963). The first six volumes of this edition are facsimiles of the original Narragansett edition of Williams's works, which was published between 1866 and 1874. The seventh volume was edited by Perry Miller and contains, along with an interpretive essay by Miller, material of Williams not included in the original Narragansett edition. The sixth volume contains selected correspondence of Williams but has been supplanted as a reference source by the excellent and more complete *Correspondence of Roger Williams*, 2 vols., ed. Glen W. LaFantasie (Hanover: Brown University Press, 1988).

2. *Minersville School District v. Gobitis,* 310 U.S. 586, 594 n.3 (1940). The Court
first adopted this interpretation of the free-exercise clause in *Reynolds v. United
States,* 98 U.S. 145 (1879) but later appeared to have repudiated it in cases such as
Sherbert v. Verner, 374 U.S. 398 (1963) and *Wisconsin v. Yoder,* 406 U.S. 205 (1972).
More recently, the Court has reinvigorated this understanding of free exercise in
Employment Division v. Smith, 494 U.S. 872 (1990).

3. Philip B. Kurland, "The Origins of the Religion Clauses of the Constitution," *William and Mary Law Review* 27 (1986): 841-42. Compare Mark DeWolfe
Howe's criticism of the Supreme Court's use of history to interpret the religion
clauses of the First Amendment: "By superficial and purposive interpretations of
the past, the Court has dishonored the arts of the historian and degraded the tal-
ents of the lawyer." Howe, *The Garden and the Wilderness: Religion and Government
in American Constitutional History* (Chicago: University of Chicago Press, 1965), 4.

4. I address Williams's views on the relation between general legal prescriptions and religious conscience in chapter 4. In *West Virginia State Board of Education v. Barnette,* 319 U.S. 624 (1943), the Supreme Court overruled *Gobitis* and
held that Jehovah's Witness children could not be forced to recite the Pledge of
Allegiance. For a useful account of the flag-salute controversy, see David Roger
Manwaring, *Render unto Caesar: The Flag-Salute Controversy* (Chicago: University
of Chicago Press, 1962).

5. *Engle v. Vitale,* 370 U.S. 421, 424 n.20 (1962).

6. *Abington School District v. Schempp,* 374 U.S. 203, 214 (1963). Justice William
J. Brennan, in a concurring opinion, also eulogized Williams by observing that
"it has rightly been said of the history of the Establishment Clause that 'our tradition of civil liberty rests not only on the secularism of a Thomas Jefferson but
also on the fervent sectarianism . . . of a Roger Williams.'" Ibid., 259-60 (Brennan, J., concurring) (quoting Paul Freund, *The Supreme Court of the United States:
Its Business, Purposes and Performance* [Cleveland: World Publishing, 1961], 84).

7. Howe, *The Garden and the Wilderness,* 5-31.

8. Ibid., 9.

9. Ibid., 11.

10. Robert Cover, "The Supreme Court, 1982 Term—Foreword: *Nomos* and
Narrative," *Harvard Law Review* 97 (1983): 19.

11. For a similar criticism of Howe's characterization of Williams, see William
Lee Miller, *The First Liberty: Religion and the American Republic* (New York: Alfred
A. Knopf, 1985), 221-22.

12. For acknowledgments by legal scholars of Williams's importance to the
history of religious liberty in the United States, see Lawrence Tribe, *American
Constitutional Law,* 2d ed. (Mineola: Foundation Press, 1988), 1158-59; Philip Kurland, "The Religion Clauses and the Burger Court," *Catholic University Law Review* 34 (1984): 3; Harold Berman, "Religion and the Law: The First Amendment
in Historical Perspective," *Emory Law Journal* 35 (1986): 784; and Arlin M. Adams
and Charles J. Emmerich, *A Nation Dedicated to Religious Liberty: The Constitu-*

tional Heritage of the Religion Clauses (Philadelphia: University of Pennsylvania Press, 1990), 39-40.

13. For scholarly commentary, see, for example, Michael Malbin, *Religion and Politics: The Intentions of the Authors of the First Amendment* (Washington, D.C.: American Enterprise Institute, 1978); Robert Cord, *Separation of Church and State: Historical Fact and Current Fiction* (New York: Lambeth Press, 1982); Thomas Curry, *The First Freedoms: Church and State in America to the Passage of the First Amendment* (New York: Oxford University Press, 1986); Leonard Levy, *The Establishment Clause: Religion and the First Amendment* (New York: Macmillan, 1986); Michael McConnell, "The Origins and Historical Understanding of Free Exercise of Religion," *Harvard Law Review* 103 (1990): 1410; Philip A. Hamburger, "A Constitutional Right of Religious Exemption: An Historical Perspective," *George Washington Law Review* 60 (1992): 915; and Steven D. Smith, *Foreordained Failure: The Quest for a Constitutional Principle of Religious Freedom* (New York: Oxford University Press, 1995), 1-54. As examples of Supreme Court opinions focusing on the historical background of the religion clauses, see *Wallace v. Jaffree,* 472 U.S. 38, 91-114 (1985) (Rehnquist, J., dissenting) and *Lee v. Weisman,* 505 U.S. 577, 610-31 (1992) (Souter, J., concurring).

14. Berman, "Religion and the Law," 779.

15. Perry Miller, *Roger Williams: His Contribution to the American Tradition* (Indianapolis: Bobbs-Merrill, 1953), 254.

16. Jefferson to Messrs. Nehemiah Dodge and Others, a Committee of the Danbury Baptist Association in the State of Connecticut, 1 Jan. 1802, in *Thomas Jefferson: Writings,* ed. Merrill D. Peterson (New York: Library of America, 1984), 510; Thomas Jefferson, "A Bill for Establishing Religious Freedom," June 12, 1779, in *The Founders' Constitution,* ed. Philip Kurland and Ralph Lerner (Chicago: University of Chicago Press, 1987), 5:77; Marvin Myers, ed., *The Mind of the Founder: Sources of the Political Thought of James Madison,* rev. ed. (Hanover: University Press of New England for Brandeis University Press, 1981), 6-13.

17. *Everson v. Board of Education,* 330 U.S. 1, 18 (1947). In the early years after *Everson,* the Court used Jefferson's metaphor liberally, with only an occasional caution that it was not self-defining. *Illinois ex rel. McCollum v. Board of Education,* 333 U.S. 203, 213 (1948) (Frankfurter, J., concurring); *McGowan v. Maryland,* 366 U.S. 420, 461 (1961). But murmurs of protest began with Justice Stewart's dissent in *Engel v. Vitale,* which argued that "uncritical invocation" of Jefferson's metaphor did not aid constitutional adjudication. 370 U.S. 421, 445 (1962) (Stewart, J., dissenting). Within a decade, a majority of the Court would confess that Jefferson's wall was "a blurred, indistinct, and variable barrier depending on all the circumstances of a particular relationship." *Lemon v. Kurtzman,* 403 U.S. 602, 614 (1971).

18. Today, in spite of Justice Stevens's desire to "resurrect" the high and impregnable wall—*Committee for Public Education v. Regan,* 444 U.S. 646, 671 (1980) (Stevens, J., dissenting)—Jefferson's metaphor has diminished to the level of a

mere signpost or useful figure of speech. *Larkin v. Grendel's Den,* 459 U.S. 116, 123 (1982); *Lynch v. Donnelly,* 465 U.S. 668, 673 (1984).

19. In *Reynolds v. United States,* 98 U.S. 145, 164 (1879), the Court relied on Jefferson's Letter to the Danbury Baptist Association as "an authoritative declaration of the scope and effect" of the free-exercise clause.

20. For the suggestion that Supreme Court justices have been "unreflective or reticent about larger issues," see Michael Smith, "The Special Place of Religion in the Constitution," *Supreme Court Review* (1983): 88.

21. Compare Jeremy Waldron's treatment of John Locke's argument for toleration as "a practical intellectual resource that can be abstracted from the antiquity of its context and deployed in the modern debate about liberal theories of justice and political morality." Waldron, "Locke: Toleration and the Rationality of Persecution," in *Justifying Toleration: Conceptual and Historical Perspectives,* ed. Susan Mendus (Cambridge: Cambridge University Press, 1988), 61.

22. See, for example, the excellent treatments in Perry Miller, *Roger Williams;* and Edmund Morgan, *Roger Williams: The Church and the State* (New York: W. W. Norton, 1967).

23. Morgan, *Roger Williams,* 62-63.

24. Smith, *Foreordained Failure,* 125.

25. John Witte, Jr., has suggested that recent years have witnessed a migration of religious liberty issues from the domain of courts to legislatures and from the federal government to the states. See "The Essential Rights and Liberties of Religion in the American Constitutional Experiment," *Notre Dame Law Review* 71 (1996): 374-75.

26. In *Employment Division v. Smith,* 494 U.S. 872 (1990), the Court held that Native Americans were not entitled to an exception from a state controlled-substance law for the religious use of peyote and were therefore not entitled to unemployment compensation after being fired for use of peyote. The Religious Freedom Restoration Act is codified at 42 U.S.C. § 2000bb to 2000bb-4 (Supp. 1993). The Supreme Court has declared the act unconstitutional in *City of Boerne v. Flores* (25 June 1997).

27. The Supreme Court's principle precedents in the area of school prayer include *Engel v. Vitale,* 370 U.S. 421 (1962); *Abington Sch. Dist. v. Schempp,* 374 U.S. 203 (1963); *Wallace v. Jaffree,* 472 U.S. 38 (1985); and *Lee v. Weisman,* 505 U.S. 577 (1992).

28. I have been especially influenced on this point by Smith, *Foreordained Failure.* Smith, however, advances a thesis more radical than that presented here by arguing that the religion clauses of the First Amendment represent only an allocation of jurisdiction over religious matters to the states. He contends that the religion clauses contain no substantive principle or limitation other than this principle of federalism.

29. An earlier generation of writers tended to make of Williams a secular hero of democracy, motivated more by political than religious impulses. Vernon

Louis Parrington, *Main Currents in American Thought* (New York: Harcourt, Brace, 1927), 1:64; James Ernst, *The Political Thought of Roger Williams* (Seattle: University of Washington Press, 1929), 25; Samuel H. Brockunier, *The Irrepressible Democrat: Roger Williams* (New York: Ronald Press, 1940), 252, 280-81. Beginning in the 1950s, however, reassessments of Williams rejected these earlier interpretations and restored his religious beliefs to a central position in his thought. Perry Miller, *Roger Williams;* W. Clark Gilpin, *The Millenarian Piety of Roger Williams* (Chicago: University of Chicago Press, 1979); Alan Simpson, "How Democratic Was Roger Williams?" *William and Mary Quarterly Review* 3d ser., 13 (1956): 55; and Edwin S. Gaustad, *Liberty of Conscience: Roger Williams in America* (Grand Rapids: William B. Eerdmans, 1991), 6. For general surveys of Williams's treatment at the hands of historians, see Gaustad, *Liberty of Conscience,* 199-203, 211-19; and LeRoy Moore, "Roger Williams and the Historians," *Church History* 32 (1976): 442.

30. Daniel Boorstin, *The Lost World of Thomas Jefferson* (Boston: Beacon Press, 1948).

31. Simpson, "How Democratic Was Roger Williams?" 53.

32. The barriers to understanding posed by Williams's prose have been a frequent matter of remark among scholars. Glen LaFantasie has observed that "at its worst, Williams's prose is tangled and convoluted. At its best it is dense and exhilarating. But only rarely is it ever crystal clear." LaFantasie, "Roger Williams: The Inner and Outer Man," *Canadian Review of American Studies* 16 (1985): 379. But for the suggestion that Williams exceeded his Puritan contemporaries in intelligibility and attraction for modern readers, see Larzer Ziff, *Puritanism in America: New Culture in a New World* (New York: Viking Press, 1973), 111.

33. Roger Williams to John Winthrop, ca. early June 1638, in *The Correspondence of Roger Williams,* ed. LaFantasie, 1:159.

Separation and Banishment

In 1631 Roger Williams arrived in Massachusetts, among the leading edge of the great migration that would deposit thousands of Puritans in New England over the next two decades.[1] John Winthrop, then governor of the colony, noted the arrival in his journal, observing simply that a ship had deposited "Mr. Williams, a godly minister, with his wife."[2] Like other Puritans who came to the New World, Williams found waiting there opportunities for "honor and preferment" that a "tender conscience" had denied him in England, where he had chaffed under the shadow of the Anglican establishment.[3] This is not to say that his life in England had not been without good fortune. Williams had worked for Sir Edward Coke, the famous jurist, and with his patronage obtained an education first at the Charterhouse Grammar School and later Pembroke College of Cambridge University. But Williams had suffered the disillusionments shared generally by Puritans confronted with a monarch hostile to their desires for reformation of the Church of England. Under Charles I and his ecclesiastical henchman Archbishop Laud, Puritans had found their situations ever more precarious and their hopes for a purified church ever more distant. Williams himself had "trod the hopefullest paths to worldly preferments" but ultimately discovered that these paths led where his conscience would not allow him to follow.[4] With a conscience more tender than most, Williams had accepted a position as chaplain for a private family rather than as minister in an Anglican pulpit.[5] But he could not endure long this limited scope for his abilities or the continued shadow cast over his prospects by the Anglican establishment. By making passage to the New World, Roger Williams—like those who preceded him and the many who would follow—seemed to have landed in a spacious place

fertile with opportunities formerly foreclosed. With a Cambridge education and his record of service as a chaplain in England, Williams was qualified to preach in one of the colony's churches. In fact, the church of
Boston immediately invited him to serve as its minister. But Williams, not
yet thirty and scarcely dry from the Atlantic passage, refused.

Separatism

Those who would locate the beginnings of a commitment to religious
liberty in America must find it partially here—in this terse rejection by a
young man of the chance to preach to the forebears of Boston Brahmins.
Yet the reasons behind this seemingly perverse repudiation of a generous
offer will seem at first contrary to the very spirit of religious toleration.
By declining to serve as minister of the Boston church, Roger Williams
showed himself to be a dogmatist of the first order. He was a paragon of
obstinacy in an obstinate century and, at least according to the Puritans
of the Massachusetts Bay Colony who eventually banished him, he was
utterly unreasonable. On this point, at least, they had correctly measured
the man. His opponents complained of the "unmoveable stiffness,""headiness," and "unlamblike frame" of his spirit.[6] They tasted the first bitter
dose of Williams's "headiness" when he rejected the offer of the Boston
church, not because he was a religious skeptic and wanted nothing to do
with the church, but because he was a religious fanatic.

Upon his arrival in Massachusetts, Roger Williams discovered at once
that the New World was not new enough—and the Puritans he found
there not pure enough—to satisfy his demanding conscience. He rebuffed
the Boston church because he found it spiritually flawed. If one were to
seek a modern label for his criticism of the Boston Puritans, it would
probably suffice to say that Williams found them too ecumenical for his
taste. He believed the New World congregation was tainted by continued
ties to the old, spiritually defiled Anglican establishment. "I dared not of-
ficiate to an unseparated people," Williams later explained, "as upon examination and conference, I found them to be."[7] "Unseparated" from
what? From that great sinkhole of abomination, the half-Catholic, wholly
defiled Church of England, he would have retorted. Williams, a Puritan,
was, more importantly, a Separatist.[8]

The word *separate* and its cognates occupy an important place in the
rhetoric of religious liberty. Normally, they signify one's belief about the
appropriate distance that ought to lie between matters of religion and
matters of the state; thus, the ever-popular references to the desirability

of a "separation of church and state." The words *Separatist* and *Separatism* in the seventeenth century meant something quite different, however. A seventeenth-century Separatist believed not so much in the separation of church and state as in the separation of true believers and churches from their polluted and false look-alikes. A Separatist was a Puritan who had asked a simple question and arrived at a disruptive answer. The question was, Is the church of England a true church? How one answered was important to Puritans because they all agreed that one must certainly separate from false churches. Under no circumstances ought the righteous to be spiritual roommates with the unrighteous. The Lord's command was stern. "Wherefore," he spoke through the apostle Paul, "come out from among them, and be ye separate, saith the Lord, and touch not the unclean thing; and I will receive you."[9]

If the Church of England was not a true church, then one was obliged to renounce it and depart from it. Yet, if the Church of England was a true church, then any separation from it would be schismatical and a sin. One had no liberty, the Puritans believed, to start a new church simply out of dissatisfaction or disagreement with an old church so long as the old church was a true church. But there was certainly precedent upon which Puritans and other Protestants could agree to suggest that not every church that called itself a church was a true church. The Roman Catholic Church, for example, headed the list of spiritual imposters as far as Puritans were concerned. With a single mind, they believed the pope to be the Antichrist and his church an abomination, the great Whore of Babylon referred to in the book of Revelation in the New Testament.[10]

Separation from this counterfeit was at the heart of the Reformation impulse, including its incarnation in English Protestantism. Puritans, to be sure, differed from other English Protestants on their estimate of how tainted the Church of England remained by traditions and trappings inherited from Rome. In fact, they gained the label of "Puritan" from a fairly hearty sense of the degree of taint with which the Church of England was still defiled. They sniffed popery in Anglican practices such as making the sign of the cross and bowing when the name of Jesus was spoken, and they were alarmed at an ascendant Armenian theology that placed, they believed, far too much emphasis on the individual believer's role in salvation and too little on God's sovereign election. Yet Puritans nevertheless believed that not every tainted church was a false church. For them, the Anglican Church was a rotten apple but still an apple all the same. On this point they parted ways with radical Separatists such as Roger Williams.

Asked if the Church of England was a true church, Williams answered emphatically, "No." How could it be? Mary Tudor had served the Church of England up as an offering to Rome during her brief and bloody reign. This betrayal, Williams thought, had not been undone by the return to Protestantism under Elizabeth. In his mind, no mere change in the religious leanings of temporal authority could cleanse the English church of the stain Mary Tudor had spilt upon it. More important, the Church of England was not a true church because it did not limit its membership to true Christians. To be English was to be a member of the Church of English, and this promiscuous membership was the chief defect that deprived the church of requisite purity in Williams's eye. He believed a true church was a community consisting solely of true believers, not simply church-attenders and their children but people who had been "born again" by the power of Christ. "Make sure thy second birth," he warned English observers prone to think of Native Americans as heathens, "else thou shalt see, / Heaven ope to Indians wild, but shut to thee."[11] It was impossible, he charged, "for a dead stone to have fellowship with the living God, and for any man to enter into the kingdom of God, without a second birth."[12] Williams was not surprised that many of his contemporaries were dead stones, but he found it inconceivable that anyone would think it appropriate to use such spiritually inferior masonry to fashion the living Church of Christ.

Williams had plenty of New England company on this matter of church membership. Massachusetts Puritans also believed that local churches should consist only of visible saints—that is, people who had given some evidence of being true believers in Christ. Not every inhabitant of Massachusetts was a church member, nor even expected to be. The saved must ever live side by side the lost, and the believer share social space with the unbeliever. Massachusetts Puritans took pains, therefore, to distinguish believers from unbelievers. They required each applicant for church membership to provide testimony tending to show that he or she was a true believer. Yet for all their carefulness in rooting out weeds from the garden of the church, Williams believed the Puritans were nevertheless derelict in their labors. He followed the Separatist impulse to a further level, and in doing so he traveled further than the New England Puritans were willing to go. He maintained that a true church consisted not only of regenerate members but also of members who had publicly repented of their former association with false churches.[13] The members of a true church "must not only be living stones, but also separated from the rubbish of Antichristian confusions and desolations."[14] Because the Church of England was by his calculation a false church, he insisted that the members of a true church must separate from the Church of England and renounce any past and future association with it. Boston church members committed what Williams viewed as the high crime of not formally and decisively repudiating all ties with the Anglican religious establishment.[15] They were ready to hear sermons from arriving Puritan ministers, even when those ministers had never publicly repented of the immense wickedness of having preached in the parish churches of England. Soon New Englanders would begin making visits back to England, and while they were there they would defile themselves by worshiping again at the corrupt parish churches.[16]

Williams would have none of this. Not for the last time he judged that the appropriate stance to be taken toward spiritual impurity was one of separation. He was not inclined to suffer patiently what he believed to be spiritual error and impurity. Like Robert Browne, the famous Separatist of the sixteenth century, Roger Williams believed in "Reformation without Tarrying for Any": no coddling the unrighteous in the church's bosom, no accommodating the unholy.[17] Severance alone defined the proper relationship between saintliness and sin. The Boston church, by its promiscuous fellowship with the Church of England, was—as Williams would later describe all the New England churches—"by the links of this mystical chain . . . still fastened to the Pope himself."[18] Boston church members failed to practice a sufficient separation from Anglican defilement, and therefore Williams deemed it expedient to separate himself from these non-Separators.

He promptly removed to Salem, north of Boston, where he imagined it possible to breath a purer spiritual air. The Salem church, itself influenced by Separatist impulses, offered to make Williams its teacher.[19] Massachusetts authorities, however, disturbed by Williams's readiness to walk a different path, persuaded the Salem church (at least for the time-being) to reconsider their offer and have nothing to do with Williams. In a letter the magistrates dispatched to the church at Salem, they "marveled" that the church would choose Williams "without advising the council" and requested the church to avoid further action until the magistrates had conferred about the matter.[20]

The magistrates' intervention succeeded in denying the Salem post to Roger Williams.[21] He then sought haven among the Pilgrims of Plymouth Colony, who, like him, believed the Church of England fit only to be abandoned like the spiritual wreck that it was. Williams, though, could not walk in harmony for long even with the Separatist Pilgrims of

Plymouth. According to William Bradford, then governor of the Plymouth Colony, Williams fell "into some strange opinions, and from opinion to practice, which caused some controversy between the church and
him. And in the end some discontent on his part, by occasion whereof he
left them something abruptly."[22]

The gist of these "strange opinions" seems to have involved Separatism
again.[23] Apparently, the stern Pilgrims of Plymouth were, for Williams at
least, not sufficiently stern in their repudiation of the Church of England.
They, like their Boston neighbors, could not resist visiting old friends at
the parish churches in England when they returned there from time to
time.[24] For this sin, Williams shook the dust of Plymouth from his clothes
and returned again to Salem. This time, allowed to stay for a while at least,
he preached Separatist reform until Massachusetts Bay authorities would
tolerate him no longer. He soon began to denounce the New Englanders
polluting themselves in the parish churches of England when they visited
there and the Massachusetts churches that tolerated such miscreants. He
protested against allowing anyone to preach in the colony who had formerly preached in Anglican parish churches until the tainted preacher had
repented of this abominable alliance with the Anglican establishment.[25]
When the colony's authorities refused to heed his jeremiad, Williams
convinced the church at Salem to renounce fellowship with all the Bay
churches still tainted with Anglican pollution.[26]

By protesting the refusal of the New England churches to sever all ties
with the Anglican establishment, Williams would have flushed into the
open what Massachusetts authorities very much wanted to remain hidden, at least from Anglican eyes across the Atlantic: the extent to which
they agreed with key premises of Williams's Separatist polemic. That, unfortunately, was the most distressing thing about the young radical: He
constantly managed to fashion the most socially destructive "wherefores"
from the Puritans' own "premises considered." He took what they believed; stretched it out like a pleasantly winding path; and then, by traveling down the path, reached the most unimaginable places. The Puritans'
vigorous repudiation of his ideas surely stemmed in part from the fact that
Williams was a mirror in which they saw images—frightening images—
of themselves.[27] They recoiled from Williams as does a man who discovers that a notorious terrorist is his son.

Williams's insistence on Separatism was a case in point. He undoubtably
touched a nerve when he asked, "what is that which Mr. Cotton and so
many hundreds fearing God in New England walk in, but a way of separation?"[28] What indeed. Massachusetts Puritans had drunk deeply from

the spring of Separatism. There was a good deal of truth to Williams's observation that one seldom found a conscientious Separatist who had not first been a Puritan.[29] The impulse of separation was a natural extension of the perception of spiritual stain and impurity, and Puritans saw stain everywhere. Central to Puritan ecclesiology was the line of demarcation between the godly and the ungodly, the holy and the profane. Shielded by distance from Anglican authorities, New England Puritans were busy redefining the nature of church membership and the nature of the church itself to emphasize this demarcation. Like Williams, they believed that church membership should be reserved for "visible saints"—true believers who had given evidence of saving faith at work in their lives. Their principal religious rites—baptism and the Lord's Supper—made visible the invisible distinctions among church attenders: those baptized and those who were not, those who shared in the Lord's supper and those who could not.[30]

Even the most godly Christians arriving in Massachusetts from England were not automatically admitted to membership in one of the colony's churches. They had to make an adequate account of their faith publicly and be willing to enter into a church covenant or else be denied membership.[31] In this regard the Puritans decisively rejected the Anglican system that essentially equated church membership with national citizenship. One might be an Anglican church member merely by virtue of being English. Massachusetts church membership was a prize awarded far more discriminately. Like Williams, New England Puritans also opposed the Anglican hierarchy of national church leaders, synods, and ecclesiastical courts. They were, moreover, quite happy to be far enough away from the eyes of Anglican authorities to practice an essentially deviant form of church government: Congregationalism.[32] The Puritans treated each of the churches founded in Massachusetts as essentially autonomous, each governed by its members rather than by an ecclesiastical hierarchy. But this Congregationalism was clearly at odds with the hierarchical structure of the Anglican establishment, and New England Puritans were well aware of their departure from the Anglican norm. On rare occasions, they admitted candidly, if somewhat disingenuously, that they had "withdrawn" from the national constitution of the Anglican Church; but they were not ready to advertise the fact.[33]

However much in common the New England Puritans may have had with Williams, though, the civil and church leaders of the Massachusetts Bay Colony were not Separatists like he was.[34] They saw no need for the stern medicine of repentance as to their ongoing ties with the Anglican establishment. They had always believed that reforms needed by the Church of England—and they believed these to be many and grave— were best obtained by working from within the church. It was true that the accession of Charles I in 1625 made the possibility of successful re- form in England seem ever more distant. Nevertheless, Massachusetts Pu- ritans, even as they were charting a path away from Anglicanism, were reluctant to make their growing deviance from Anglican patterns a mat- ter of public record. They had, in fact, sound political reasons for main- taining public association with the Church of England. In the way of separation lay "political madness."[35]

The Puritans' celebrated "City upon a Hill" had as a chief cornerstone the royal patent granted by Charles I, and what Charles had given, Charles, lately encouraged by Anglican hostility to Puritanism, might yet take away. In the years following Charles's accession, he demonstrated lit- tle sympathy with, and growing antipathy toward, reformers both within and without the Church of England. If New England Puritans were to sustain their errand into the wilderness, then they must appear in word, if not in deed, loyal servants of Charles and the Anglican establishment. Massachusetts authorities had already had to fend off charges that the colony "intend[ed] rebellion, to . . . cast off . . . allegiance, and to be wholly separate from the church and laws of England; that [its] ministers and people did continually rail against the state, church, and bishops there."[36] To refute such charges, Massachusetts authorities deemed it necessary to deal sternly with publicly displayed inclinations toward Separatism. Had Williams been allowed to continue his Separatist ravings from within the shelter of the Massachusetts Bay Colony, he undoubtedly would have fueled the energies of the colony's Anglican opponents.[37]

Apart from these pragmatic realities, Massachusetts Puritans were sim- ply more interested in spiritual harmony than in Roger Williams's fan- tastic demands for exacting ecclesiastical purity. When, nearly two decades later, the Puritan clergy got around to summarizing their essential beliefs in the Cambridge Platform of 1648, they explicitly repudiated the Sepa- ratist cure for spiritual impurity. Individuals were not to separate from a church, nor even to refuse to partake of the sacraments in such a church, merely because it tolerated among its numbers "profane and scandalous livers."[38] For the sake of spiritual and civil unity the Puritans were ready to tolerate a fair amount of dirt on the robes of righteousness. Their dif- ference with Williams in this regard was a matter of degree, of course. To the modern eye they may seem mostly a stern lot, excessively occupied with the requirements of godliness, with a dour air made famous by H. L. Mencken's barbed definition of Puritanism as the "haunting fear that someone, somewhere, may be happy." But matters of degree are often the most decisive matters. In the controversy between Roger Williams and Massachusetts orthodoxy, this differing sensitivity to ecclesiastical stain and the Puritans' relatively expansive attitude toward the weaker brethren among their churches formed the heart of the controversy that would ultimately hurl Williams in a winter's flight from the shelter of Massachusetts to the wilderness of Narragansett Bay.

The colony witnessed the infancy of Roger Williams's Separatist pilgrimage, for when he arrived in Massachusetts he still believed that a pure church might be found if only he were to search for it diligently enough. In later years, though, Williams abandoned the search altogether.[39] He became convinced that churches could not be established willy-nilly just because a band of individuals decided to form one. To found a church one needed a properly ordained minister, and—here was the rub—so far as Williams could tell, no such ministers existed any longer. To be ordained, one had to receive ordination from someone properly ordained by a minister of a true church. Now this chain of ordination had proceeded in an orderly fashion during the early years of the church. Christ had ordained apostles; they, in turn, had ordained church ministers; the ministers had ordained their successors; and so on. But eventually, Williams thought, the chain had been disrupted. The line of apostolic succession had been severed by Constantine's nationalization of Christianity in the fourth century. At that point, Williams believed, the true church had died, and with it the chain of ordinations that kept the ministry alive. Thereafter, the world was ruled by the anti-Christian Roman Catholic Church and had become a wilderness in which true believers roamed as pilgrims, without benefit of ministry or sacrament.[40] God had torn down the wall separating his garden—the church—from the world's wilderness, and the wilderness had overgrown the garden. The "Christian world (so called)" had "swallowed up Christianity."[41] Williams's great rhetorical adversary, the Boston church teacher John Cotton, summed up the natural progression of Williams's Separatism as well as anyone.

> Time was, when of all Christian churches, the churches of New-England were accounted, and professed by him, to be the most pure: and of all the churches in New-England, Salem (where himself was teacher) to be the most pure. But when the churches of New-England took just offense at sundry of his proceedings, he first renounced communion with them all: and because the

church of Salem refused to join with him in such a groundless censure, he then renounced communion with Salem also. And then fell off from his ministry, and then from all church-fellowship, and then from his baptism, (and was himself baptized again) and then from the Lords Supper, and from all ordinances of Christ dispensed in any church-way, till God shall stir up himself, or some other new apostles to recover, and restore all the ordinances, and churches of Christ out of the ruins of Antichristian apostasy.[42]

Legal scholars have sometimes claimed that Williams's view of church-state relations made protection of the garden from the wilderness—or the church from the state—the principal aim.[43] But that characterization fails to discern the true extent of his radical Separatism. According to Roger Williams, there was no garden to be protected any longer. Weeds grew where cultivated flowers once bloomed. He did not advocate a wall between church and state, he mourned the wall's destruction and the destruction of the church. There was no church left to be separated from the state. The most that true believers could do was wait in expectation that God would one day send apostles who would replant the garden. Until that time, the world would be inhabited by Christians without a church.

Driven by this radical Separatism, Williams eventually abandoned any hope of finding a pure church. He associated for a few months with an infant congregation of Baptists but ultimately separated from them because even they could not claim to have preserved the legacy of the apostolic church.[44] How could they baptize anyone without a properly ordained minister to perform the baptism, and where could they find such a minister? In forming the Baptist church, one of the founding members had baptized Williams, who had baptized the remaining members.[45] But now, Williams saw, he was not a true minister and could not conduct the ordinance of baptism. He saw no alternative but to withdraw from his so recently acquired Baptist brethren. They were trying to create a garden out of the barren wilderness of the world and had set upon an illusive quest for a church that had died and would remain dead until God resurrected it in the last days.

> In the poor small span of my life, I desired to have been a diligent and constant observer, and have been my self many ways engaged in city, in country, in court, in schools, in universities, in churches, in old and New-England, and yet cannot in the holy presence of God bring in the result of a satisfying discovery, that either the begetting ministry of the apostles or messengers to the nations, or the feeding and nourishing ministry of pastors and teachers, according to the first institution of the Lord Jesus, are yet restored and extant.[46]

Williams saw no alternative but to wait patiently until God at length sent apostles who had the power to start new churches. Until that time, there was no one available either to start a church or to sustain it.[47] John Cotton certainly exaggerated, but he captured the essential direction of Williams's thinking when he reported that Williams ultimately refused spiritual communion with everyone, including his wife.[48] Once again, Williams had followed his Separatist impulses as far as they would lead him—and they had led him to renounce fellowship with every church in the world.

Separatism and Toleration

Modern readers expecting to find in Roger Williams an early champion of religious toleration may find his rigid Separatism inexplicable. He was a fervent advocate of civil toleration in religious matters, but if by toleration one means ecumenism, then Williams was relentlessly intolerant. The Puritans of New England, who steadfastly refused to call their establishment of churches in Massachusetts a separation from the Church of England, were virtual bastions of ecumenism compared to Williams. Their faith, rigid as it may appear from a distance of more than three centuries, was in reality quite at home with pragmatic compromise.[49] Puritans believed the Church of England to be riddled with impurity but were unwilling to fracture all ties with the Anglican establishment. They did not imagine that every Massachusetts inhabitant was a Christian, but they welcomed (in fact, required) the presence of unbelievers at church services. Williams, on the other hand, was a straight-backed enemy of accommodation in matters relating to religious doctrine and spiritual purity, and he branded the Puritans' indiscriminate fellowships with false churches and unbelievers an impermissible accommodation: "by compelling all within their jurisdiction to an outward conformity of the church worship, of the word and prayer, and maintenance of the ministry thereof, they evidently declare that they still lodge and dwell in the confused mixtures of the unclean and clean, of the flock of Christ, and herds of the world together, I mean in spiritual and religious worship."[50]

Williams would not bend on the subject. His conscience quivered at the slightest stain and the most insignificant spiritual error. The spiritual world he inhabited contained sharp divisions between the saved and the lost, the holy and the unholy, the good corn and the worthless chaff, the rose and the weeds of the wilderness, the sheep and the goats (or wolves or swine).[51] A crisp distinction between "within" and "without" the true Church of Christ organized his thought: "within" were the people of God, "without" were the worshipers of idols—some civilized, others uncivilized, but all heathen.[52]

Williams's Separatist scruples were a product of confidence in his ability to discern spiritual truth and a heightened sensitivity to contamination with spiritual stain. His Separatism was sustained by frank epistemological confidence. He found in the Scripture a basis for certainty rather than for doubt. His faith took root in the confidence of truth discovered, and he was not willing to yield on matters of spiritual truth: "we must not let go for all the flea bitings of the present afflictions, having bought truth dear, we must not sell it cheap, not the least grain of it for the whole world, no not for the saving of souls, though our own most precious; least of all for the bitter sweetening of a little vanishing pleasure."[53] Being right mattered, according to Roger Williams. He could admire the conscience of the "Jew or Turk, or Papist, or who ever that steers no otherwise then his conscience dares."[54] Yet his admiration for expressions of sincere conscience did not prevent him from believing that all consciences were ultimately subject to the claims of truth and would stand or fall according to their recognition of that truth.[55]

Williams, moreover, was confident in making his preliminary judgments about who would stand and who fall before the "bar" of God. For example, he judged the Church of England to consist mostly of people who were not true Christians because their outward professions of faith concealed unregenerate hearts.[56] Moreover, although he spent years in close association with various Native Americans in New England and demonstrated great understanding of their cultural strengths, he doubted not but that they were "lost"—that is, unbelievers.[57] Even when they prayed, they did not necessarily enter into the community of faith. To the declaration of a dying Indian that "me much pray to Jesus Christ," Williams replied severely, "I told him so did many English, French, and Dutch, who had never turned to God, nor loved him."[58] Williams had no doubt but that most of his contemporaries would ultimately suffer judgment at the hands of a God to whom they had never turned.[59] Yet a few would "see him, reign with him, eternally admire him, and enjoy him, when he shortly comes in flaming fire to burn up millions of ignorant and disobedient."[60] Williams was willing to leave faiths that differed from his own free from civil disabilities and punishments, but that did not mean he respected those differing faiths as either true or valuable. The pluralism he embraced was tragic rather than celebratory. He thought most of the world's inhabitants were hell-bent and saw no reason to rejoice in this fact.

An overriding constant in the career of Roger Williams as New England gadfly was his repeated rejection of spiritual communion with beliefs and forms of worship he found erroneous or unholy. As William Miller aptly put it, he was "known more for leaving churches than for founding them."[61] Williams was relentlessly intolerant when it came to matters of worship and sharply distinguished between "toleration in the Church," which he abhorred, and "toleration in the world," which he championed.[62] He saw a bright line of demarcation between "fellowship with the Lord Jesus in his sufferings" and "fellowship with sinners."[63] He sniffed refusal at the offer to pastor the church in Boston, declined to tarry long with the Plymouth Pilgrims, and persuaded the Salem brethren to splinter from the other New England churches. He was a Baptist for a few months but ultimately gave up fellowship with them because they could not claim the proper apostolic succession necessary to validate the ordinance of baptism they practiced. Each new renunciation of spiritual communion was fueled by Williams's confidence in his ability to distinguish the holy from the unholy, the orthodox from the heretical. His opponents marveled at the arrogance of this certainty: "conceiving himself to have received a clearer illumination and apprehension of the estate of Christ's kingdom, and of the purity of holy communion, than all Christendom . . . he therefore takes it to be his duty, to give public advertisement, and admonition to all men . . . of the corruptions of religion, which himself observes in their judgment, and practice."[64]

Nor did Williams think that toleration required believers in different faiths to simply leave one another alone. Proselytization, for him, was entirely consistent with religious liberty. He believed in a militant faith, although one whose militancy expressed itself through spiritual weapons such as preaching and persuasion and prayer rather than through civic violence. The religious toleration Williams advocated was one that would leave believers free to undertake spiritual warfare against spiritual error. He sought to sheath the civil sword so that the sword of spiritual truth could be wielded against apostasy and unbelief: "It is . . . necessary, yea . . . honorable, godly, and Christian, to fight the fight of faith, with religious and spiritual artillery, and to contend earnestly for the faith of Jesus, once delivered to the saints against all opposers, and the gates of earth and hell, men or devils, yea against Paul himself, or an angel from heaven, if he bring any other faith or doctrine."[65]

Not a few historical observers have misunderstood Williams on this point. For example, late in his life Roger Williams seized the chance to engage in a public debate with three Quakers in which he tried to demonstrate their manifold errors.[66] The spectacle of the seventy-year-old Williams rowing alone all day to wage debate against three Quakers near the end of his life has seemed to some an abdication of principles he had earlier announced.[67] But the debate was a picturesque example of exactly that liberty for which Roger Williams had long prophesied. The Quakers were wrong, he believed. They ought to be opposed, although not with the civil sword but with persuasive words, and the debate ought to be civil, carried on in an orderly fashion so that truth would out.[68]

A heightened sensitivity to spiritual stain also fueled Roger Williams's Separatism.[69] In contrast with those who view the self as essentially impenetrable, the Separatist self is at constant risk of contamination in the presence of evil. The only way to avoid contamination is to avoid contact with evil by enforcing a spiritual quarantine on the healthy self to preserve it from the ravages of spiritual infection. Williams's impulse toward spiritual sequestration was most vivid in his dealings with the nonseparating Puritans of the Massachusetts Bay Colony, with whom he constantly maintained the necessity of separation from spiritual pollution, especially when it took the form of the Anglican Church. His commitment to avoid spiritual stain also demonstrated itself in his vigorous protest against true believers associating with unbelievers in any acts of worship, even in the formalized invocations of divine oversight contained in the various oaths that Massachusetts Puritans thought essential to social stability. And, to cite one further example, it also surfaced in his relations with the Native Americans, with whom he had many years of close association as an informal ambassador from the New England Colonies, as a trader, and as a sometime missionary.

In 1643 Roger Williams published an account of Native American language, *A Key into the Language of America*. The book contains a wealth of observations about Native American culture. In particular, Williams's *Key* displays a significant familiarity with Native American religious beliefs. It also suggests, however, that Williams did not gain this familiarity by observing or participating in Native American religious rites. The sequestered soul could have nothing to do with such idolatry. Williams stated his reasoning: "after once being in their houses and beholding what their worship was, I dared never be an eye witness, spectator, or looker on, lest I should have been partaker of Satan's inventions and worships."[70] Williams's account of his reasons for avoiding certain Native American "games" illustrates a similar concern with spiritual stain: "Their public games are solemnized with the meeting of hundreds; sometimes thousands, and consist of many vanities, none of which I dared ever be present at, that I might not countenance and partake of their folly, after I once saw the evil of them."[71]

The spiritual sequestration whose rigid enforcement Roger Williams demanded did not extend to purely civil intercourse. He was not an advocate of insular Christian communities barricaded against all contact with a sinful world. Christians, he believed, could neither escape the world nor its sinful inhabitants. To avoid all contact with unbelievers would require one to leave the world entirely, and Williams saw no evidence that God had either commanded or even made possible such a spiritual exodus. Consequently, Christians could expect to find themselves in all kinds of civil relationships with unbelievers, and these relationships did not inevitably expose believers to spiritual stain. Only when believers participated in polluted acts of spiritual fellowship were they contaminated with spiritual stain. When believers encountered unbelievers in other contexts, God himself provided ample defenses against contamination.

In one sense, Williams differed from his Puritan contemporaries by seeing far more possibilities than they to pollute oneself in unholy fellowships. For example, he viewed civil oaths made in the name of God as acts of spiritual worship—as prayers, essentially. He accordingly concluded that a believer who called upon an unbeliever to swear an oath entered into a soul-staining spiritual fellowship with unbelief.[72] He also disagreed with other Puritans over the appropriateness of inviting (in fact, compelling) unbelievers to attend church services. Massachusetts Puritans sequestered unbelievers from the ordinances of communion and baptism, believing them to be unfit to participate in these holy rites. But the Puritans welcomed unbelievers to hear sermons preached by Puritan ministers, concluding that no unholy fellowship was created by the mere fact that believers and unbelievers listened to the same sermon. Williams, on the other hand, insisted that preaching was a holy ordinance and instituted a spiritual fellowship between preacher and listeners no different from the fellowship created when a church celebrated the ordinances of communion and baptism.[73] Thus, forcing unbelievers to attend church services not only violated their rights of conscience but also polluted believers who welcomed these nonbelievers in a spiritual embrace.[74]

In another sense, however, Williams insisted that believers were far more insulated than the Puritans imagined from contaminating contacts with unbelievers. He drew a sharp distinction between spiritual fellowship and civil fellowship and maintained that civil intercourse with unbelievers did not threaten believers with contamination.[75] The soul, he seems to have thought, only became permeable to stain when it exposed itself to God in acts of worship. Williams was driven to that conclusion partially by a frank appraisal of worldly wickedness. Evil was, as far as he could see, the order of the day. "The world lies in wickedness, is like a wilderness or a sea of wild beasts innumerable, fornicators, covetous, idolaters," he judged.[76] Williams, moreover, saw little possibility of taming either wilderness or beasts. Wickedness was here to stay, and the righteous could not escape it. Either believers were allowed to "converse and cohabit in cities, towns," or else "must they not live in the world, but go out of it."[77] God had commanded "a continuance in all relations of government, marriage, service, notwithstanding that the grace of Christ had appeared to some."[78]

Williams's rigorous distinction between believer and unbeliever, and his conviction that believers were the rarer of the two, led him to conclude that unbelievers were as common as weeds in a wilderness.[79] He charged that Massachusetts Puritans had busied themselves with the senseless work of trying to weed the wilderness rather than focusing, as they should have, on weeding the garden.[80] Williams, on the other hand, was willing to let the weeds alone. The severe demarcation he made between the unregenerate and the righteous—between nature and grace— carved out for lost souls a place of civil habitation unmolested by the righteous.[81]

Massachusetts Puritans also saw distinctions between the godly and the ungodly. Nevertheless, their view of sacred history tended to treat this distinction as one that would shortly be obliterated in the appearance of Christ's kingdom on earth. They clung to the belief that the visible rule of Christ might yet be planted—with their assistance—in the work-a-day world. There were, of course, constant evidences to challenge this belief. But even in the face of bleak reminders that the kingdoms of the world had not yet become the kingdom of Christ, the Puritans looked about them and saw—if not the reality of Christ's kingdom—then at least the possibility of it. They were therefore prepared to harry the ungodly a bit if doing so advanced the dominion of the garden—that is, Christ's kingdom—over the world. Williams, however, saw matters in precisely the opposite light. The garden was not advancing upon the worldly wilderness, it had been overrun by weeds and forced into retreat. He looked about him for signs of true belief and saw only "the little flock of Jesus . . . scattered, routed and laid waste and desolate."[82] Thicket and bramble were the order of the day, and Christ's kingdom would not be planted in the world until God sent new apostles to do the planting. Moreover, he believed, John Cotton and the other New England ministers, no matter how wondrously learned and eloquent, were not apostles. Therefore, because the world was a wilderness and would be until God decided that it should be otherwise, the scattered godly seedlings from the garden had no business tormenting the ungodly weeds.

Banishment

By 1634 Massachusetts authorities realized that Williams threatened to unravel the social tapestry they were so busily weaving and that he had laid an axe to the foundations of the New Jerusalem the Puritans sought to plant in the New England wilderness. The colony was beginning to reverberate to the sound of his blows, and its protectors were not content to sit idly by while Williams destroyed the work of their hands.

They had been patient before. Williams, after all, had barely set foot in the colony before announcing that the church of Boston was not fit for his communion. He had, moreover, declared at the same time that the civil magistrates had no authority to punish Sabbath-breakers, "as it was a breach of the first table."[83] By this charge, Williams seems to have given the first hint of thinking that would later be linked to his name in American history: Government had no business superintending purely religious affairs. Furthermore, in December 1633 civil authorities had pondered the contents of a treatise he had written, alleging, among other things, that the king's patent was an insufficient basis for claiming title to lands in the New World. No one, Williams declared, could assert legitimate title unless he had "compounded with the natives."[84] Williams also maintained that King James was a liar for claiming that he was the first Christian prince to have discovered the New World and that it was blasphemous to call Europe "Christendom."[85] When Massachusetts authorities moved to censure Williams for these and other assertions, he quickly offered to burn his book and, appearing penitently before the General Court, convinced the governor and his assistants of his loyalty.[86]

By 1634, though, Williams had abandoned his penitential garments and was again busy assaulting the pillars upon which the Puritans were at work constructing their experiment in holy commonwealth. Ultimately, Massachusetts authorities found four propositions advanced by Williams capable of jeopardizing the fragile social order so recently planted in the Bay Colony.[87] His insistence on visible acts of separation from the

Anglican establishment in England headed the list of troubling errors. Massachusetts authorities had ample reason to believe that their political future hinged on pledging at least the appearance of loyalty to the Church of England, and Williams's Separatist rantings threatened the appearance of that loyalty.

He had also renewed his objections to the king's asserted authority to grant patents in the New World in contravention of Indian rights and the "sinful opinion among many that Christians have right to heathens' lands."[88] According to John Winthrop, Williams's return to this theme was a repudiation of his previous representation that he would forswear such accusations. Williams, though, was adamant on the point and could not keep silent. "We have not our land by patent from the King," Williams maintained, "but . . . the Natives are the true owners of it, and . . . we ought to repent of such a receiving it by patent."[89]

The Massachusetts Bay Colony, which claimed its tenuous existence from such a patent and labored under fears that Anglican opponents would yet succeed in having that patent annulled, was unreceptive to Williams's argument. Five years earlier, when the officers of the Massachusetts Bay Company were still overseeing the colony from England, the company had warned Governor Endicott not to "render yourself or us distasteful to the state here, to which (as we ought) we must and will have an obsequious eye."[90] For the colony to tolerate an attack on the king's authority to grant the patent would be to endorse the cause of its opponents seeking to have the Massachusetts patent annulled. Moreover, the charge seemed absurd to Massachusetts authorities. It was not as though arriving English settlers had torn down Native American abodes and driven the hapless occupants into the wilderness. There was plenty of land for everyone, Governor Winthrop maintained, and he urged that land that "lies in common, and has never been replenished or subdued is free to any that possess or improve it."[91] John Cotton concurred: "We did not conceive that it is a just title to so vast a continent, to make no other improvement of millions of acres in it, but only to burn it up for pastime."[92] Williams, they thought, had a penchant for finding grand theological issues in matters that ought to be resolved with a simple dose of good sense and fairness. For Winthrop and Cotton, the colonization of Massachusetts Bay was not really a grand saga about a Christian prince conquering the heathen. They had just moved onto vacant land and were entitled, they believed, to put it to good use without having to endure the frettings of Roger Williams.

Williams, however, had metamorphosed into a full-blown critic of Massachusetts society and soon found something new against which to prophesy. In April 1634 magistrates ordered all adult male residents of the colony who did not have the franchise to take an oath of loyalty or else be banished.[93] Williams, having already earned the magistrates' displeasure over his objections to the colony's patent, immediately attacked the requirement. Once again his Separatist convictions blazed at the Puritans' unholy marriage of sacred and profane. The oath, he said, was in reality a prayer. "I do here swear, and call God to witness," the oath-taker intoned and summoned divine assistance to guard the oath's solemnity: "So help me God."[94] What was this, Roger Williams asked, but a sacred conversation with the Almighty, orchestrated by the Puritans to secure domestic tranquility? They were, in effect, forcing Massachusetts inhabitants to pray. Because Williams judged that most of those inhabitants were unbelievers, he concluded in good Separatist style that their so-called prayers were nothing but religious hypocrisy dressed in the garb of civil ceremony.

By mandating these prayers, Massachusetts believers had stained themselves with the same hypocrisy, and the spectacle of a government-sponsored mockery of God was simply more than Williams could stomach in silence.[95] Thomas Hooker, one of the most important preachers in Massachusetts, was quick to point out what he believed to be the absurdity of Williams's position: "If it be unlawful to call an unregenerate person to take an oath, or to pray, as being actions of God's worship, then it is unlawful for your unregenerate child, to pray for a blessing upon his own meat. If it be unlawful for him to pray for a blessing upon his meat, it is unlawful for him to eat it, (for it is sanctified by prayer, and without prayer unsanctified, I Tim. 4:4,5.) If it be unlawful for him to eat it, it is unlawful for you to call upon him to eat it, for it is unlawful for you to call upon him to sin."[96] Williams, though, took the matter seriously in spite of this criticism. Some years later he traveled to England and there suffered defeat in a chancery court action he was prosecuting because he refused to take an oath.[97]

The authorities could have hardly seen Williams's scruples about oaths as anything but profoundly threatening to the civil order. Their use of oaths to secure truthfulness and loyalty among Massachusetts inhabitants was, by current standards, extravagant. In addition to oaths to guarantee faithful service by important government officials such as the governor, the Puritans reinforced almost all social responsibilities with the severity of oaths. The earliest codification of Massachusetts law, adopted in 1648, specified oaths for positions as varying in rank as governor and appraiser of property. The oath for the latter office represents a specimen common to numerous other civil occupations: "Whereas you . . . are chosen to be appraisers of such lands or goods as are now to be presented to you, you do here swear by the Living God, that all partiality, prejudice and other sinister respects laid aside, you shall appraise the same, and every part thereof, according to the true and just value thereof at this present, by common account, by your best judgment and conscience. So help you God."[98]

But one need not have been engaged in government responsibilities to be called upon to swear an oath of fidelity. In addition to public officials, both citizens, called freemen, and other inhabitants registered assent to the social contract by swearing an oath of subservience to the lawful authorities of the colony. "I freely and sincerely acknowledge my self to be subject to the Government [of the colony]," inhabitants affirmed, "and do here swear by the great and dreadful name of the Ever-living God, that I will be true and faithful to the same."[99] Freemen swore a similar oath.[100] Oath-taking appears to have been such a popular device for securing trust and fidelity that the General Court ultimately felt constrained to put an end to indiscriminate compulsions to swear an oath. In 1641 the court ordered that "no man shall be urged to take any oath, or subscribe any articles, covenants, or remonstrance of public and civil nature but such as the General Court hath considered, allowed and required."[101]

Williams's challenge to the use of oaths, had it been heeded, would have deprived the colony of what its authorities viewed as an essential social cement. The courts could not be expected to fulfill their function of rendering justice without the assurance of having truthful testimony before them, and governments could not purge themselves of potential insurgents without the use of loyalty oaths, which were made reliable by the threat of divine punishment for perjury.[102] Williams's position would have eliminated the use of the inhabitant's oath, because this was mainly for the non-freemen of the colony, a category largely consisting of non-church members, whom Williams would have classed unregenerate and therefore not appropriate candidates for an oath. It would have also jeopardized the colony's ability to secure truthful testimony in judicial proceedings, because unregenerate witnesses would, by William's lights, be forbidden to swear an oath of truthfulness.

The complaints Roger Williams lodged against the use of oaths paled in audacity beside one final claim, more pernicious in Puritan eyes than all the rest: that the civil magistrate's power extended only to the "bodies and goods, and outward state of men, etc."[103] Here lay the infectious corruption for which banishment was the only purgative. By so defining the scope of the civil magistrate's authority, Williams had deliberately excluded the spiritual affairs from civil superintendence, an exclusion that

Puritans in the Massachusetts Bay Colony found utterly at odds with their ideas of history and government. Describing the potential effect of Williams's contention more than half a century later, Cotton Mather maintained that it would have opened the door "unto a thousand *profanities*" and would have prevented authorities from seeing that the land did not become "such a *sink of abominations,* as would have been the *reproach and ruin of Christianity* in these parts of the world."[104]

For New England Puritans, the meaning of the American experience was "an exegetical, not a historical question."[105] Reading the Old Testament, they believed that they had entered into a covenant with God and had become a new nation of Israel. They were, or thought themselves to be, a people of God, recipients of divine favor so long as they fulfilled their covenantal obligations. Those obligations they found written in the Old Testament, especially in the descriptions of the nation of Israel and its moral (as opposed to ceremonial) laws. They gleaned from Old Testament accounts of Israel that the nation in covenant with God was responsible for seeing that all of God's commands, not just those relating to the "bodies and goods" of citizens, were obeyed. The Ten Commandments recorded in the book of Exodus, for example, contained two "tables" or sections. The first related to the covenant community's responsibilities toward God, and the second related to affairs of people with one another.[106] Among the commands of the first table were those prohibiting idolatry and blasphemy. The second table included the commandments against murder, adultery, and covetousness.[107] Puritans contended that God had commissioned government to enforce both tables. The Cambridge Platform, adopted by the leaders of Massachusetts churches in 1648 as a statement of belief, declared that "it is the duty of the magistrate, to take care of matters of religion, and to improve his civil authority for the observing of the duties commanded in the first, as well as for observing of duties commanded in the second table."[108] Williams, however, maintained that the civil government in Massachusetts had authority only to enforce the commands of the second table—which contained "the law of nature, the law moral and civil"—and had no legitimate power to enforce the obligations of the first.[109]

Cotton Mather later said of Williams that "there was a whole country in *America* like to be set on *fire* by the *rapid motion* of a *windmill,* in the head of one particular man."[110] Neither civil nor ecclesiastical leaders in New England were inclined to sit idly by while their City upon a Hill went up in smoke. They viewed Williams as a wild man and concluded that he ought to be caged.[111] The colony's church leaders petitioned civil authorities for permission to make an assay at bringing Williams back within the fold of orthodoxy before the civil sword was unsheathed, but they hammered against Williams's flintiness in vain.[112]

Although he may have given up further challenges to the patent, he persevered in his other claims.[113] Church leaders, called upon by the General Court for advice, suggested that if Williams continued in his obstinate error he should be removed from his leadership position in the church at Salem.[114] The General Court accordingly gave Williams time to ponder the matter and informed him that at the next session of the court he was "either to give satisfaction to the court, or else to expect the sentence."[115] Shortly thereafter, the General Court used its civil jurisdiction to further its exercise of spiritual jurisdiction in the Williams affair. The inhabitants of Salem had petitioned the court to secure certain lands they claimed were owned by the town. The General Court, however, denied the petition "because they had chosen Mr. Williams their teacher, while he stood under question of authority, and so offered contempt to the magistrates."[116] Williams countered this move by persuading the Salem church to join him in writing "letters of admonition" to the various churches in which the magistrates were members, urging the churches to admonish the magistrates for "their open transgression of the rule of justice."[117] The General Court, in turn, refused to receive the deputies to the court sent by Salem until a majority of the Salem freemen disavowed these letters.[118]

The Salem church's brief tenure of rebellion collapsed before the General Court's pressure, and Williams climaxed his Massachusetts sojourn with one final display of Separatist zeal.[119] According to John Cotton, he renounced communion with the Salem church for its failure to renounce communion with the other churches of the Bay Colony, which themselves refused to renounce communion with the parish churches of England. He stopped attending meetings of the Salem church and settled for preaching to his family at home.[120] The General Court had run out of patience, though, and in September 1635 entered the sentence of banishment against Williams.

Whereas Mr. Roger Williams, one of the elders of the church of Salem, has broached and divulged divers new and dangerous opinions, against the authority of magistrates, as also wrote letters of defamation, both of the magistrates and churches here, and that before any conviction, and yet maintains the same without retraction, it is therefore ordered, that the said Mr. Williams shall depart out of this jurisdiction within six weeks now next ensuing, which if he neglect to perform, it shall be lawful for the Governor and two of the magistrates to send him to some place out of this jurisdiction, not to return any more without licence from the Court.[121]

Shortly after the beginning of 1636, Williams, sentenced to the "dry pit of banishment," fled to the wilderness that became Rhode Island rather than be shipped forcibly back to England.[122] His exile from Massachusetts would last until the third decade of the twentieth century, when Massachusetts finally relented and expunged from its laws the sentence of banishment against Williams. House Bill Number 488, enacted in 1936, welcomed Williams back to the place he had been forced to leave. The bill stated simply, "Resolved, that the sentence of expulsion passed against Roger Williams by the General Court of Massachusetts Bay Colony in the year sixteen hundred and thirty-five be and hereby is revoked."[123]

Notes

1. I have restricted biographical details in the text to those that I think help illuminate Roger Williams's theory of religious liberty. For fuller biographical accounts, the best modern sources are Edwin S. Gaustad, *Liberty of Conscience: Roger Williams in America* (Grand Rapids: Eerdmans, 1991); Samuel Hugh Brockunier, *The Irrepressible Democrat: Roger Williams* (New York: Ronald Press, 1940); and Ola E. Winslow, *Master Roger Williams* (New York: Macmillan, 1957). For other biographical material, see Cyclone Covey, *The Gentle Radical: A Biography of Roger Williams* (New York: Macmillan, 1966); Emily Easton, *Roger Williams: Prophet and Pioneer* (Boston: Houghton, Mifflin, 1930); James Ernst, *Roger Williams: New England Firebrand* (New York: Macmillan, 1932); and John Garrett, *Roger Williams: Witness beyond Christendom, 1603-1683* (New York: Macmillan, 1970). I have modernized the spelling and capitalization of selections from the seventeenth and eighteenth centuries, except in titles. I have eliminated the overly copious italizations used by Williams, as well as the frequent "&c." with which he ended sentences and clauses. Finally, although I have left Williams's punctuation generally unchanged, I have added possessive apostrophes where appropriate.

2. John Winthrop, *The History of New England from 1630 to 1649*, 2 vols., ed. James Savage (Boston: Phelps and Farnham, 1825, repr. New York: Arno Press, 1972), 1:41-42.

3. Roger Williams to Lady Joan Barrington, ca. April 1629, in *The Correspondence of Roger Williams*, 2 vols., ed. Glen W. LaFantasie (Hanover: Brown University Press, 1988), 1:2. In the dating of Williams's correspondence, I have followed LaFantasie throughout.

4. Roger Williams, *The Hireling Ministry None of Christs*, in *The Complete Writings of Roger Williams*, 7 vols. (New York: Russell and Russell, 1963), 7:153.

5. W. Clark Gilpin, *The Millenarian Piety of Roger Williams* (Chicago: University of Chicago Press, 1979), 30-31.

6. John Cotton, *A Reply to Mr. Williams His Examination*, in *The Complete Writings of Roger Williams*, 7 vols. (New York: Russell and Russell, 1963), 2:14.

7. Roger Williams to John Cotton, 25 March 1671, in *The Correspondence of Roger Williams*, ed. LaFantasie, 2:630.

8. For general introductions to Separatism in colonial America, see Philip F. Gura, *A Glimpse of Zion's Glory: Puritan Radicalism in New England 1620-1660* (Middletown: Wesleyan University Press, 1984), 31-48; and Edmund Morgan, *Visible Saints: The History of a Puritan Idea* (Ithaca: Cornell University Press, 1963), 1-32. The roots of Separatism in England are explored in B. R. White, *The English Separatist Tradition: From the Marian Martyrs to the Pilgrim Fathers* (New York: Oxford University Press, 1971). For a comparison of Roger Williams's Separatist beliefs with those of other roughly contemporaneous Separatists, see Hugh Spurgin, *Roger Williams and Puritan Radicalism in the English Separatist Tradition* (Lewiston: Edwin Mellen Press, 1989).

9. 2 Corinthians 6:17 (KJV).

10. See, for example, Roger Williams, *The Bloudy Tenent, of Persecution*, in *The Complete Writings of Roger Williams*, 7 vols. (New York: Russell and Russell, 1963), 3:182.

11. Roger Williams, *A Key to the Language of America*, in *The Complete Writings of Roger Williams*, 7 vols. (New York: Russell and Russell, 1963), 1:141.

12. Roger Williams, *Queries of Highest Consideration*, in *The Complete Writings of Roger Williams*, 7 vols. (New York: Russell and Russell, 1963), 2:261-62.

13. Roger Williams, *Mr. Cottons Letter Lately Printed, Examined and Answered*, in *The Complete Writings of Roger Williams*, 7 vols. (New York: Russell and Russell, 1963), 1:350.

14. Williams, *The Bloudy Tenent, of Persecution*, 67.

15. See Winthrop, *History*, ed. Savage, 1:53, which notes Williams's refusal to join the Boston church "because they would not make a public declaration of their repentance for having communion with the churches of England, while they lived there."

16. John Cotton, Boston's imminent pastor and rhetorical opponent of Williams, admitted that the New England ministers did not forbid members of their congregations "to hear the word of God preached by godly ministers in the parish churches" when those members visited England. Cotton, *Reply to Mr. Williams*, 66.

17. Robert Browne, *A Treatise of Reformation without Tarrying for Anie, and of the Wickednesse of Those Preachers which will not Reforme till the Magistrate Commande or Compelle Them* (1582).

18. Roger Williams, *The Bloudy Tenent Yet More Bloudy*, in *The Complete Writings of Roger Williams*, 7 vols. (New York: Russell and Russell, 1963), 4:205.

19. John Winthrop described the incident in Winthrop, *History*, ed. Savage, 1:52-53. On the Separatist inclinations of the Salem church, see Morgan, *Visible Saints*, 80-87.

20. Winthrop, *History*, ed. Savage, 1:52-53.

21. LaFantasie, ed., *The Correspondence of Roger Williams*, 1:13 (editorial note).

22. William Bradford, *Of Plymouth Plantation*, ed. Samuel Eliot Morison (New York: Alfred A. Knopf, 1952), 257.

23. Samuel Brockunier suggested that Williams and the Plymouth colonists differed on the extent of their Separatism, Williams being the more aggressive sectarian. *Irrepressible Democrat*, 45.

24. Spurgin, *Roger Williams and Puritan Radicalism*, 25-26.

25. Williams, *Mr. Cottons Letter*, 325.

26. Winthrop, *History*, ed. Savage, 1:166, 170-71, 176.

27. The point is regularly made by Puritan commentators that Williams forced the Puritans "to recognize the full implications of their own thinking." Andrew Delbanco, *The Puritan Ordeal* (Cambridge: Harvard University Press, 1989), 167. See, for example, E. Brooks Holifield, *Era of Persuasion: American Thought and Culture, 1521-1680* (Boston: Twayne Publishers, 1984), 112; and Gilpin, *The Millenarian Piety of Roger Williams*, 51.

28. Williams, *Mr. Cottons Letter*, 393.

29. Ibid., 381.

30. David D. Hall, *Worlds of Wonder, Days of Judgment: Popular Religious Belief in Early New England* (New York: Alfred A. Knopf, 1989), 117-18.

31. Williams, *Mr. Cottons Letter*, 348-49.

32. Perry Miller, *Orthodoxy in Massachusetts, 1630-1650* (Cambridge: Harvard University Press, 1933), chs. 5-6. For the principal New England defenses of Congregationalism, see John Cotton, *The Way of the Congregational Churches Cleared* (London: Matthew Simons for John Bellamie, 1648, repr. in *John Cotton on the Churches of New England*, ed. Larzer Ziff [Cambridge: Harvard University Press, 1968]); Thomas Hooker, *A Survey of the Summe of Church-Discipline* (London: A. M. for John Bellamy, 1648, repr. New York: Arno Press, 1972).

33. John Cotton admitted to Williams that the New England churches had separated themselves from the "National Constitution" of the Anglican church, which consisted of national church leaders, synods, and ecclesiastical courts. *Reply to Mr. Williams*, 133. For a useful discussion of the New England struggle to achieve ecclesiastical purity short of formal separation from the Church of England, see David D. Hall, *The Faithful Shepherd: A History of the New England Ministry in the Seventeenth Century* (Chapel Hill: University of North Carolina Press, 1972), 72-86.

34. On Massachusetts Puritans' objections to Separatism, see especially Miller, *Orthodoxy in Massachusetts*.

35. Ibid., 83.

36. Winthrop, *History*, ed. Savage, 1:102-3.

37. Edmund Morgan, *Roger Williams: The Church and the State* (Boston: Little Brown, 1958), 25-26.

38. Williston Walker, ed., *The Creeds and Platforms of Congregationalism* (New York: Scribner's, 1892, repr. Philadelphia: Pilgrim Press, 1960), 229, 231. The Platform allowed separation of Bay Colony churches, acting collectively as a synod, from deviant congregations.

39. For an excellent discussion of this progression in Roger Williams's thought, see Gilpin, *The Millenarian Piety of Roger Williams*, 50-134.

40. Williams, *The Bloudy Tenent, of Persecution*, 184; Williams, *The Bloudy Tenent Yet More Bloudy*, 442.

41. Williams, *The Bloudy Tenent, of Persecution*, 174.

42. Cotton, *Reply to Mr. Williams*, 11.

43. See, for example, Mark DeWolfe Howe, *The Garden and the Wilderness*, 7; and Philip B. Kurland, "The Religion Clauses and the Burger Court," *Catholic University Law Review* 34 (1984): 1, 3.

44. On Williams's brief career as a Baptist, see Winthrop, *History*, ed. Savage, 1:293, 307. Samuel Brockunier provides a useful discussion of the reasons for Williams's separation from the Baptists in *Irrepressible Democrat*, 120-23.

45. Winthrop, *History*, ed. Savage, 1:293.

46. Williams, *The Hireling Ministry*, 160.

47. Williams, *The Bloudy Tenent, of Persecution*, 293-94.

48. Cotton, *Reply to Mr. Williams*, 20. John Winthrop suggested that Williams for a time refused communion with everyone but his wife, although he later "would preach to and pray with all comers." *History*, 1:307.

49. For the Puritans' "pragmatic compromise" and Williams's rejection of it, see Delbanco, *Puritan Ordeal*, 100. Brockunier attempted to resolve the irony of Puritan liberality and Williams's sectarianism by arguing that the conflict was between "the sectarian principle which tended toward a free church system and toleration and the ideal of one authoritarian church which included the whole society." Brockunier, *Irrepressible Democrat*, 43. Gilpin treats Williams's "contentious life" in Massachusetts as inconsistent with "the large-minded tolerance today popularly associated with his name." *The Millenarian Piety of Roger Williams*, 16. I think the more accurate understanding of Williams requires a frank acknowledgment of his tolerant dogmatism. This dogmatism was not inconsistent with the tolerance but rather the chief fount of it. Because Roger Williams was a profound Separatist, he was an advocate for complete liberty of the righteous to avoid polluting alliances with the unrighteous.

50. Williams, *The Bloudy Tenent, of Persecution*, 234.

51. Williams, *Mr. Cottons Letter*, 376.

52. Roger Williams, *Christenings Make Not Christians*, in *The Complete Writings of Roger Williams*, 7 vols. (New York: Russell and Russell, 1963), 7:32-33.

53. Williams, *The Bloudy Tenent, of Persecution*, 13.

54. Roger Williams to John Whipple, Jr., 8 July 1669, in *The Correspondence of Roger Williams*, ed. LaFantasie, 2:586.

55. When one of his long-time acquaintances became a Quaker and chastised Williams in a series of letters for his opposition to the Quakers, Williams mourned the bitterness of the chastisement but concluded that "the most High and only Wise will have it so, and your judgment and conscience (and mine) will have it so, yet that will not acquit us, we both say we must come to another bar, and there stand or fall eternally." Roger Williams to John Throckmorton, 30 July 1672, in *The Correspondence of Roger Williams*, ed. LaFantasie, 2:671.

56. Williams, *Queries of Highest Consideration*, 261. Williams acknowledged, however, that many individuals who were the captives of false ideas about the nature of the Church were nevertheless Christians: "yet far be it from any pious breast to imagine that they are not saved, and that their souls are not bound up in the bundle of eternal life." *The Bloudy Tenent, of Persecution*, 64.

57. Williams, *Key*, 85.

58. Ibid., 87.

59. Williams, *Queries of Highest Consideration*, 261.

60. Williams, *Mr. Cottons Letter*, 318.

61. William Lee Miller, *The First Liberty: Religion and the American Republic* (New York: Alfred A. Knopf, 1985), 155.

62. Williams, *The Bloudy Tenent Yet More Bloudy*, 118-19.

63. Williams, *Mr. Cottons Letter*, 342.

64. Cotton, *Reply to Mr. Williams*, 11-12. Hugh Spurgin's suggestion that Williams was a skeptic concerning truth mistakenly focuses on a single quotation from Williams's writings and misses the more prominent tenor of his thought. See *Roger Williams and Puritan Radicalism*, 41. Although there were aspects of Scripture that Williams thought were cloaked in mystery and thus should deter the arrogant use of the civil sword to punish supposed error, Williams was in the main quite confident in his own scriptural exegesis and the truths he uncovered from it.

65. Williams, *The Bloudy Tenent, of Persecution*, 59.

66. For a description of the event, see Winslow, *Master Roger Williams*, 272-80. For a useful summary of the issues covered in the debate, see David S. Lovejoy, "Roger Williams and George Fox: The Arrogance of Self-Righteousness," *William and Mary Quarterly*, 3d ser., 62 (1993): 199-225.

67. John Camp sees less a betrayal of principles, perhaps, than an increasing devotion to orthodoxy. "Though in his old age Williams found the strength to hunt with the orthodox hounds, in his even more vigorous youth he was far more inclined to run with the foxes." *Out of the Wilderness: The Emergence of an American Identity in Colonial New England* (Middletown: Wesleyan University Press, 1990), 133. This evaluation, though, fails to attend sufficiently the measure of theological difference between Williams and the Quakers and the consistency of vigorous debate over such difference with his general principles of religious liberty.

68. When another rhetorical opponent, John Cotton, complained that Williams had unfairly made public a private debate between them and thus deprived Cotton of liberty of conscience, Williams was puzzled: "I never heard that disputing, discoursing and examining men's tenents or doctrines by the word of God, was . . . persecution for conscience." Williams, *The Bloudy Tenent Yet More Bloudy*, 55-56. For the suggestion that Williams's argumentative contest with the Quakers was consistent with his principles of religious liberty, see Miller, *The First Liberty*, 193.

69. For the phenomenology of stain in religious experience, see Paul Ricoeur, *The Symbolism of Evil* (Boston: Beacon Press, 1967). Andrew Delbanco has explored the development in American thought, beginning with the Puritans, of the concept of evil as a positive essence rather than a deficiency of the good. Roger Williams, observes Delbanco, viewed evil as possessing a positive essence in the form of stain. Delbanco, *Puritan Ordeal*, 169.

70. Williams, *Key*, 212.

71. Ibid., 254.

72. Williams, *The Bloudy Tenent, of Persecution*, 253-54.

73. Ibid., 203, 234.

74. Jesper Rosenmeier went so far as to suggest that Roger Williams's dedication to "soul liberty" was not so much "a driving conviction about man's inherent right to freedom of worship as it is the consequence of a more deeply held belief in the necessity to keep his soul pure and free from contact with the world until the establishment of Christ's kingdom." Rosenmeier "The Teacher and the Witness: John Cotton and Roger Williams," *William and Mary Quarterly*, 3d ser., 25 (1968): 413. This overstates the matter, but it is certainly the case that Williams's Separatism enhanced, rather than impeded, his commitment to religious liberty.

75. For Williams's distinction between spiritual and civil fellowship, see Williams, *The Bloudy Tenent, of Persecution*, 117.

76. Ibid., 104.

77. Ibid.

78. Williams, *The Bloudy Tenent Yet More Bloudy*, 208.

79. On the relative scarcity of true believers, see Williams, *The Bloudy Tenent, of Persecution*, 245, 325; and Williams, *The Bloudy Tenent Yet More Bloudy*, 335.

80. Williams, *The Bloudy Tenent, of Persecution*, 95; Williams, *The Bloudy Tenent Yet More Bloudy*, 436-37.

81. Larzer Ziff, *Puritanism in America: New Culture in a New World* (New York: Viking Press, 1973), 100-102. Williams never convinced Massachusetts Puritans to abandon Nathaniel Ward's theorem that one who tolerates another's religion must inevitably doubt his own. But he labored strenuously to prove Ward mistaken. He challenged Ward's view by suggesting that the toleration of and endorsement of evil were separate matters: "It must be remembered, that it is one thing to command, to conceal, to counsel, to approve evil, and another thing to

permit and suffer evil with protestation against it, at least without approbation of it." Williams, *The Bloudy Tenent, of Persecution,* 165.

82. Roger Williams, *Experiments of Spiritual Life and Health, and Their Preservatives,* in *The Complete Writings of Roger Williams,* 7 vols. (New York: Russell and Russell, 1963), 7:48. On the church's "routed" state, see also Williams, *The Hireling Ministry,* 158.

83. Winthrop, *History,* ed. Savage, 1:53.

84. Ibid., 1:122.

85. Ibid.; Cotton, *Reply to Mr. Williams,* 46.

86. Winthrop, *History,* ed. Savage, 1:122-23.

87. Williams reproduced the charges, and acknowledged that the particulars were "rightly summed up," in *Mr. Cottons Letter,* 324-25.

88. Williams, *Key,* 180; Williams, *The Bloudy Tenent Yet More Bloudy,* 461-62.

89. Williams, *Mr. Cottons Letter,* 324-25.

90. Nathaniel B. Shurtleff, ed., *Records of the Governor and Company of the Massachusetts Bay in New England (1628-86),* 5 vols. (Boston: W. White, 1853-54), 1:408 (hereafter cited as *Mass. Records*).

91. John Winthrop, *Winthrop Papers,* 6 vols., ed. Allyn Bailey Forbes and Malcolm Frieberg (Boston: Massachusetts Historical Society, 1929-92), 2:140-41.

92. Cotton, *Reply to Mr. Williams,* 47.

93. *Mass. Records,* 1:115-16. A year later the General Court restated the oath requirement and extended its application to residents sixteen years of age and older. Ibid., 137.

94. Ibid., 1:115-16. The oath eventually added even more sacred severity to ensure truthfulness: "I . . . do here swear by the great and dreadful name of the ever-living God," the oath declared, and ended with the more emphatically Christian request, "So help me God in our Lord Jesus Christ." *The Laws and Liberties of Massachusetts* (Cambridge, 1648, repr. Cambridge: Harvard Unitersity Press, 1929), 56.

95. Williams, *The Bloudy Tenent, of Persecution,* 12, 138; Winthrop, *History,* ed. Savage, 1:158; Cotton, *Reply to Mr. Williams,* 47-48. On the religious grounds for Williams's opposition to the oath, see generally Gilpin, *The Millenarian Piety of Roger Williams,* 44-45. For an examination of the use of the oath in legal proceedings in another Puritan colony, see Marcus, " 'Due Execution of the General Rules of Righteousnesse': Criminal Procedure in New Haven Town and Colony, 1638-1658," in *Saints and Revolutionaries: Essays in Early American History,* ed. David D. Hall, John M. Murrin, and Thad W. Tate (New York: W. W. Norton, 1984), 112-14. For a discussion of Williams's views concerning the sinfulness of worship with the unconverted, see Morgan, *Roger Williams,* 31-33.

96. Cotton, *Reply to Mr. Williams,* 52.

97. Brockunier, *Irrepressible Democrat,* 152. For Williams's continued criticism of oath requirements, see *The Hireling Ministry,* 178, 188.

98. *Laws and Liberties,* 59.

99. Ibid.

100. Ibid.

101. Ibid., 43.

102. The Puritans were not alone, of course, in believing that loyalty oaths were critical threads in the social fabric. John Locke, for example, denied religious liberty to atheists for the very reason that they could not be expected to be bound by oaths, which, Locke said, were the "bounds of human society." John Locke, "A Letter Concerning Toleration," in *John Locke: On Politics and Education*, ed. Howard R. Penniman (Toronto: D. Van Nostrand, 1947), 58. Loyalty oaths were ultimately enshrined in the Constitution itself. Sanford Levinson, *Constitutional Faith* (Princeton: Princeton University Press, 1988), 90-121.

103. Williams, *Mr. Cottons Letter*, 325.

104. Cotton Mather, *Magnalia Christi Americana* (London, 1702, repr. New York: Arno Press, 1972), 430.

105. Sacvan Bercovitch, *The Puritan Origins of the American Self* (New Haven: Yale University Press, 1975), 99.

106. Exodus 20:1-11, 12-17.

107. The "two tables" have been arranged and numbered differently within various Jewish and Christian traditions. Harold Berman and John Witte, "The Transformation of Western Legal Philosophy in Lutheran Germany," *Southern California Law Review* 62 (1989): 1619n114.

108. The Cambridge Platform (1648), reprinted in *The Creeds and Platforms of Congregationalism*, ed. Williston Walker (New York: Scribner's, 1892, repr. Philadelphia: Pilgrim Press, 1960), 236. For a brief description of the Cambridge Synod and the platform adopted at the synod, see Sidney Ahlstrom, *A Religious History of the American People* (New Haven: Yale University Press, 1972), 155-56. On the magistrates' power to enforce both tables, see also Thomas Cobbet, *The Civil Magistrates Power in Matters of Religion* (London: W. Wilson, 1653, repr. New York: Arno Press, 1972), 54.

109. Williams, *The Bloudy Tenent, of Persecution*, 358, 355; Williams, *The Bloudy Tenent Yet More Bloudy*, 144, 263.

110. Mather, *Magnalia*, 430.

111. On the general view of Williams as "divinely mad," as Cotton Mather denominated him, see John Camp, *Out of the Wilderness: The Emergence of an American Identity in Colonial New England* (Middletown: Wesleyan University Press, 1990), 126-27.

112. Cotton, *Reply to Mr. Williams*, 62.

113. Brockunier, *Irrepressible Democrat*, 57-58.

114. Winthrop, *History*, ed. Savage, 1:163.

115. Ibid.

116. Ibid., 164.

117. Cotton, *Reply to Mr. Williams*, 50.

118. *Mass. Records*, 1:158 (3 Sept. 1635).

119. According to Williams, most church members were "swayed and bowed (whether for fear of persecution or otherwise) to say and practice what to my knowledge, with signs and groans many of them mourned under." *Mr. Cottons Letter,* 321.

120. Cotton, *Reply to Mr. Williams,* 50-51. John Winthrop timed this final separation as having occurred in the wake of the General Court's pronouncement of the sentence of banishment against Williams. Winthrop, *History,* ed. Savage, 1:170-71.

121. *Mass. Records,* 1:160-61.

122. Roger Williams to John Cotton, Jr., March 1671, in *The Correspondence of Roger Williams,* ed. LaFantasie, 2:629. On Roger Williams's frequent allusion to the harshness of his banishment, Perry Miller observed that no other New England writer "who also endured great hardships so loves to expatiate on them." Miller, *Roger Williams,* 52. For examples of Williams's complaints concerning his banishment, see Williams, *Mr. Cottons Letter,* 315, 319, 337, 338, 340, 371.

123. Edwin Powers, *Crime and Punishment in Early Massachusetts, 1620-1692* (Boston: Beacon Press, 1966), 119.

The Premises of Religious Establishment in the Massachusetts Bay Colony

Religious persecution is a creature of logic as much as passion and inhabits the realm of ideas as comfortably as the domain of feeling. The zeal that harries an unbeliever with scourge and banishment is rooted in a syllogism of premises and deductions. Although raw animosity and fear may charge this syllogism with special fervor, its logic can thrive as well in the cool light of reason. So long as its premises are reckoned true and its deductions agreed valid, persecution remains a real social possibility.

Beginning in the 1630s and continuing well past the middle of the seventeenth century, governing authorities of the Massachusetts Bay Colony regularly exercised civil power to punish religious dissenters. Roger Williams was neither the first nor the last to feel the sting of Puritan orthodoxy wielded by the colony's governing arm, although he would pronounce the most sustained judgments upon Massachusetts for its devotion to what he termed "the bloudy tenet of persecution, for cause of conscience." For his religious and political heresies, he was banished from the colony and fled to the wilds of Narragansett Bay in what is now Rhode Island. There were other temporal punishments meted out for offenses against ecclesiastical orthodoxy. In 1631, for example, Philip Ratcliff earned a whipping, a fine, and—after having his ears cut off—banishment for uttering "scandalous speeches" against the government and church at Salem.[1] Three decades later, Quakers anxious to illuminate Massachusetts Bay Colony with their inner light received similar treatment.

After initial attempts to warn the Quakers away from the colony failed, Massachusetts authorities turned for aid to the deterring power of physical mutilation and revived the practice of cropping the ears of

incorrigible religious dissidents who would not stay out of Massachusetts. A 1657 statute made Quaker men who returned to the colony after banishment subject to losing an ear. For a second offense the statute
prescribed loss of the other ear, and Quaker males who made a third
attempt to enter the colony after banishment were to have their tongues
bored with a hot iron. The Puritans of Massachusetts Bay seemed to
have quickly perceived, however, that even these punishments were not
likely to blunt the Quakers' persistence. After 1658, Massachusetts authorities abandoned physical mutilation for the more certain sentence
of death for Quakers who reentered the colony after banishment. Even
this threat did not deter the Quakers, however, and in 1659 and 1660
the Puritans executed three men and a woman on the Boston Common for defying their sentence of banishment.[2]

Williams's banishment, the Quaker executions of the mid-seventeenth
century, and scores of other civil punishments meted out against religious
dissenters during the colony's first half-century represented the successful implementation of considered principle rather than mere aberrations
of momentary hysteria. Social premises had formed the basis of social deductions, and from these flowed—especially in the case of four Quakers—sober conclusions.[3] The logic of these events manifested itself not
only in particular instances of civil punishments meted out against religious dissenters but also in a complex web of relations between civil and
ecclesiastical authority.

Puritans who planted themselves in Massachusetts self-consciously set
about to order both their civil and spiritual institutions in a manner consistent with a profoundly religious view of social relations. They could not
jettison the entire structure of social practices that had ordered their pre-
Massachusetts lives, however, and thus they anchored the colony's life and
laws to an intricate array of practices transported from England.[4] Nevertheless, the Puritans of Massachusetts Bay deliberately pondered the making of—and took concrete steps to establish—a "due form of government,
both civil and ecclesiastical" in which abstract theological principles took
on the garb of legal and political reality.[5] The secular became servant to
the sacred. The eminent church teacher of Boston, John Cotton, insisted
that Puritans were just getting their priorities straight. "No man," he
wrote to Lord Say and Seale in 1636, "fashions his house to his hangings,
but his hangings to his house. It is better that the commonwealth be fash-
ioned to the setting forth of God's house, which is his church: than to accommodate the church frame to the civil state."[6] Because the Puritans set
out to build a house in which the church occupied the master suite, they

made sure that its accommodations were comfortable and that its gardens
were keep free of weeds.

For all his long and obstreperous career as Massachusetts critic, Roger
Williams challenged the establishment premises of the New England Puritans. He waged war with the ideas that mutilated Phillip Ratcliff's ears
and that noosed the necks of the Quakers executed on the Boston Common. He noisily dissected the Puritans' social syllogism and declared it
invalid. In this chapter and the next, I examine the attempts by New
England Puritans to defend, and by Roger Williams to refute, the establishment syllogism that joined Massachusetts church and state in an elaborate partnership.

Those who believe that the relation between religion and civil government ought to be ruled by simple metaphors such as the wall of separation may find the debate between Williams and the Massachusetts
Puritans tedious. Nevertheless, both sides in this rhetorical battle viewed
the issues in terms more complicated than a single metaphor could ever
capture. They wrestled with the political relevance of the Bible, a sacred
text in which they and their contemporaries shared common reverence,
and they argued about the extent to which an individual's religious beliefs might have consequences for the body politic that would justify
government superintendence of those beliefs. For these issues, and others like them, no single metaphor or concept seemed adequate to either
the Puritans or Roger Williams. Their debate ranged across a multitude
of scripture passages, learned quotations, historical observations, and
sociological deductions. Although Williams did not convince the Puritans of his day to repudiate their attempt to construct a holy commonwealth, the ideas he helped plant in the soil of the New World ultimately
germinated and by steady growth cracked the foundations of the religious establishments that originally dominated the colonies. These
eventually toppled not so much because Americans suddenly became
convinced in Jefferson's wall of separation but because they gradually
came to repudiate at least some of the premises that had supported the
Puritans' establishment syllogism.

I begin by considering the premises of the Puritan establishment.
The account that follows, by focusing on the theocratic visions of leading colonists such as John Winthrop and John Cotton, risks creating
the impression that the colony was dominated by a single, monolithic
ideology.[7] In fact, modern colonial scholars have repeatedly emphasized
the heterogeneity of New England society, a fact exhibited chiefly by

the complex web of motives that fired the great migration to the New World, the possibilities of material advancement that encouraged individualism, distinct differences among various New England towns, and the religious differences that Puritan orthodoxy never quite muzzled.[8] Leaders such as Winthrop cannot always, or perhaps even frequently, be said to represent a consensus of the colonists' views.[9] Nevertheless, they remain the principal source for understanding the social logic that engineered the punishment of religious dissent during the first four decades of the Massachusetts Bay Colony's existence. Moreover, these leaders were the principle adversaries in Williams's long controversy with New England, and their arguments structured his attempt to articulate a new relationship between the civil magistrate and religion.

A Certain Guide

A fundamental premise of New England social logic was that God had spoken, that his words could be understood, and that the substance of his speaking was relevant to the governance of human affairs. God had spoken, the Puritans believed, chiefly in the Bible. It was therefore inevitable—in fact, it was reasonable—that New England Puritans, like their English contemporaries, should look to the Bible as a source of law.[10]

The incorporation of scriptural precepts into colonial law was not simply the work of elite theocrats who drummed an unbelieving populace with biblical texts. New England clergy and laity participated jointly in a scripturally saturated community of discourse that found in the Bible a host of metaphors, exemplars, and principles available to address the issues encountered in their lives.[11] No atheists were about to threaten this consensus, and, during the early colonial days, Massachusetts had no non-Christian presence to speak of.[12] Thus, the Puritans possessed a sacred text whose authority was universally recognized within the colony. Why should they not rely upon the Bible to find at least some of the answers needed to resolve the problems of their common lives? Of course, they had to interpret the Bible, but the fact that they might disagree over interpretive issues did not seem to them fatal to their enterprise. A first principle does not forfeit its communal authority simply because reasonable members of the community may differ over its application. Every principle, whether or not scripturally rooted, must be situated in specific contexts, and the work of situating principles will inevitably create its own contests. Massachusetts Puritans were familiar with these, but contests over particular interpretations occurred within a community of discourse at home with the language of Scripture.

Eventually, the accessibility of Scripture to all New Englanders would itself subvert the Puritans' dream of brotherly commonwealth and justify John Dryden's dismay: "The book thus put in every vulgar hand, / Which each presumed he best could understand, / The common rule was made the common prey / And at the mercy of the rabble lay."[13] The rabble did not always find in the Bible the same treasures as their spiritual leaders, and, having located different veins for prospecting, they showed no hesitation about departing from the claims staked out by those leaders.[14] Moreover, New England Puritans would ultimately be required to address the appropriate civil sanctions to be levied on those who threatened their scriptural foundation by denying the infallibility of or otherwise impugning the Bible.[15] But for a time, at least, Scripture yielded more grounds for agreement than otherwise, and when Puritans encountered occasional miscreants who saw in the glass of Scripture a different reflection, they could marshal sufficient consensus among the faithful to drive these deviants away or at least persuade them to keep silent.

Massachusetts Puritans looked to the Bible as a source of law primarily because they believed its prescriptions to be relevant to their circumstances. They would have rejected as rank nonsense what strikes the modern ear as a incontestable axiom of reality: that religious belief is a purely private affair. They embraced, in contrast, a settled conviction that "the obligations of piety knew no bounds"—that is, that obligations of obedience to divine will extended across the range of human experience, both public and private.[16] The Almighty was sovereign over all of life and had shown himself to be a public God rather than a merely private icon. Puritans saw the God of the Old Testament as one who strode across the face of history, choosing Israel to be his chosen people and schooling that people in how to conduct themselves, both with one another and with other nations. The God of the New Testament instructed the church in obligations that were clearly social in nature: of husbands to wives, children to parents, masters and slaves to one another, and believers to unbelievers. What, the Puritans would have asked, is private in all of this? Holy Writ, they believed, was imminently relevant to the circumstances of public life.

The Puritans found in the scriptural texts not only intelligibility and relevance but also a basis for certainty.[17] Because they were certain about both the fundamental tenets of their faith and the social prescriptions it enjoined, they were poor candidates to accept a notion of toleration based on religious doubt. Nathaniel Ward, an English lawyer turned New England minister, summed up the commonly perceived connection between toleration and doubt: "He that is willing to tolerate any religion, or discrepant way of religion, besides his own, unless it be in matters merely indifferent, either doubts of his own, or is not sincere in it."[18] Massachusetts Puritans believed themselves to be in possession of the truth and would have had little use for Justice Oliver Wendell Holmes's suggestion that truth can be best discovered in a "marketplace of ideas."[19] The cacophony of liberalism lay muffled in a future where the consensus possessed briefly by the New England commonwealths had collapsed. One need not shop for goods already in one's bag, and Puritans saw themselves emphatically as possessors rather than seekers. In this, they mirrored their age. Such religious liberty as was grudgingly granted by Massachusetts and the other American colonies over the next century and a half would be wrested from the grasp of believing certainty rather than skeptical doubt.

The Puritans' reliance on Scripture as bearing the intelligible word of God eventually came to be supplemented by a conviction that God had spoken directly to them. John Winthrop argued that the Puritans' safe passage across the Atlantic demonstrated that God had agreed to enter into a covenant with them like the one he had entered into with Israel.[20] Although Winthrop's vision of the Massachusetts colony as a successor to the nation of Israel may not have been widely shared at first, as the seventeenth century progressed New Englanders seem to have been drawn increasingly to a comparison of their lives with those of the Israelites.[21] Having made this identification, they naturally looked to the covenant obligations of the Old Testament for principles relevant for discerning their social obligations to the Almighty. Thus, Winthrop declared that "the officers of this body politic have a rule to walk by, in all their administrations, which rule is the *Word of God,* and such conclusions and deductions, as are, or shall be regularly drawn from thence."[22]

The alliance of church and state in Puritan New England came to rely increasingly on a view of history that saw colonists as at the center of God's penultimate activity in sacred history. In fact, they would not have recognized a distinction between sacred and secular history. There was only one history, governed by the Almighty and proceeding according to his purpose.[23] New England Puritans came to see themselves as being in the forefront of that history and that purpose. A sense of spiritual

destiny would ultimately sustain their dogged persistence in perpetuat-
ing the "City upon a Hill." When England after the middle of the seventeenth century moved in the direction of greater religious toleration,
New England saw no need to copy that example. Had God not chosen
New England to be a new Zion? Why, then, should it attend to the patterns of those whom sacred history had left behind in its irresistible
plunge forward?[24]

Although New England Puritans were more literal in their appeals to
Scripture as a basis for social obligations than non-Puritans and perhaps
more optimistic about the prospects of enforcing a biblically rooted system of moral precepts, even they did not simply copy the laws contained
in the Pentateuch into Massachusetts statute books.[25] They viewed biblical history as relevant precedent for contemporary practice but perused
the sacred register with a selective eye, believing that many biblical examples had lost their exemplary force in the wake of Christ's coming.[26]
Puritans lifted some laws almost verbatim from Old Testament texts, but
these instances occupied a relatively small portion of the overall body of
positive law in the Massachusetts Bay Colony.[27] Magistrates such as
John Winthrop tended to treat Scripture primarily as a source of first
principles from which legal deductions could be made that took into
account the concrete particularity of New England circumstances. The
"matter of the scripture," Winthrop declared, was "always a rule to us,
yet not the phrase."[28]

The "matter" of the Scripture possessed a generative essence suitable
for application to future cases. The *Laws and Liberties,* a collection of
Massachusetts law adopted in 1648, was prefaced with an acknowledgment of this kind of scriptural deduction: "So soon as God had set up
political government among his people Israel he gave them a body of
laws for judgment both in civil and criminal causes. These were brief
and fundamental principles, yet withal so full and comprehensive as
out of them clear deductions were to be drawn to all particular cases
in future times."[29] Similarly, when on one occasion Winthrop responded
to charges that he and the other magistrates dispensed justice too arbitrarily, he reminded Massachusetts inhabitants of their obligations
under the social covenant made explicit by an oath of allegiance: "The
covenant between you and us is the oath you have taken of us . . . that
we shall govern you and judge your causes *by the rules of God's laws and
our own.*"[30] The laws Winthrop referred to as "our own" no doubt included those deduced from biblical principles but not explicitly set
forth in the scriptural text. He and the other magistrates saw no reason

not to fashion laws appropriate to the New England condition, even when these laws found no precise parallel in the "matter" of Scripture. Thus, they felt free to borrow from the extensive body of English civil and ecclesiastical law so long as these borrowings did not actually conflict with Scripture.[31]

The sacred history in which Massachusetts Puritans saw themselves as participants was neither static nor cyclical but linear. They saw in the biblical texts evidence of a progressive unfolding of divine will.[32] The theocratic history of Israel in the Old Testament was not for them a rigid mold out of which the present was to be framed, but one point along a continuous unfolding of God's superintendence of history, history that would climax in the establishment of his visible kingdom.[33] These times, Winthrop observed, "have the advantage of all that have gone before us in experience and observation."[34] John Cotton could also refer to Mosaic law as "primitive" and could speak of the task of translating these laws for contemporary use in terms of making such "explications" and "applications" of them that were suitable according to "necessary consequence" or "just proportion."[35] Thus, not all God's commands at a specific time were applicable to other times. Nevertheless, Puritans believed that God's character was unchanging and that he had stamped the world with a moral order that reflected his immutable character. Accordingly, they read the Scripture to include both descriptions of segments of sacred history not necessarily pertinent to their own condition in the New World and prescriptions relating to immutable principles of morality and human conduct. Looking beneath the positive law of scriptural prescriptions such as those contained in the Decalogue, Puritans found a "moral equity." What God had spoken by command in the pages of Leviticus and Deuteronomy, he had also spoken in the breast of each human heart.[36]

Covenanted and Closed Communities

Massachusetts Puritans, like so many immigrants to the New World who would follow, crossed the North Atlantic in pursuit of liberty. But the liberty they sought was instrumental rather than substantive, liberty for something quite specific rather than simply liberty for various individuals to pursue private visions of the good.[37] New England Puritans sought liberty to create a holy commonwealth, and those who partook of their vision could be partakers of the same liberty. But the only freedom guaranteed by the Puritans to religious dissenters was, as Nathaniel Ward put it succinctly, the freedom "to keep away from us."[38] By ignoring this generous liberty to stay away from the Massachusetts Bay Colony, spiritual deviants such as Baptists risked fines, whippings, and imprisonments. Quakers, far more radical in the eyes of Puritans, risked ear croppings or death. When accused of persecuting religious dissenters, Puritans turned for their defense to the ideas of contract and consent, ideas that formed a second critical premise of their establishment logic.

Puritans of Massachusetts Bay organized the major facets of their social life—colony, town, and church—on a plane that was at least formally consensual.[39] The colony's inhabitants, whether freemen or not, swore an oath of allegiance to this common vision.[40] Those not inclined to bind themselves to the vision were free to find some other place of habitation. Both towns such as Dedham and churches organized themselves around similar covenants.[41] The church at Salem, the first in the colony to gather itself as a community of visible saints, erected its spiritual edifice on mutual promises made by its members "in the presence of God, to walk together in all his ways."[42] Agreements to uphold a common orthodoxy thus supported the colony at every level, and Puritans took the not outrageous position that a repudiation of these agreements by religious dissenters justified covenanting communities—whether colony, town, or church—in excluding the dissenters from continued association. In the case of churches, exclusion took the form of excommunication. In the case of the colony or towns, exclusion entailed physical banishment.

Within its first decade the Massachusetts Bay Colony had recognized that communal freedom to pursue a holy vision required some restraint on the migration of inhabitants into the colony. Arrivals required screening if this vision was to triumph, and in 1637 the General Court ordered that "no town or person shall receive any stranger" or "allow any lot or habitation to any, or entertain any such above three weeks, except such person shall have allowance under the hands of some one of the counsel, or of two other of the magistrates."[43] Once an individual had gained admission to the civil community or, in far rarer circumstances, to one of the Bay Colony's churches, the problem of how to preserve the holy commonwealth in the face of deviation became more problematic.

The sanctions levied by both church and state against deviance were rooted in a perception of the intimate relatedness of the various members of these communities. For example, the Cambridge Platform of 1648 discussed the sanctions available to churches to deal with wrongdoers, and these sanctions focused overwhelmingly on restoring and preserving the health of particular relational structures.

> The censures of the church, are appointed by Christ, for the preventing, removing, and healing of offenses in the Church: for the reclaiming and gaining of offending brethren; for the deterring others from the like offences: for purging out the leaven which may infect the whole lump: for vindicating the honor of Christ, and of his church, and the holy profession of the gospel: and for preventing the wrath of God, that may justly fall upon the church, if they should suffer his covenant, and the seals thereof, to be profaned by notorious and obstinate offenders.[44]

Four uses of ecclesiastical censure are suggested here: deterrence, reformation, exclusion, and vindication. These uses have their parallel in correlative civil punishments. Deterrence, of course, is a familiar aim of penal systems. The Puritans, both through civil and church censures, sought to deter the occurrences of inappropriate conduct. Here, though, as elsewhere in the Puritan morphology of punishment, the evil sought to be deterred was a relational one: "offenses in the Church." But more important than the value of church and civil censures to deter wrongdoing was their value in restoring the wrongdoer to fellowship within the community, whether a particular church or the civil commonwealth. With respect to religious deviance, Puritans in general emphasized the reformative aspects of punishment, reformation of an individual not simply in the sense of restoring the inclination to act appropriately but as a member of the holy commonwealth.[45] This emphasis occurred in the civil as well as the spiritual context. Social sanctions generally endeavored to rescue deviant souls and restore them to the bosom of the community.

Occasionally, efforts at censure were ineffective to accomplish healthy restoration. In these cases, both civil and spiritual communities exercised power to exclude particular wrongdoers from social intercourse. Puritans could argue that in inflicting the sentence of banishment on religious dissenters they were exercising their right to associate only with those who voluntarily submitted to a common vision concerning the colony. Although dissenters such as Roger Williams might complain of the hardships that banishment visited upon them, Puritans could with some reasonableness respond that Williams and his ilk could erect their civil visions in plenty of other places. John Cotton, for example, responded to Williams's complaints about forced exile by questioning whether banishment was even punishment: "Banishment is a lawful, and just punishment: if it be in proper speech a punishment at all in such a country as this is, where the jurisdiction (whence a man is banished) is but small, and the country round about it, large, and fruitful: where a man may make his choice of a variety of more pleasant, and profitable seats, than he leaves behind him. In which respect, banishment in this country, is not counted so much a confinement, as an enlargement, where a man does not so much loose civil comforts, as change them."[46]

Public Consequences of Spiritual Error

Massachusetts authorities justified their exercise of jurisdiction over matters pertaining to religion by emphasizing the public consequences of spiritual error and dissent. The Puritans recognized a distinction between that which was public—therefore subject to legal and ecclesiastical censure—and that which was private. But they envisioned the public domain to occupy a relatively spacious territory bounded by extensive cords of community. They dwelt within a cognitive universe that perceived elaborate chains of relatedness joining individuals to the community in which they were situated and joining the community to God. They viewed the community as having intrinsic value and thus as a suitable object for protection by civil and ecclesiastical authorities. It was not simply a harbor for the pursuit of individual visions of the good; it was the good that Puritans had already overwhelmingly chosen. The bonds of community were not necessary evils but positive values in their own right.

The chief public consequence of religious dissent for New England Puritans was its disruption of this peace. Certainly, John Cotton argued, the civil government acted within its proper sphere when it took steps to preserve or restore the public peace.[47] And Massachusetts authorities had every reason to believe that political stability and civil order were blessings that did not drop from heaven like the gentle rain but had to be fought for continually. They did not trust men and women to live peaceably together without stern supervision from civil authority. In fact, a strong dose of sensitivity to humanity's inherent sinfulness bred pessimism about the prospect of spontaneous civil order rather than the more optimistic mood that would guide fledgling liberals a century and a half later.[48] They, like almost all of their contemporaries of whatever political stripe, accepted as an incontestable axiom the necessity of religious uniformity as a basis of political stability.[49] Just as the state had an interest in moderating the disputes of corporate shareholders, for example, because these disputes could easily spill over into the wider commonwealth, it had an interest in supervising the disputes in which churches might find themselves embroiled.[50] That was especially so when one of the parties to the dispute urged a particular viewpoint in an "arrogant and impetuous way."[51] Governing authorities of the Massachusetts Bay Colony thus made it their business to secure civil peace by securing ecclesiastical peace, and in this business they were largely successful.[52]

Massachusetts Puritans saw public concerns in religious error beyond those relating to civil peace, however. Religious error also adorned itself with public consequences when a dissenter "infected" others with false doctrine. Cotton argued that quarantine was the appropriate response to infectious spiritual error: "If they be infectious, and leprous, and have plague sores running upon them, and think it their glory to infect others; It is no want of mercy, and charity, to set such at a distance: It is a merciless mercy, to pity such as are incurably contagious, and mischievous, and not to pity many scores or hundreds of the souls of such, as well be infected and destroyed by the toleration of the other."[53] Similarly, Puritans likened those who propagated erroneous religious views not only to a contagion but also to thieves and murderers who stole the purity of true believers and seduced them to follow the way of spiritual death. For such spiritual criminals, Cotton asserted that "moral equity," a kind of spiritual "eye for an eye," or *lex talionis,* demanded that the life of the soul-stealer and the soul-killer be forfeited.[54] "When therefore the corruption, or destruction of souls, is a destruction also of lives, liberties, estates of men, *lex talionis* calls for, not only soul for soul, but life for life."[55] Massachusetts Puritans drew short, however, of enforcing this law of the soul-killer except in the case of four Quakers who refused to stay out of the colony after they were banished. Their more common approach to steadfast religious error was either to discourage its proliferation through the use of fines or to treat it as a contagion and banish it "into solitary tabernacles," for example, the wilds of Narragansett Bay where such notorious dissenters as Roger Williams and Anne Hutchinson ultimately fled.[56]

The toleration of notorious wickedness, including notorious heresy, also created the possibility that not only the evildoer but also those who tolerated the evil would suffer God's judgment. New England Puritans found frequent evidence that God did not necessarily reserve righteous judgments until the world's end. So far as they could see, he visited evildoers with stern doses of present wrath. Heretical women bore deformed children or were killed by Indians.[57] Lewd men drowned.[58] Scoffers suffered death in fiery explosions.[59] The sting of a wasp might chastise those recalcitrant in worship.[60] It required no immense step for Massachusetts Puritans to see the divine hand of judgment poised over the community when it harbored wickedness. Portents of God's judgment were ever close at hand. A drought could prompt New Englanders to consider "such things as were amiss, which might provoke God against us."[61] The colony's civil leaders sometimes found "cause to fear least our sins may provoke the Lord to lay more heavy corrections upon us."[62]

Men such as John Winthrop were alert to turn aside God's wrath from the New England community; it was partially to avoid the anticipated rain of that wrath upon England that he and others had fled to the New World.[63] New England preachers regularly roused the faithful to a holy watchfulness over civil affairs lest the City upon a Hill become a lightning rod for divine blasts of punishment and suffer "an inundation of ruinating judgments."[64] Churches, of course, would be held accountable by God for wickedness winked at.[65] But the state as well would be judged for tolerating religious error: "For if the Church and people of God, fall away from God, God will visit the city and country with public calamity, if not captivity for the churches' sake."[66] Wickedness polluted the land with spiritual stain, and God, the Puritans believed, punished the nation that tolerated such stain. Accordingly, they invested the law with a fundamental role in cleansing the land. In this role, the law need not always administer punishments simply to exact retribution or effect deterrence against like-minded wrongdoers. For example, the rite of confession played an important part in the judicial mechanism for dealing with deviance. Notorious sinners sometimes escaped punishment, or received diminished punishments, when they confessed wrongdoing.[67] Exposure of sin—through confession—rid the land of its stain as though the very act of acknowledging publicly a wicked deed then blanketed that deed under the righteous judgment of God acknowledged by the community.[68]

New England Puritans found a further reason to justify civil oversight of religious matters by pointing to spiritual "liberties" comparable to civil liberties. John Cotton observed that magistrates were justified in preserving each individual's civil liberties. The protection of such liberties was part of the recognized responsibility of government. Magistrates, he maintained, were also justified in defending spiritual rights and liberties. Purity of doctrine, worship, and church government he found to be "righteous privileges of the churches" and therefore entitled to protection by the civil magistrate.[69] The New England preacher Thomas Cobbet similarly portrayed the orthodox faithful as innocent victims of marauding religious heretics and entitled to civil protection. Disturbers of spiritual rights included those

> such as by open violence combine together to hinder the godly from meeting together publicly or privately to worship the Lord according to his mind, or such as profanely rise up in their assemblies or families, and openly disturb them in that worship, or interrupting them by unseemly and inconvenient gestures; talking, shouting, singing or the like; or such as openly revile them, rail upon them, or at least rashly censure and condemn them, and openly protest against them, and the worship and ways of God held forth and practiced by them, and by the rest of the assemblies and families of the saints among them, or take any other ways, undermining and striking at them quiet and peaceable living in all godliness or honesty.[70]

The Puritans' focus on the public consequences of religious error rather than on the innate perniciousness of that error resulted in their generally leaving religious error undisturbed so long as it kept its head low. They launched no inquisition to ferret out heresy from its hiding places in the hearts of Massachusetts inhabitants. Puritans, John Cotton said, had learned the virtue of meekness, which required them to "suffer one another in differences of weakness."[71] The weight of civil authority only came to bear upon deviations from orthodoxy when those deviations took a public form, as, for example, when heresy compounded its wickedness with "blasphemy, or idolatry, or seducement of others to . . . heretical pernicious ways."[72] Even at that point, the state was not entitled to proceed immediately to punish religious error. To do so would have been persecution for the cause of conscience. Only after a dissenter had been "convinced"—presented with arguments the authorities deemed convincing—of his erroneous ways and had openly persisted in them was the state free to discipline the error. At that point, "weakness" proved itself to be "wilfulness" and deserved punishment because it would not "suffer truth to live in peace."[73] "We approve no persecution for conscience," Cotton declared, "neither conscience rightly informed . . . nor conscience misinformed with error: unless the error be pernicious, and unless the conscience be convinced of the error and perniciousness thereof, that so it may appear, the erroneous party suffers, not for his conscience, but for his sinning against his conscience."[74]

Church and State: Distinct but Compact

No one much remembers the Puritans of the Massachusetts Bay Colony as exemplars of religious tolerance. The banishments of Roger Williams and Anne Hutchinson, and especially the hanging of the four Quakers on the Boston Common, did much to sully the Puritans' record on rights of conscience. But to agree with Gary Wills that the only real invention of the American political experience was disestablishment is also to admit that the first sputtering coughs of that invention were heard in Massachusetts.[75] The social order the Puritans of New England created would not have satisfied Jefferson or Madison to be sure. But they made an important beginning by sowing the seeds of disestablishment with their notion that church and state were distinct.

New England Puritans, who would have rejected out of hand any assertion that church and state ought to be kept separate by anything like a "high and impregnable wall," believed that the two were at least distinct.[76] Although they viewed the destinies of ecclesiastical and civil power as linked in the sovereign plan of God, they insisted that these two spheres of power held separate offices and exercised "distinct and due administrations."[77] They desired to assure that the boundaries between church and state were maintained free from erosion "either by giving the spiritual power which is proper to the church into the hand of the civil magistrate . . . or by giving civil power to church officers, who are called to attend to spiritual matters and the things of God."[78] Their aim was to fashion a relationship between the spheres of temporal and church authority that "may be close and compact, and co-ordinate to one another, and yet not confounded," in which church and state were "distinct, yet agreeing and helping the one to the other."[79] The lawyer Thomas Lechford described the appropriate balance as requiring "a just and equal correspondence in jurisdictions, not to intrench one on the other."[80] The Puritans thus saw church and state as separate entities whose existences were nevertheless inextricably intertwined. Church and state were, according to common understanding, "like Hippocrates twins, they are born together, grow up together, weep together, sicken and die together."[81]

For modern observers accustomed to classifying the Puritans as stern theocrats, their constant assertion of the importance of the distinction between civil and ecclesiastical authority is baffling. But Puritan assertions on this point were rooted in their understandings of the Reformation itself. The general Protestant explanation for why civil governments need not accede to the wishes of the Roman Church was that God had ordained both the church and the state, and each operated on the basis of a separate grant of divine authority.[82] Puritans could not help seeing that the Reformation might well have been stillborn had there not been civil governments capable of withstanding the commanding influence of the papacy.[83] As heirs of the Reformation, therefore, they saw significant reason to keep the church out of the business of the state. They had learned from John Calvin that "Christ's spiritual kingdom and the civil jurisdiction are things completely distinct."[84] Delegates to the Cambridge Synod gave voice to the general distinction between church and state in 1648 by declaring: "As it is unlawful for church-officers to meddle with the sword of the magistrate, so it is unlawful for the magistrate to meddle with the work proper to church-officers."[85] A decade earlier, the colony's most famous preacher had asserted allegiance to this rule in a letter to an English observer: "Magistrates are neither chosen to office in the church, nor do govern by directions from the church, but by civil laws, and those enacted in general courts, and executed in courts of justice, by the governors and assistants. In all which, the church (as church) has nothing to do."[86]

The distinction between church and state also reflected pessimism regarding human nature. Concentration of human power inevitably bred tyranny, Puritans believed. "What ever transcendent power is given," John Cotton preached, "will certainly over-run those that give it, and those that receive it: There is a strain in a man's heart that will sometime or other run out to excess, unless the Lord restrain it, but it is not good to venture it."[87] Puritans were not inclined to test the Lord's restraining power. To avoid the conception of tyranny, they judged it necessary to fragment and segregate spheres of power. All power on earth, including ecclesiastical power, had to be limited. And those who operated within the resulting spheres of limited power had to take care that they did not trespass beyond their allotted field. "It is therefore fit for every man to be studious of the bounds which the Lord hath set. . . . And it is meet that magistrates in the Commonwealth, and so officers in churches should desire to know the utmost bounds of their own power, and it is safe for both."[88]

Conclusion

Of all the varied alliances between church and state established in the American colonies, the one planted in Massachusetts proved to have extraordinary durability. Basic elements of the Congregational establishment survived the American Revolution and the enactment of the Constitution, including the First Amendment's religion clauses. The alliance between Massachusetts civil authority and the heirs of the Puritans endured, in fact, well into the nineteenth century, when the state finally abandoned its official establishment of the Congregational Church. But by noting the durability of Massachusetts religious establishment, I do not mean to underestimate the erosion this establishment suffered during the seventeenth and eighteenth centuries. The Quaker hangings of the 1640s became an embarrassment and the banishments of religious dissenters a page of history rather than a present social practice. The relentless agitations of Baptists and Quakers subverted the City on a Hill, upsetting its fondly imagined thoroughfares.

It is not always easy to determine when Puritans deliberately abandoned particular premises that had supported the original errand into the wilderness and when they simply lost the power to actualize that logic.[89] But even in its infancy the Massachusetts establishment had to contend with polemical assaults on the social premises that sustained the alliance between church and state. Of those assaults, Roger Williams's was the most comprehensive. The next chapter turns to his attempt to deconstruct the Puritans' social logic by challenging its fundamental premises.

Notes

1. Nathaniel B. Shurtleff, ed., *Records of the Governor and Company of the Massachusetts Bay in New England (1628–86)*, 5 vols. (Boston: William White, 1853–54), 1:88 (hereafter cited as *Mass. Records*); John Winthrop, *The History of New England from 1630 to 1649*, 2 vols., ed. James Savage (Boston: Phelps and Farnham, 1825, repr. New York: Arno Press, 1972), 1:56. The severe punishment visited on Philip Ratcliff drew criticism from some English observers. A year after Ratcliff's banishment, an English correspondent wrote to John Winthrop, then governor of the colony, with a word of warning: "I have heard diverse complaints against the severity of your government . . . about cutting off the lunatic man's ear, and other grievances." In the spirit of solidarity, however, Howe assured Winthrop,

"Fear not, there are more with you than against you." Edward Howes to John Winthrop, Jr., 1636, *Winthrop Papers*, 6 vols., ed. Allyn Bailey Forbes and Malcolm Freiberg (Boston: Massachusetts Historical Society, 1929-92), 3:76. For the suggestion that the punishment inflicted on Ratcliff and other actions taken by the General Court of the Massachusetts Bay Colony were reminiscent of the Star Chamber, see Thomas G. Barnes, "Law and Liberty (and Order) in Early Massachusetts," in *The English Legal System: Carryover to the Colonies* (Los Angeles: William Andrews Clark Memorial Library, University of California, 1975), 73-76, 78-80; and Edgar J. McManus, *Law and Liberty in Early New England: Criminal Justice and Due Process, 1620-1692* (Amherst: University of Massachusetts Press, 1993), 6.

2. Philip F. Gura, *A Glimpse of Sion's Glory: Puritan Radicalism in New England, 1620-1660* (Middletown: Wesleyan University Press, 1984), 150. For descriptions of the Puritans' attitude toward and treatment of the Quakers, see Carla Gardina Pestana, *Quakers and Baptists in Colonial Massachusetts* (New York: Cambridge University Press, 1991); and Jonathan M. Chu, *Neighbors, Friends, or Madmen: The Puritan Adjustment to Quakerism in Seventeenth-Century Massachusetts Bay* (Westport: Greenwood Press, 1985). For the attempts by the Massachusetts Puritans to fashion criminal laws to deal with the Quakers, see Edwin Powers, *Crime and Punishment in Early Massachusetts, 1620-1692* (Boston: Beacon Press, 1966), 321-66; and Bradley Chapin, *Criminal Justice in Colonial America, 1606-1660* (Athens: University of Georgia Press, 1983), 104-6.

3. I do not mean to dispute that passion had its role in the punishment of religious dissent in New England. See, for example, the suggestion that anger at perceived violations of goodwill fueled attacks on dissenters and the witch-hunts of the late seventeenth century in Christine L. Heyrman, *Commerce and Culture: The Maritime Communities of Colonial Massachusetts, 1690-1750* (New York: W. W. Norton, 1983), ch. 3.

4. David Grayson Allen, *In English Ways: The Movement of Societies and the Transferal of English Local Law and Custom to Massachusetts Bay in the Seventeenth Century* (Chapel Hill: University of North Carolina Press, 1981); David Cressy, *Coming Over: Migration and Communication between England and New England in the Seventeenth Century* (New York: Cambridge University Press, 1987); David Thomas Konig, *Law and Society in Puritan Massachusetts: Essex County, 1629-1692* (Chapel Hill: University of North Carolina Press, 1979); George L. Haskins, "Precedents in English Ecclesiastical Practices for Criminal Punishments in Early Massachusetts," in *Essays in Legal History in Honor of Felix Frankfurter*, ed. Morris D. Forkosch (Indianapolis: Bobbs-Merrill, 1966), 321-36; George Lee Haskins, *Law and Authority in Early Massachusetts: A Study in Tradition and Design* (New York: Macmillan, 1960), 6-8.

5. Winthrop, *Winthrop Papers*, ed. Forbes and Freiberg, 2:293.

6. John Cotton to Lord Say and Seal, 1636, in *The Puritans: A Sourcebook of Their Writings*, 2 vols., ed. Perry Miller and Thomas H. Johnson (New York: Harper and Row, 1963), 1:209.

7. Cotton maintained that "theocracy" was "the best form of government in the commonwealth, as well as in the church." John Cotton to Lord Say and Seal, in *The Puritans: A Sourcebook of Their Writings,* ed. Miller and Johnson, 1:209.

8. On the "great migration" of Puritans to the New World, see Francis J. Bremer, *The Puritan Experiment: New England Society from Bradford to Edwards* (New York: St. Martin's Press, 1976), 39-40. The complexity of motives prompting this migration is explored in Cressy, *Coming Over,* 74-106; Allen, *In English Ways,* 164-65; and T. H. Breen and Stephen Foster, "Moving to the New World: The Character of Early Massachusetts Immigration," *William and Mary Quarterly,* 3d ser., 30 (1973): 189-222. For an account of the great migration acknowledging the complex motivations that flooded the New World with colonists but arguing that religious concerns were predominant, see Virginia DeJohn Anderson, *New England's Generation: The Great Migration and the Formation of Society and Culture in the Seventeenth Century* (New York: Cambridge University Press, 1991). On individualism, see Darrett B. Rutman, *Winthrop's Boston: Portrait of a Puritan Town, 1630-1649* (Chapel Hill: University of North Carolina Press, 1965); and on differences among towns, see T. H. Breen, "Persistent Localism: English Social Change and the Shaping of New England Institutions," in *Puritans and Adventurers: Change and Persistence in Early America* (New York: Oxford University Press, 1980), 3-24.

For elaborations of the theme of religious differences, see Gura, *Glimpse of Zion's Glory;* Patricia U. Bonomi, *Under the Cope of Heaven: Religion, Society, and Politics in Colonial America* (New York: Oxford University Press, 1986), 14, 18-19; Paul R. Lucas, *Valley of Discord: Church and Society along the Connecticut River,* 1636-1725 (Hanover: University Press of New England, 1976); and David D. Hall, *The Faithful Shepherd: A History of the New England Ministry in the Seventeenth Century* (Chapel Hill: University of North Carolina Press, 1972), 89. David Hall has argued that religious dissent, although it existed, was not representative of most popular religious belief in New England; see David D. Hall, *Worlds of Wonder, Days of Judgment: Popular Religious Belief in Early New England* (New York: Alfred A. Knopf, 1989), 7. For a similar perspective, see Timothy H. Breen and Stephen Foster, "The Puritans' Greatest Achievement: A Study of Social Cohesion in Seventeenth-Century Massachusetts," in *Puritan New England: Essays on Religion, Society, and Culture,* ed. Alden T. Vaughan and Francis J. Bremer (New York: St. Martin's Press, 1977), 110-11.

9. On the extent to which Winthrop's views were not always representative, see Konig, *Law and Society in Puritan Massachusetts,* 24; and Breen, "Persistent Localism," 21-24.

10. For the suggestion that Massachusetts Puritans were joined by their English contemporaries in a common belief that the Bible was an important guide to human affairs, see Haskins, *Law and Authority in Early Massachusetts,* 142-45; and McManus, *Law and Liberty in Early New England,* 21.

11. For the importance of the Bible to both church leaders and laity, see Hall, *Worlds of Wonder, Days of Judgment,* 21-38, 242; Harry S. Stout, *The New*

England Soul: Preaching and Religious Culture in Colonial New England (New York: Oxford University Press, 1986), 19, 32; and Harry S. Stout, "Word and Order in Colonial New England," in *The Bible in America: Essays in Cultural History,* ed. Nathan O. Hatch and Mark A. Noll (New York: Oxford University Press, 1982), 19-38.

12. James Turner, *Without God, without Creed: The Origins of Unbelief in America* (Baltimore: Johns Hopkins University Press, 1985), 26; Hall, *Worlds of Wonder, Days of Judgment,* 17, 162. For the presence of atheists in seventeenth-century England, see G. E. Aylmer, "Unbelief in Seventeenth-Century England," in *Puritans and Revolutionaries: Essays in Seventeenth-Century History Presented to Christopher Hill,* ed. Donald Pennington and Keith Thomas (New York: Oxford University Press, 1982), 22-46.

13. Quoted in Hall, *Worlds of Wonder, Days of Judgment,* 66.

14. Ibid., 119.

15. *Mass. Records,* 3:259-60 (1652).

16. Andrew Delbanco, *The Puritan Ordeal* (Cambridge: Harvard University Press, 1989), 43. For the Puritans' recognition of a relatively expansive "archetypal jurisdiction" of Scripture over the Christian life, see Theodore Dwight Bozeman, *To Live Ancient Lives: The Primitivist Dimension in Puritanism* (Chapel Hill: University of North Carolina Press, 1988), 43.

17. Delbanco, *The Puritan Ordeal,* 30-31.

18. Nathaniel Ward, *The Simple Cobler of Aggawam in America,* ed. P. M. Zall (Lincoln: University of Nebraska Press, 1969), 10.

19. *Abrams v. United States,* 250 U.S. 616, 630 (1919) (Holmes, J., dissenting).

20. John Winthrop, "A Modell of Christian Charity," in *The Puritans: A Sourcebook of Their Writings,* 2 vols., ed. Perry Miller and Thomas H. Johnson (New York: Harper and Row, 1963), 1:198.

21. For an argument that a sense of special destiny took a generation to find a secure place in the American identity, see Delbanco, *Puritan Ordeal,* 8; see also Bozeman, *To Live Ancient Lives,* 115-16.

22. Winthrop, *Winthrop Papers,* ed. Forbes and Freiberg, 4:472.

23. Harold J. Berman, "Law and Belief in Three Revolutions," *Valparaiso University Law Review* 18 (1984): 594. Amy Lang describes the myth of New Israel as having brought together "the personal and the historical, the private and the public, the individual and the communal, in such a way as to demonstrate that all of these were bent toward one and the same end: the fulfillment of God's errand in the New World." Amy Schrager Lang, *Prophetic Woman: Anne Hutchinson and the Problem of Dissent in the Literature of New England* (Berkeley: University of California Press, 1987), 47.

24. For a general account of New England's refusal to follow the trend in England toward greater toleration beginning in the fourth decade of the seventeenth century, see Perry Miller, *Orthodoxy in Massachusetts, 1630-1650* (Cambridge: Harvard University Press, 1933), 263-313.

25. Haskins, *Law and Authority in Early Massachusetts*, 145. Compare David Hall's comment that the New England Puritans were "more Protestant than most, more ready to eliminate old customs and to liberalize the structure of the church." *Worlds of Wonder, Days of Judgment*, 10. On moral precepts, see David H. Flaherty, "Law and the Enforcement of Morals in Early America," in *Law in American History*, ed. Donald Fleming and Bernard Bailyn (Boston: Little, Brown, 1971). For a useful summary of the many ways in which the laws of Massachusetts and the other New England colonies departed from Scripture, see McManus, *Law and Liberty in Early New England*, 21-37.

26. Bozeman, *To Live Ancient Lives*, 42; McManus, *Law and Liberty in Early New England*, 4.

27. For an attempt to calculate the relative influences of English and Biblical law on the laws of the Massachusetts Bay Colony, see Chapin, *Criminal Justice in Colonial America*, 5. Chapin suggests that 41.2 percent of the colony's substantive criminal law was derived from English law and 38.8 percent from the Bible. He calculates that 20 percent of the colony's criminal provisions were indigenous.

28. Winthrop, *Winthrop Papers*, ed. Forbes and Freiberg, 4:348. See James G. Mosely, *John Winthrop's World: History as a Story; the Story as History* (Madison: University of Wisconsin Press, 1992), 42, describing Winthrop as one who had "learned to see his personal religious covenant less as a code of moral rules than as a mode of relationship with a gracious God."

29. See the foreword to *The Laws and Liberties of Massachusetts* (Cambridge, 1648). For a general discussion of the *Laws and Liberties*, see Thorp L. Wolford, "The Laws and Liberties of 1648: The First Code of Laws Enacted and Printed in English America," *Boston University Law Review* 28 (1948): 426-63.

30. Winthrop, *History*, ed. Savage, 2:238 (emphasis added).

31. Haskins, *Law and Authority in Early Massachusetts*, 56; Wolford, "The Laws and Liberties of 1648," 430.

32. Delbanco, *Puritan Ordeal*, 31.

33. For a discussion of the New England Puritan concept of history, see Sacvan Bercovitch, *The Puritan Origins of the American Self* (New Haven: Yale University Press, 1975), 35-71.

34. Winthrop, *History*, ed. Savage, 2:35.

35. John Cotton to John Winthrop, ca. 1648, *Winthrop Papers*, ed. Forbes and Freiberg, 5:192-93.

36. Haskins, *Law and Authority in Early Massachusetts*, 204; John D. Eusden, "Natural Law and Covenant Theology in New England, 1620-1670," *Natural Law Forum* 6 (1960): 21.

37. Stout, *The New England Soul*, 15.

38. Ward, *The Simple Cobler of Aggawam*, 6.

39. Breen and Foster, "The Puritans' Greatest Achievement," 115; John Witte, Jr., "How to Govern a City on a Hill: The Early Puritan Contribution to American Constitutionalism," *Emory Law Journal* 39 (1990): 47; Kermit L. Hall, *The*

Magic Mirror: Law in American History (New York: Oxford University Press, 1989), 15. On the importance of covenants in Puritan thought, see generally Perry Miller, *The New England Mind: The Seventeenth Century* (Cambridge: Harvard University Press, 1939), chs. 13-15.

40. *Laws and Liberties,* 56.

41. For the Dedham Covenant, see Kenneth A. Lockridge, *A New England Town: The First Hundred Years* (New York: W. W. Norton, 1970), 4-7.

42. Williston Walker, ed., *The Creeds and Platforms of Congregationalism* (New York: Scribner's, 1892, repr. Philadelphia: Pilgrim Press, 1960), 116.

43. *Mass. Records,* 1:196.

44. The Cambridge Platform, in *The Creeds and Platforms of Congregationalism,* ed. Walker, 227.

45. Haskins, *Law and Authority in Early Massachusetts,* 204.

46. John Cotton, *A Reply to Mr. Williams, His Examination,* in *The Complete Writings of Roger Williams,* 7 vols. (New York: Russell and Russell, 1963), 7:8.

47. John Cotton, *The Bloudy Tenent, Washed, and Made White in the Bloud of the Lambe* (London: Matthew Symmons, 1647, repr. New York: Arno Press, 1972), 10.

48. On the contrast between Puritanism's pessimism regarding human nature and liberalism's "extraordinary confidence in the possibility of both a firm sense of human reasonableness and of the ease with which order might be attained," see Michael Walzer, "Puritanism as a Revolutionary Ideology," in *Puritan New England: Essays on Religion, Society, and Culture,* ed. Alden T. Vaughan and Francis J. Bremer (New York: St. Martin's Press, 1977), 22. On the general significance to the Puritans' political thought of their belief in human sinfulness, see Witte, "How to Govern a City on a Hill," 58-62.

49. Miller, *Orthodoxy in Massachusetts,* 5, 12, 54, 72.

50. Cotton, *The Bloudy Tenent, Washed,* 13.

51. Ibid., 14-15.

52. Breen and Foster, "The Puritans' Greatest Achievement," 110-11.

53. Cotton, *The Bloudy Tenent, Washed,* 35.

54. Ibid., 55.

55. Ibid., 64.

56. *Mass. Records,* 2:177. On the use of banishment, see Anderson, *New England's Generation,* 121.

57. Winthrop, *History,* ed. Savage, 1:261-64.

58. See John Winthrop's account of one such example and his confidence that "an evident judgment of God" was upon the drowning victims. Ibid., 106. For a recent account of Puritan understandings of Providence, see Michael P. Winship, "Encountering Providence in the Seventeenth Century: The Experiences of a Yeoman and a Minister," *Essex Institute Historical Collections* (Jan. 1990): 27-36.

59. Winthrop, *History,* ed. Savage, 2:11.

60. Winship, "Encountering Providence," 34.

61. Winthrop, *History,* ed. Savage, 1:305.

62. *Mass. Records,* 2:230.

63. Avihu Zakai, *Exile and Kingdom: History and Apocalypse in the Puritan Migration to America* (New York: Cambridge University Press, 1992); Bozeman, *To Live Ancient Lives,* 96-99, 194-96; Kai T. Erickson, *Wayward Puritans: A Study in the Sociology of Deviance* (New York: John Wiley, 1966), 37.

64. Thomas Cobbet, *The Civil Magistrates Power in Matters of Religion* (London, 1653, repr. New York: Arno Press, 1972), 33.

65. Cotton, *The Bloudy Tenent, Washed,* 50.

66. Ibid., 67, 150-51. See also Cobbet, *The Civil Magistrates Power,* 24. For the Puritans' desire to avoid God's wrath against the civil community as a basis for punishing moral offenses, see Flaherty, "Law and the Enforcement of Morals," 217.

67. Haskins, *Law and Authority in Early Massachusetts,* 207. David Hall recounts the instance of John Underhill, an antinomian who had been accused of adultery, who returned to the colony from exile and, after confessing this sin to his former church and to the General Court, was released from his excommunication and most of the civil penalties that had been assessed against him. Hall, *Worlds of Wonder, Days of Judgment,* 172-73. Some stains, however, such as that produced by the crime of bestiality, were too indelible to be cleansed by such means. Death was the only solvent. Ibid., 175-76, 178.

68. Ibid., 175 (a discussion of confession as a means of removing stain). Ironically, alleged deviants from the community's norms could characterize their treatment at the hands of the community as a stain itself. Anne Hutchinson, banished for obstinate antinomianism in 1638, warned Massachusetts leaders that their treatment of her had earned calamity for the colony. William K. B. Stoever, *'A Faire and Easie Way to Heaven': Covenant Theology and Antinomianism in Early Massachusetts* (Middletown: Wesleyan University Press, 1978), 32. In 1644 a man was executed for having allegedly mistreated a servant so that he died. The accused denied any guilt, however, and died "professing assurance of salvation, and that God would never lay the boy his death to his charge, but the guilt of his blood would lie upon the country." Winthrop, *History,* ed. Savage, 2:187-89, quoted in Hall, *Worlds of Wonder, Days of Judgment,* 180. Similarly, the Quakers executed in the 1650s prophesied that God would exact vengeance against New England for their martyrdom. Ibid., 188.

69. Ibid., 104, 106.

70. Cobbet, *The Civil Magistrates Power in Matters of Religion,* 28.

71. Cotton, *A Reply to Williams* 2:28.

72. Cotton, *The Bloudy Tenent, Washed,* 27.

73. Cotton, *A Reply to Williams* 2:28.

74. Cotton, *The Bloudy Tenent, Washed,* 21-22; see also Cobbet, *The Civil Magistrates Power in Matters of Religion,* 39.

75. Gary Wills, *Under God: Religion and American Politics* (New York: Simon and Schuster, 1990), 383.

76. *Everson v. Board of Educ.*, 330 U.S. 1, 18 (1947).

77. The Cambridge Platform, in *The Creeds and Platforms of Congregationalism*, ed. Walker, 235.

78. This statement by John Cotton is quoted in Williams G. McLoughlin, *New England Dissent, 1630-1883*, 2 vols. (Cambridge: Harvard University Press, 1971), 1:12.

79. John Cotton to Lord Say and Seal, in *The Puritans: A Sourcebook of Their Writings*, ed. Miller and Johnson, 1:209; Edward Johnson, *Wonder-Working Providence of Sion's Saviour in New-England* (London, 1654, repr. Delmar: Scholars' Facsimiles, 1974), 3.

80. Thomas Lechford, "Plain Dealing: or Newes from New-England," *Massachusetts Historical Society Collections*, 3d ser., 3 (1833): 74.

81. See Roger Williams, *The Bloudy Tenent, of Persecution*, in *The Complete Writings of Roger Williams*, 7 vols. (New York: Russell and Russell, 1963), 4:333, which summarizes the common perception and refers to it as "a most dangerous fiction."

82. Edmund S. Morgan, *Roger Williams: The Church and the State* (New York: W. W. Norton, 1967), 65.

83. Morgan, *Roger Williams*, 64.

84. John Calvin, *Institutes of the Christian Religion*, 2 vols., trans. Ford L. Battles, ed. John T. McNeill (Philadelphia: Westminster Press, 1960), 2:1486.

85. The Cambridge Platform, in *The Creeds and Platforms of Congregationalism*, ed. Walker, 235-36.

86. John Cotton to Lord Say and Seal, in *The Puritans: A Sourcebook of Their Writings*, ed. Miller and Johnson, 1:210.

87. John Cotton, *An Exposition upon the Thirteenth Chapter of the Revelation* (London, 1656), reprinted in part in *The Puritans: A Sourcebook of Their Writings*, ed. Perry Miller and Thomas H. Johnson (New York: Harper and Row, 1963), 1:213.

88. Cotton, *An Exposition*. For a discussion of the Puritans' belief in a separation of spiritual and civil power to avoid tyranny, see Stout, *The New England Soul*, 16. On the Puritans' belief in the necessity of limits on power, see Marci A. Hamilton, "The First Amendment's Challenge Function and the Confusion in the Supreme Court's Contemporary Free Exercise Jurisprudence," *Georgia Law Review* 29 (1994): 85-86; and Eusden, "Natural Law and Covenant Theology," 23.

89. For the suggestion that the greater religious toleration evidenced in the colonies of the New World toward the end of the seventeenth century was "more opportunistic than ideological, more a case of helpless acquiescence than an endorsement of the principle of religious freedom," see Bonomi, *Under the Cope of Heaven*, 37.

3

Challenging the Logic of the
Puritan Establishment

Beginning almost immediately after his banishment and continuing for the next forty years, Roger Williams challenged the social logic that engineered his exile from the Massachusetts Bay Colony. In a vigorous stream of letters and books he assaulted the premises upon which New England Puritans had erected their New Zion. Along the way, he branded the Puritans "persecutors," but his criticisms of the Massachusetts alliance between church and state were more than a mere stream of ad hominem arguments. Williams located the root of persecution in bad thinking rather than in malevolent will or perverted emotion. For him, the contest for religious liberty took place in the mind, where ideas grappled for preeminence.

In 1644, the same year that John Milton published *Areopagetica*, his argument for freedom of the press, Roger Williams published his first major attack on the New England way. He titled his book *The Bloudy Tenent, of Persecution for cause of Conscience, discussed in a Conference betweene Truth and Peace*. Printed in England, and immediately burnt there, the volume launched an inquisition against the bloody yet sacred tenet that social stability required religious uniformity.

New England, of course, was not of a mind to suffer the rhetorical blows of Williams in silence. John Cotton, the Boston preacher who ultimately occupied the preaching post that Williams had turned down upon his arrival in Massachusetts, responded to the attack in 1647 with *The Bloudy Tenent, Washed, and made White in the Bloud of the Lambe: Being Discussed and Discharged of Bloud-Guiltiness by Just Defence*. As though to an unruly child, Cotton set forth to Williams—and to the world—the premises and deductions by which New England justified its efforts to create and sustain a holy commonwealth.[1] Williams, in turn, managed to slip in a weighty rebuttal just before Cotton spoiled the debate by dying in 1652. The Providence renegade damned again "the bloody tenent of persecution for cause of Conscience: (a notorious and common pirate, that takes and robs, that fires and sinks the spiritual ships and vessels) the consciences of all men, of all sorts, of all religions and persuasions whatsoever."[2] He titled his new book *The Bloudy Tenent Yet More Bloudy: By Mr Cottons Endevour To Wash it White in the Blood of the Lambe; of Whose Precious Blood, Spilt in the Blood of His Servants; and of the Blood of Millions Spilt in Former and Later Wars for Conscience Sake, That Most Bloudy Tenent of Persecution for Cause of Conscience Sake, Upon a Second trial, is Found Now More Apparently and More Notoriously Guilty.*

In *The Bloudy Tenent, of Persecution* and *The Bloudy Tenent Yet More Bloudy,* as well as in several shorter tracts, Roger Williams challenged three central ideas that undergirded the New England way: the belief that Old Testament law was relevant to the creation of New England law, the contractual imagery that invigorated the Puritans' justifications for excluding religious dissenters from their communities, and the alleged public consequences of spiritual error that supported the New England magistrates' superintendence of religious matters.

Divorcing the Old Testament Past

The image of Israel in the Old Testament, delivered by God from Egyptian bondage and led by the Divine Hand into the land of promise, has had a powerful effect on the American imagination. Not only aspiring theocrats have found the image suggestive. Thomas Jefferson, for example, proposed to enshrine on the Great Seal of the United States a picture of "The Children of Israel in the Wilderness, led by a Cloud by day, and a Pillar of Fire by night."[3] In his Second Inaugural Address, Jefferson also described the founding of the colonies by using the metaphor of the biblical exodus and conquest of Canaan. "I shall need, too," he told his audience, "the favor of that Being in whose hands we are, who led our forefathers, as Israel of old, from their native land, and planted them in a country flowing with all the necessaries and comforts of life."[4]

For Jefferson, the Old Testament Nation of Israel functioned as a convenient metaphor to encapsulate American colonial and revolutionary experience. In his hands, though, the metaphor existed at an elevated level of abstraction—one that did not involve perusing Old Testament texts for guidance in creating either a nation or its legal structures. But for

Massachusetts Puritans, Israel's history provided far more tangible instruction for their own errand into the wilderness. The holy commonwealth conceived by New England Puritans drew sustenance from an umbilical cord that linked their lives with the history of Israel. Puritans found more than metaphor in Old Testament texts. They discovered there something like a rough social diagram, adaptable to their particular circumstances but still reflecting the mind of the Divine Architect. They did not seek to reanimate Old Testament laws and social practices indiscriminately because they believed that at least some of these had been supplanted by Christ's coming. But they found an ample residuum of law and practice that they considered applicable to their circumstances.

Although Roger Williams vehemently protested the Puritans' attempt to establish a new Zion, he did not challenge their experiment in biblical commonwealth by challenging the importance of the Bible. Like the Massachusetts authorities who banished him, Williams believed that the Bible was the word of God, and—rightly understood—relevant to the circumstances of New England. "The scriptures or writings of truth," he declared, "are those heavenly righteous scales, wherein all our controversies must be tried."[5] His writings are saturated with scriptural references: Williams could scarcely pen a sentence without either referring to scripture directly or transmitting biblical echoes through the words he wrote. He repeatedly turned to the New Testament and the "first and most ancient path" illustrated there as a measure by which to judge contemporary practice.[6] Moreover, he found in the texts of the Old Testament a rich source of moral and spiritual exemplars for individuals seeking to live godly lives.[7] Yet his key stratagem in undermining the Puritans' holy commonwealth was to sever the link between Massachusetts law and the law of Israel, and he argued across three decades that most of the Old Testament patterns Puritans had adopted were inapplicable to the business of civil government.

To shatter the Old Testament mold in which the Puritans sought to create New England society, Williams faced a difficult hurdle. Worshipers of an eternal God might well begin with a presumption against change. Viewed through the lens of eternity, divine legislation delivered to Israel through Moses could scarcely be said to have been amended or repealed without some very clear indication of that fact by its author. Although New England Puritans found some such indications, they nevertheless concluded that much of the substance of Old Testament law had endured to their own generation. The Puritans saw, of course, evidence that particular matters in the Old Testament involved provisional arrangements that Christ's coming had displaced. For example, Christ's sacrifice on the cross had repealed the laws commanding sacrifices in the Old Testament. God had preserved scriptural accounts of these sacrifices not because he expected Christians to imitate Levitical rites literally, but so they might discover that Christ's death was part of God's eternal plan prefigured in the sacrifices carried out in the Old Testament.

The Old Testament sacrifices were "types" or prefiguring representations of Christ's supreme sacrifice, and Christ was the "antitype" of these sacrifices. These types were more than symbols or allegories because they had a real historical existence and significance in addition to their typological one. For example, Puritans saw typological significance in the account of Moses' crafting a bronze snake to deliver the Israelites from a plague of venomous snakes.[8] According to the Old Testament, those who were bitten by the snakes but looked upon Moses' bronze emblem were saved from a venomous death. For the Puritans, the bronze snake was real and had a significant effect on the lives of the Israelites who looked upon it. But the bronze snake was also a type of Christ, who, by being lifted up on a cross, would bring salvation to those who looked to him for grace.[9]

These typological interpretations of the Old Testament allowed Puritans to distance themselves from at least some of the religious and social practices described there. They did not believe it necessary to bloody their hands with Levitical offerings: Christ had supplanted allegory with reality and abolished the need for any further prefiguring sacrifices. After making this concession to change, however, the Puritans of New England generally retreated to their original presumption against any biblical interpretation that would attribute fundamental changes of the divine mind as to other matters of Old Testament law. They were comfortable speaking of types and antitypes, but more often than not these allegorical parallels between Old and New Testament happenings supplemented more literal readings of Old Testament texts, especially when it came to crafting laws appropriate to a godly society. Generally, Puritan typological interpretations made distant Old Testament happenings appear closer to the lives of seventeenth-century Puritans. Through such interpretations the thundering voice of Jehovah on Mount Sinai rattled in their ears.

Roger Williams was also at home with typological interpretations of scripture. In his hands, however, typology drove a deep wedge between Old Testament law and seventeenth-century society, pushing the Old Testament further away from Massachusetts rather than drawing it closer.[10] He saw Christ's coming as having fixed an impassable gulf between Israel and every other nation of the world. He challenged attempts to find legal blueprints in the Old Testament by arguing that the Nation of Israel had been dissolved as a theocracy at the coming of Christ and that God had removed its pattern forever as a thing to be copied.[11] "The pattern of the national church of Israel, was a none-such, inimitable by any civil state," Williams observed.[12] Israel was now a type whose antitype was not another nation or nations but the church of Christ.[13] The literal events of the Old Testament had figurative applications in the church. In the Old Testament, for example, punishment of heretics by death was a type of the church's punishment of the heterodox by excommunication: "It is true in the national church of Israel (the then only Church and Nation of God) he that did ought presumptuously was to be accursed and to be put to death, . . . a figure of the spiritual putting to death an obstinate sinner in the church of Christ, who refusing to hear the voice of Christ, is to be cut off from Christ and Christians, and to be esteemed as an Heathen, that is, a Gentile or Publican."[14]

Williams made two important deductions from the severance that Christ had wrought between Old Testament Israel and the modern world. First, he concluded that God had gotten out of the business of awarding favored nation status to any modern nation. He thus attacked the Puritans' tendency to imagine themselves to be Israel's favored successor as God's people. Of course, New England colonists were not alone in imagining that the eye of divine favor had smiled particularly upon them. More than a few English citizens thought that England occupied an especially prominent place in God's good graces. Williams, however, scoffed at these pretensions. Since the coming of Christ, no place was better, or more holy, than another.[15] There were no holy commonwealths, only profane ones; no Christian nations, only the world.[16] All nations were "merely civil."[17] Although the Almighty had indeed entered into a covenant with the Nation of Israel, he had given up deal-making after Christ's coming. Show me another nation, Williams challenged, for whom God has parted a sea and provided manna from heaven and I will show you a nation qualified to make Old Testament law its own.[18] John Winthrop had argued that the safe passage granted to the Puritans traveling to Massachusetts signified God's ratification of a covenant with the Puritans.[19] Williams, however, repudiated that attempt to bind God contractually by his silence. The Massachusetts Bay Colony's covenant with God was a worthless scrap of paper in Williams's eyes, a presumptuous attempt to create by unilateral fiat an agreement with a God who had never agreed to the Puritans' terms.

Second, Williams concluded that no modern civil power possessed the authority of the Israelite rulers to enforce laws relating to religious matters. The first table of the Ten Commandments, having to do with obligations Israel owed to God, had no further civil application after the coming of Christ.[20] Thus, for example, Williams denied that civil governments had any authority to require Sabbath observance.[21] He argued that Old Testament texts authorizing death for offenses against spiritual orthodoxy had to be understood typologically. The literal import of these texts had expired with the coming of Christ. Now, only a figurative sense remained: The church punished spiritually by excommunication and rebuke the sins that Israelite rulers had formerly punished with the sword. As to the second table of the Ten Commandments, Williams believed that part of Mosaic law articulated moral principles of continuing legal force. The laws against theft and adultery, for example, did not simply express special covenantal obligations that the covenanting people of Israel owed to the covenanting God but were moral imperatives applicable to all civil societies. Nevertheless, although Williams believed that the civil government could enforce the commands of the second table, including the prohibition against adultery, even these commands could not sustain the kind of punishments—for example, death—with which the Nation of Israel had enforced them.[22]

Excising Religion from the Social Contract

Roger Williams and New England Puritans agreed on at least two things about the civil magistrate's authority. First, they both asserted that the magistrate derived his power from the people. According to Williams, "All true civil magistrates, have not the least inch of civil power, but what is measured out to them from the free consent of the whole."[23] Civil authority was thus a matter of delegation from the ruled to the ruler. Second, the people's power to delegate authority to the civil magistrate had to be exercised in keeping with divine limitations on that delegation. As the Puritans put it, the people, being not "free lords of their own estates" but "stewards under God," could not transfer power to the magistrate according to their personal desires, but only as God dictated.[24]

From these common premises, however, Williams and his rhetorical opponents traveled to widely different conclusions. Because Puritans had already concluded that biblical "laws and rules" prescribed the Massachusetts version of a godly commonwealth, citizens had only one choice: to submit themselves to rule of the saints. The parties—citizens and magistrates—were not free to bargain concerning the New England version of the social contract; they could only sign it. God had previously established the terms. Nevertheless, Puritans were convinced that they were not mistreating religious dissenters by harrying them with various civil punishments. No one was forced to migrate to Massachusetts or to abide there once arrived, they insisted. The errand into the wilderness was, they believed, an utterly voluntary affair. Souls not inclined to submit themselves to the rule of the Massachusetts saints were free to settle elsewhere—free, as the simple cobbler of Aggawam pointed out, "to keep away from us."[25]

Williams, in contrast, turned the notion of delegated political authority to a different conclusion. If one desired to determine whether the civil magistrate had authority to superintend matters relating to the church, he reasoned, one must first determine whether the people had delegated such authority. Before that, though, one had to learn whether the people had any authority themselves to manage church affairs and thus any authority to delegate. Here Williams had a ready answer. Contrary to the Puritans, he believed that God had not invested the people of any civil state with power to rule the church or keep it pure.[26] Thus, the people, lacking power to superintend religious affairs in civil contexts, could not transmit such power to the magistrates.

Williams argued that God would have been foolish to delegate to civil rulers any authority over the church. Most of the world was, after all, unregenerate and lost, he believed. To subject religion to the superintendence of civil magistrates was to subject the church to governments all over the world. "Is not this to subject this holy nation," he asked, "this heavenly Jerusalem, the wife and spouse of Jesus, the pillar and ground of truth, to the vain uncertain and changeable mutations of this evil present world?"[27] If God had intended to provide his church with civil fathers, Williams suggested, then God had shown himself to have made rather poor appointments. History provided abundant testimony to the incompetence of civil magistrates over spiritual affairs. Rulers had not tended to treat what Williams and the Puritans would have generally agreed was the true faith with benevolent regard; had God wanted the civil magistrate to tend to spiritual affairs, he would have appointed angels to be rulers rather than the likes of Nero.[28] Williams, therefore, refused to be persuaded by the Puritans' "love it or leave it" variation of the New England social contract. In his eyes, the Massachusetts compact was tainted by incorporation of an illegal term. It did not matter that inhabitants may have consented in some fashion to that term. Their consent to have government superintend the church was void.

Denying the Public Consequences of Spiritual Error

By championing religious liberty, Roger Williams did not propose to leave conscience free of all social restraints. He objected to the Massachusetts version of the civil magistrate but not to all magistrates. The "wildest of the sons of men," he declared, had found it necessary "to cast themselves into some mold or form of government."[29] God himself had countenanced the resulting civil arrangements. The "ordinance of magistracy" had been "properly and adequately fitted by God, to preserve the civil state in civil peace and order."[30] Therefore, the civil magistrate need not, and should not, allow disobedience to parents or magistrates, murder, quarreling, uncleanness, lasciviousness, theft, extortion, adultery, oppression, sedition, or mutiny.[31] The civil magistrate possessed a "civil sword . . . for the defense of persons, estates, families, liberties of a city or civil state, and the suppressing of uncivil or injurious persons or actions."[32] Williams argued that civil government had authority in two broad areas: keeping the civil peace and maintaining what he referred to as "civility."[33] Civility, the opposite of "barbarism," was for Williams both the state of relations in which no man harmed another and the maintenance of certain fundamental moral precepts.[34]

This summary of Williams's principles would not have been wholly disagreeable to New England Puritans. In the civil magistrate's legitimate concern for peace and civility, they saw a gate sufficiently wide to admit their experiment in holy commonwealth. Because Puritans conceived matters of religious doctrine and church governance to be social in nature, they could easily justify New England's alliance of church and state as a necessary means of preserving civil peace and order. Thus, unlike Williams, they saw breaches of the civil peace lurking behind every schismatical doctrine. They contended that "civil peace cannot stand entire, where religion is corrupted."[35] Moreover, they argued that false doctrine, when held forth with an arrogant or "boisterous" manner, caused a breach of civil peace that could be punished "to the quality and measure of the disturbance caused."[36] To Williams's argument that the civil magistrate could only punish offenses that injured civility—that is, caused some harm to other members of the community—Puritans responded that false doctrine harmed others in two respects. It created the possibility that others would be infected by the same error and increased the likelihood that God would punish the community as a whole for allowing the error to flourish.[37] Therefore, under Williams's rule, spiritual error could be punished because it tended to harm others besides its possessor. As a matter of "moral equity," an individual whose error led another individual to suffer spiritual death could be punished with physical death.[38] Puritans thus proclaimed a hybrid *lex talionis* in which the soul-killer was punished with physical execution.[39]

Williams was well aware that the argument concerning liberty of conscience was critically linked to the definition of civil peace. "It is too lamentably known," he reminded readers of *The Bloudy Tenent Yet More Bloudy*, "how the furious troops of persecutors in all states, cities, towns have ever marched under . . . the white colors of peace, civil peace, public peace."[40] The heart of his response to the Puritan concept of civil peace was therefore to envision for the civil government a place of existence that religious conflicts could not trouble. In an important passage from *The Bloudy Tenent, of Persecution* he compared government to a great city and churches to those myriad businesses and associations whose formation and dissolution left the city's essential peace undisturbed because the city's existence was distinct from theirs.

> The Church or company of worshipers (whether true or false) is like unto a body or college of physicians in a city; like unto a corporation, society, or company of East India or Turkish merchants, or any other society or company in London: which companies may hold their courts, keep their records, hold disputations; and in matters concerning their society, may dissent, divide, break into schisms and factions, sue and implead each other at the law, yea wholly break up and dissolve into pieces and nothing, and yet the peace of the city not be in the least measure impaired or disturbed; because the essence or being of the city, and so the well-being and peace thereof is essentially distinct from those particular societies; the city courts, city laws, city punishments distinct from theirs. The city was before them, and stands absolute and entire, when such a corporation or society is taken down.[41]

Here was the central thrust of Williams's argument: The agitation occasioned by religious controversy did not threaten the peace of the civil state. Although Williams coached his argument as a description, he had no real experience as a model. In fact, Williams's description was egregiously flawed. In a world in which religious ideas were realities as tangible as one's house and tools, religious conflict could not help but disturb the peace of the city. Religious disagreements were real disagreements and capable of igniting tempers and incubating distrust. The anger and ill-will generated by lively religious disputes would inevitably effect social interaction. To assert otherwise was not to describe experience but to superimpose a new vision upon a centuries-old reality. The city and its religious corporations were—or Williams imagined they could be—of such distinct character that conflict in the one would not cause a ripple in the other.

In part, Williams defined the "peace of the city" so as to accommodate a fair amount of rowdiness. How else could he defend prophetic witnesses from the inevitable charge that their preaching disrupted civil peace? "God's people," he admitted, "by their preaching, disputing, etc. have been (though not the cause) yet accidentally the occasion of great contentions and divisions, yea tumults and uproars in towns and cities where they have lived and come."[42] Such "tumults and uproars" were the natural consequence of truth encountering falsehood. Prophets tend to disturb those who hear them. One ought not be surprised, Williams thought, "if sore eyes be troubled at the appearance of the light, be it never so sweet."[43] He therefore sought to preserve civil freedom for the witness of truth by denying a heckler's veto to unbelief. Because the civil state was distinct from the various corporate entities that made up the spiritual commonwealth, the civil peace was not disturbed by the mere arrogance and boisterousness of idolaters. It was breached, rather, by "that wrong and preposterous way of suppressing, preventing, and extinguishing such doctrines or practices by weapons of wrath and blood, whips, stocks, imprisonment, banishment, death, by which men commonly are persuaded to convert heretics, and to cast out unclean spirits."[44]

According to Williams's vision, the city and the religious corporations that inhabited it were not brothers who grew up together, intertwined like Siamese twins as the Puritans maintained, but separate islands with separate histories and discrete destinies. The civil commonwealth was a thing separate from the religious corporations that inhabited it, and the key actors within the civil commonwealth—the citizen and the magistrate—need not profess and practice true religion to fulfill their roles.[45] God had furnished citizens with the abilities necessary to perform public service, even when they did not know him.[46] A Jew, a Turk, a Papist, or an "Antichristian" could both govern and be governed in spite of their erroneous religious views. They frequently made better neighbors than did Christians.[47] In addition, their conversion to true Christianity added not a whit to their civil abilities.[48] Moreover, Williams insisted, a commonwealth could "flourish" even though it contained no Christian influence at all.[49]

The underlying premise of Williams's argument was that "a moral virtue, a moral fidelity, ability and honesty" was accessible to both Christians and non-Christians and could form the basis of a stable society.[50] He had seen in his frequent contacts with Native Americans that the flower of civility bloomed in places where the light of Christian truth had never beamed.[51] He favorably compared their habits of hospitality to those of Jews and Christians who had often sent "Christ Jesus to the Manger."[52] Native American courtesy could become a counterpoint in a strident fugue on the inhumanity of persecutions carried out by "civilized" people.

> The courteous pagan shall condemn
> Uncourteous Englishmen,
> Who live like foxes, bears and wolves,
> Or lion in his den.
> Let none sing blessings to their souls,
> For that they courteous are:
> The wild barbarians with no more
> Than nature, go so far:
> If nature's sons both wild and tame,
> Humane and courteous be:
> How ill becomes it sons of God
> To want humanity?[53]

In his attempt to untangle the web of New England relations between church and state, Williams was a father to the modern "Secular City" to a degree not frequently recognized.[54] And on this point it is necessary to challenge the view of Williams that has dominated legal discussions of religious liberty since the 1970s, a view advanced most eloquently in Mark DeWolfe Howe's *The Garden and the Wilderness.* According to Howe, "When the imagination of Roger Williams built the wall of separation, it was not because he was fearful that without such a barrier the arm of the church would extend its reach. It was, rather, the dread of the worldly corruptions which might consume the churches if sturdy fences against the wilderness were not maintained."[55] Howe derived his thesis, and the title of his book, from a famous passage in one of Williams's early works in which he set forth the image of a wall separating church and state:

> The faithful labors of many witnesses of Jesus Christ, extant to the world, abundantly proving, that the Church of the Jews under the Old Testament in the type, and the Church of the Christians under the New Testament in the

antitype, were both separate from the world; and that when they have opened a gap in the hedge or wall of separation between the garden of the Church and the wilderness of the world, God has ever broke down the wall itself, removed the candlestick, and made his garden a wilderness, as at this day.[56]

Under Howe's reading, the wall of separation between church and state—between the garden and the wilderness—mainly protects encroachments from the state into the church. Because this view does not read the First Amendment's establishment clause to operate in the opposite direction, it is more sympathetic to incursions of the church into the state.

Williams's writings, however, do not lend themselves to Howe's portrayal of an aggressive partisan of the church's liberty who is otherwise uninterested in the fate of the state. Williams defined for the state a sphere of existence untroubled by religious disputes. He envisioned a notion of the secular as not antagonistic to religion but occupied with fundamentally different concerns from religion. He respected the secular city because he believed that God had instituted it and that its existence was not hostile to the existence of the church.[57] Moreover, Williams viewed it as a sign of disrespect for the secular city when the church usurped the authority God had granted to the civil magistrate. He thus complained that the clergy, relying on state support, had made civil magistrates "but steps and stirrups to ascend and mount up into their rich and honorable seats and saddles."[58]

In *The Bloudy Tenent, of Persecution* Williams compared the treatment of civil authority by Puritan ministers with the soldiers' cruel and demeaning treatment of Christ before the crucifiction.[59] "The Minister (though a blind guide) he is the seer," he argued, "but wanting legs and strength of civil power, he is carried upon the civil magistrate's shoulders, whose blindness the subtle clergy abuse, but both together, rob the orchard of the most high and sure-avenging God."[60] Persecution, he said, threatened not only to take true Christianity out of the world but also to take the "world out of the world."[61] It was a "body-killing, soul-killing, and state-killing doctrine" that was a "danger to every civil state."[62] Williams denied the legitimacy of any religious test for public office or civil right: "It is not lawful to deprive Caesar the civil magistrate, nor any that belong to him of their civil and earthly rights. . . . although . . . a man is not godly, a Christian, sincere, a church member, yet to deprive him of any civil right or privilege, due to him as a man, a subject, a citizen, is to take from Caesar, that which is Caesar's, which God endures not though it be given to himself."[63]

Williams sought not only to strip the civil magistrate of powers he believed the Puritans had illicitly delegated to it but also to restore superintendence of certain matters of social life that Puritans had cloaked in the rhetoric of privacy. They had labeled as private concerns, and therefore beyond civil cognizance, complaints by children against parents, wives against husbands, and servants against masters. Williams was ready to lay these kinds of disputes at the feet of the civil magistrate for judgment according to the dictates of civil law.[64] He chastised the Puritans for their disrespect of civil authority in such areas: "I have long observed that such as have been ready to ascribe to the civil magistrate and his sword more than God has ascribed, have also been most ready . . . to spoil him of the robe of that due authority with which it has pleased God and the people to invest and clothe him."[65] Roger Williams therefore championed both a vigorous concept of religious liberty and something like magisterial liberty—freedom of civil government from the encroachments of clerical power. He thus described the thirteenth chapter of Paul's letter to the Romans, which commands obedience to general civil law, the "Magna Charta for the civil magistrate."[66]

Williams was convinced that the path to salvation was narrow and that most of the world's inhabitants—including those of its "civilized nations"—had failed to find it. From this perspective, the Puritans' claim of a public interest in treating spiritual infection found a skeptical hearing. Williams doubted in the first place that the risk of spiritual infection was great. "Dead men cannot be infected," he argued, and most of the world was spiritually dead, its inhabitants beyond even the possibility of sickness.[67] He also maintained that those few who were spiritually alive, although exposed to possible spiritual infection, were nevertheless amply protected from contagion by the power of Christ. They had no need of the civil magistrate's arm of steel to enforce a quarantine on spiritual error. "A false religion out of the church will not hurt the church, no more than weeds in the wilderness hurt the inclosed garden."[68] The righteous had spiritual weapons ample to wage warfare against error, and these weapons did not require the support of the civil magistrate. The New Testament metaphor of spiritual armor and weaponry (Eph. 6:11-18) made Williams's point: "Will the Lord Jesus . . . join to his breastplate of righteousness, the breastplate of iron and steel? To the helmet of righteousness and salvation in Christ, a helmet and crest of iron, brass, or steel, a target of wood to his shield of faith? [To] his two edged sword coming forth of the mouth of Jesus, the material sword, the work of smiths and cutlers? Or a girdle of shoes leather to the girdle of truth?"[69]

Williams also rejected the alleged right of the civil community to protect itself from divine judgment by punishing spiritual error. In part he responded to the Puritans' position with the historical argument that God does not appear to have punished nations for idolatry.[70] So far as he could tell, idolatry did a pretty good business—stable and secure. He pointed to pagan nations that had existed for hundreds and even thousands of years without suffering the destroying wrath of God.[71] In fact, although Williams agreed that God sometimes judged nations for their conduct, he accused the Puritans of promoting the kinds of conduct most likely to encourage divine wrath. Williams elaborated two kinds of behavior that risked divine punishment. First, God judged those nations that persecuted his saints.[72] Williams suggested, for example, that the Massachusetts Bay authorities who banished him had brought down God's judgment on the colony. He referred to "the many evils which it pleased God to bring upon some chief procurers of my sorrows, [and] upon the whole state after them, which many of their own have observed and reported to me."[73] Similarly, he declared "soul yokes, soul oppression, plunderings, ravishings" to be "the chief of England's sins, unstopping the vials of England's present sorrows."[74] Second, Williams believed that God's wrath would visit nations that set up a national church (by Williams's definition a false church).[75] Of course, once Roger Williams admitted that God sometimes judged nations in the here and now, he was thrust into a tedious dissection of history in which first he, then the Puritans, tried to trace civil calamities to either persecution of the righteous (as Williams thought) or heresy (as the Puritans believed).

By challenging Puritan concepts of civil peace and cognizable civil wrongs, Roger Williams deconstructed the argument for civil jurisdiction over religious matters. Although he shared with the Puritans an understanding of God as sovereign over all of life, including all the affairs of humanity, both civil and ecclesiastical, he urged that God had not transferred this all-encompassing sovereignty to the civil magistrate. The magistrate's delegated authority, he contended, was of a far more limited sphere than the Puritans envisioned. Williams also resisted the Puritan effort to expand the scope of the magistrate's limited authority through broad concepts of civil peace and civil wrong. His definitions of these concepts laid the theoretical basis for a fragmented world in which Cain's question—"Am I my brother's keeper?"—was answered, at least with respect to government involvement in matters of religion, "No."

The Bloody Tenent of Persecution

For half a century, Williams repeated and amplified his contention that civil governments possessed no power to direct spiritual affairs. Persecution for cause of conscience was the "bloudy tenent" that robbed the world of peace.[76] Williams grasped what would require almost two more centuries for others to acknowledge, that civil peace was attainable only by "sheathing" the sword of persecution: "He that reads the records of truth and time with an impartial eye, shall find [persecution for cause of conscience] to be the lancet that has pierced the veins of kings and kingdoms, of saints and sinners, and filled the streams and rivers with their blood."[77]

Persecution destroyed the peace chiefly because it underestimated the perseverance of dissenting religious consciences. One religious establishment after another in England had imagined that by strength of law it could guarantee religious uniformity and therefore civil peace. But Williams saw clearly that the conscience could not be so readily coerced and that the result of demanding from the consciences of citizens that which they could not surrender was endless bloodshed and mutiny by those who would not bow to the civil magistrate's claim of divine authority.[78] During the decade from 1547 to 1558, England had endured first the militantly conservative Protestantism of Edward VI, with its enforced preeminence of the Book of Common Prayer, and then the equally militant Catholicism of "Bloody" Mary Tudor. Even during the relatively settled years of Elizabeth's reign, Catholics continued to suffer martyrdom under a restored Protestant establishment. "The fathers made the children heretics, and the children the fathers," wrote Williams.[79] Persecution subjected the world to the bitter irony of a holy war in which "he that kills, and he that's killed, they both cry out, 'It is for God, and for their conscience.' "[80] The only hope for securing civil peace, Williams insisted, lay in "taking counsel of the great and wisest politician that ever was, the Lord Jesus Christ."[81]

Persecution was a grievous violation of conscience, and Williams could think of no more vivid metaphor to describe this horrible intrusion into the sacred precinct of the soul than the metaphor of rape. Persecution inflicted a "soul or spiritual rape" more abominable in the eyes of God than "to force and ravish the bodies of all the women in the world."[82] And, "The forcing of a woman, that is, the violent acting of uncleanness upon her body against her will, we count a rape: by proportion that is a spiritual or soul-rape, which is a forcing of the conscience of any person, to acts of worship."[83]

For Williams, the odiousness of religious persecution was aggravated by the futility of using force to effect religious change. Force could not accomplish conversion, he said, because conscience was of such a nature that "although it be groundless, false, and deluded, yet it is not by any arguments or torments easily removed."[84] The act of persecution would signify to the persecuted that "that religion cannot be true which needs such instruments of violence to uphold it."[85] Moreover, because religious conversion for Williams was more than simply a matter of mental reorientation but a change of heart and of the soul's affections, he denied that "the arm of flesh" or the "sword of steel" could ever "reach to cut the darkness of the mind, the hardness and unbelief of the heart, and kindly operate upon the soul's affections to forsake a long continued father's worship, and to embrace a new, though the best and truest."[86]

The most that persecution could accomplish was to manufacture a dissembled worship. The sword—government coercion—"may make . . . a whole nation of hypocrites."[87] God, however, looked upon the heart and could not be honored by such hypocrisy as the arm of the state could create. "Forced worship stinks in God's nostrils" and made hypocrites of the unbelievers forced to mouth words that had not taken root in their hearts and lives.[88] Because such worship was without faith, it was sin.[89] Moreover, for Williams, who believed that the soul's salvation was a matter of more pressing urgency than any political consideration, the hypocrisy spawned by a "dissembled uniformity" had a further, tragic consequence.[90] It was worthless as well as harmful. It "hardened" the souls of unbelievers "in a dreadful sleep and dream of their own blessed estate, and [sent] millions of souls to hell in a secure expectation of a false salvation."[91]

Williams's abhorrence of "forced worship" reflected a more general conviction that true worship always began with the heart's turning to God and the corollary certainty that acts of worship that did not arise out of a believing heart were sinful.[92] In the case of the Native Americans with whom he spent much time, for example, Williams was reluctant to encourage them to adopt Christian practices before they had turned to the true God. Thus, he did not attempt to convince them to keep the Sabbath, even though he averred that he could have easily done so: "I was persuaded, and am, that God's way is first to turn a soul from its idols, both of heart, worship, and conversation, before it is capable of worship, to the true and living God."[93] Ignorance of this spiritual truth, Williams maintained, was the bane of millions in England and elsewhere who had been baptized and admitted to the church's other ordinances without having ever experienced "the saving work of repentance, and a true turning to God."[94]

But the effect of "forced worship" on unbelievers was not the only manifestation of its perniciousness. The fostering of such hypocrisy in the name of maintaining "Christendom" polluted every Christian involved in the hypocrisy. Williams believed that swearing an oath in the name of God or uttering a prayer were acts of worship and reserved for Christians only. He further believed that no Christian could, without defiling conscience, participate in an act of worship with the unregenerate. This promiscuous worship was the chief stain of the Church of England, where every citizen was essentially a church member, and the failure to renounce this sin was a defilement of all non-Separatist churches in New England.

Moreover, perhaps the most grievous consequence of attempts to coerce worship and maintain uniformity of religion was that true believers were invariably caught in the zeal of the state's persecution.[95] God's children became "sweet prey to all," hunted and devoured.[96] The bloody tenet of persecution was "proved guilty of all the blood of the souls crying for vengeance under the altar."[97] Upon hearing in 1651 that two Baptists had been fined, and one whipped, for venturing into the Massachusetts Bay Colony, Roger Williams wrote to John Endicott, then governor of the colony: "Sir, I must be humbly bold to say, that it is impossible for any man or men to maintain their Christ by the sword, and to worship a true Christ! To fight against all consciences opposite to theirs, and not to fight against God in some of them, and to hunt after the precious life of the true Lord Jesus Christ."[98] Of course, persecutors never admitted that the blood they spilt was the blood of Christ. "Search all scriptures, histories, records, monuments, consult with all experiences, did ever Pharaoh, Saul, Ahab, Jezebel, Scribes and Pharisees, the Jews, Herod, the bloody Neroes, Gardiners, Boners, Pope or Devil himself, profess to persecute the Son of God, Jesus as Jesus, Christ as Christ, without a mask or covering?"[99]

Roger Williams was not a skeptical reader of Scripture. He found much clarity in its pages and was ever ready to do rhetorical battle with one opponent or another using the truths he found there as his principal weapons.[100] Nevertheless, he found not only certainty in the Holy Writ but sometimes "mystery" as well, and he believed the presence of such mystery ought to blunt the edge of persecuting arrogance.[101] Williams saw the possibility of error in matters pertaining to spiritual truth as too

THE LOGIC OF THE PURITAN ESTABLISHMENT

great to risk the state's persecuting zeal: "How easy, how common, how dreadful" the mistakes made by the persecuting sword.[102] Spiritual humility counseled a different course: "The experience of our fathers' errors, or own mistakes and ignorance, the sense of our own weaknesses and blindness in the depths of the prophesies and mysteries of the kingdom of Christ, and the great professed expectation of light to come which we are not now able to comprehend, may abate the edge, yea sheath up the sword of persecution toward any."[103]

Williams, of course, believed that truth was precious and should be sought after with all one's might. Unlike the Puritans, though, who tended to think of truth as a visible treasure in need of protection, Williams saw it more frequently as a hidden jewel in need of discovery. With that image in mind, he proposed an explicitly Christian version of the "marketplace of ideas" metaphor that Justice Oliver Wendell Holmes would give famous expression three centuries later. "It is the command of Christ Jesus to his scholars, to try all things: And liberty of trying what a friend, yea what an (esteemed) enemy presents, has ever (in point of Christianity) proved one special means of attaining to the truth of Christ."[104] In the present world, Williams suggested, the truth of Christ might not be easily discovered, and reasonable believers might differ in their apprehension of it. Thus, Williams challenged Massachusetts Puritans to acknowledge frankly the fact of religious pluralism or, as he described it, "the present differences even among them that fear God."[105]

For Roger Williams, the Puritans' readiness to inflict upon others the civil penalties they had themselves suffered under the Anglican establishment was a violation of the Golden Rule. "Mr. Cotton measures to others, which himself when he lived in such practices, would not have had measured to himself," he observed.[106] Williams found the Puritans' arguments in favor of this "partiality" completely unconvincing.[107] They insisted that God had granted generally to governments everywhere authority to act as a "nursing father" toward true religion. But, they also insisted, most magistrates—particularly non-Christians—lacked the knowledge of true religion necessary to perform this God-given role of spiritual oversight. Accordingly, Puritans argued that such magistrates should refrain from undertaking any supervisory role over religion until they had become rightly informed as to the substance of true religion.

The Puritans' argument put God in a rather poor light, Williams argued. After all, according to the Puritans, God had appointed civil magistrates to the role of "nursing father" to the churches. Yet because most magistrates could not exercise this role for lack of knowledge of true religion, God had apparently appointed mostly incompetents to tend to his church.[108] In fact, he had frequently chosen magistrates who believed themselves compelled to persecute the church. God, it would seem, had hired as babysitters the equivalent of a gang of axe-murderers.[109] The very thought that "any servant of Christ Jesus, should cry out to the Caesars of this world to help the eternal God to get his due" was more than Williams could stomach.[110] "Is the religion of Christ Jesus so poor and so weak and feeble grown," he demanded, "so cowardly and base . . . that neither the soldiers nor commanders in Christ's army have any courage or skill to withstand sufficiently in all points a false teacher, a false prophet, a spiritual cheater or deceiver?"[111]

Finally, Williams stated what seems today obvious but what was peculiarly invisible to his age: Persecution defied ordinary notions of humane treatment and, moreover, was contrary to the character and teachings of Christ.[112] Persecution was "irreligious and inhumane," Williams insisted, and denied the principles of both Christianity and civility.[113] When a follower of Christ advocated persecution, he presented the tragic irony of "the language of the Dragon in a lamb's lip" and failed to comprehend that "it was no ordinance for any disciple of Jesus to persecute the Pharisees at Caesar's bar."[114] It was contrary to the nature of Christ that "throats of men . . . should be torn out for his sake, who most delighted to converse with the greatest sinners." "The Christian Church," Williams maintained, "does not persecute; no more than a lily does scratch the thorns, or a lamb pursue and tear the wolves, or a turtle dove hunt the hawks and eagles, or a chaste and modest virgin fight and scratch like whores and harlots." Persecution for cause of conscience was, he said in the final sentence of his most important tract, "most evidently and lamentably contrary to the doctrine of Christ Jesus the Prince of Peace."[115]

In a preface addressed to Parliament at the beginning of *The Bloudy Tenent Yet More Bloudy*, Williams summarized the essence of persecution: "All violence to conscience turns upon these two hinges. First, of restraining from that worshiping of a god or gods, which the consciences of men in their respective worships (all the world over) believe to be true. Secondly, of constraining to the practicing or countenancing of that whereof their consciences are not persuaded."[116] Persecution, thus, might take the form of fines, whippings, or banishments arising out of matters relating to conscience and worship. Punishing people for not coming to church constituted persecution for cause of conscience, as did withdrawing civil privileges or rights on account of one's religious beliefs.[117] And, importantly, requiring individuals to support with taxes a religion or worship in which they did not believe was also a violation of religious freedom.[118] The combined effect of compulsory church attendance and compulsory support of ministers was to require unbelievers to pay for the privilege of having preachers try to convert them.[119] Like his contemporary John Milton, Williams sought to protect the individual conscience from "the paw / Of hireling wolves, whose Gospel is their maw."[120]

Williams, however, would have permitted the civil magistrate to encourage true religion, although he did not specify what kinds of encouragement would have been consistent with his view of religious liberty. He often declared that the civil magistrate ought to "countenance" and "encourage" the church.[121] He also suggested that magistrates should give "honorable testimony and approbation" to churches, and even "endeavor to win and save whom possibly he may, yet far from the appearance of civil violence."[122] By "countenancing" and "encouraging" the church Williams seems to have had in mind the use of civil authority to protect believers from would-be persecutors and permit them to exercise their religions freely.[123] The chief responsibility of the magistrate was to "break the teeth of the Lions."[124]

Roger Williams would have stripped civil government of power to superintend religious affairs. He chastised as offshoots of the "bloudy tenent of persecution" all deliberate attempts to wield the civil magistrate's sword in service of religious purity or religious uniformity. But conflicts between religious practice and government power do not always involve deliberate attempts by civil authorities to govern religious faith. Sometimes, in pursuit of public purposes unrelated to the suppression of religious practice, government power may collide with the perceived demands of religious belief. Government may command that from which religious belief requires abstention, or it may forbid that which religious duty requires. Although Williams directed most of his polemic against deliberate attempts by government to muzzle religious dissent, he was also familiar with unintended clashes between law and religious practice. The next chapter considers his efforts to referee these contests between the needs of public order and the demands of religious conscience.

Notes

1. Williams was happy to point out the awkwardness that must have attended Cotton's defense of persecuting principles with which English observers found themselves ever less in sympathy: "Some say Master Cotton is wise, and knows in what door the wind blows of late; he is not ignorant what sad complaints in

letters, printings, conferences, so many of God's people (and of his own conscience and judgment of Independency) have poured forth against New England's persecuting. He knows what bars New England's bloody tenet and
practice may put to his brethren's just desires and suits for moderation and toleration, to non-conforming consciences." Roger Williams, *The Bloudy Tenent Yet
More Bloudy,* in *The Complete Writings of Roger Williams,* 7 vols. (New York: Russell and Russell, 1963), 4:51.

2. Williams, *The Bloudy Tenent Yet More Bloudy,* 5.

3. Thomas Buckley, "The Political Theology of Thomas Jefferson," in *The
Virginia Statute for Religious Freedom: Its Evolution and Consequences in American History,* ed. Merrill D. Peterson and Robert C. Vaughan (New York: Cambridge University Press, 1988), 80. See William Miller's suggestion that the disposition to link
Israel with one's own nation triumphed over Williams's contrary vision and ultimately influenced even the deists of the founding period. William Lee Miller,
The First Liberty: Religion and the American Republic (New York: Alfred A. Knopf,
1985), 190.

4. Thomas Jefferson, *Thomas Jefferson: Writings,* ed. Merrill D. Peterson (New
York: Library of American, 1984), 523.

5. Roger Williams, *Mr. Cottons Letter Lately Printed, Examined and Answered,*
in *The Complete Writings of Roger Williams,* 7 vols. (New York: Russell and Russell, 1963), 1:359-60.

6. Roger Williams to John Winthrop, 24 Oct. 1636[?], in *The Correspondence
of Roger Williams,* 2 vols., ed. Glen W. LaFantasie (Hanover: Brown University
Press, 1988), 1:68.

7. For examples of Williams's use of the Old Testament to illustrate traits of
personal virtue he believed of continuing relevance, see Jesper Rosenmeier, "The
Teacher and the Witness: John Cotton and Roger Williams," *William and Mary
Quarterly,* 3d ser., 25 (1968): 416-17.

8. Numbers 21:4-9.

9. For useful discussions of typology in the Christian tradition, see Ursula
Brumm, *American Thought and Religious Typology,* trans. John Hoaglund (New
Brunswick: Rutgers University Press, 1970), 20-33; and Thomas M. Davis, "The
Traditions of Puritan Typology," in *Typology and Early American Literature,* ed. Sac-
van Bercovitch (Amherst: University of Massachusetts Press, 1972), 11-95.

10. Perry Miller argued that Roger Williams's use of typological interpretation of scripture was unorthodox; see *Roger Williams: His Contribution to the American Tradition* (Indianapolis: Bobbs-Merrill, 1953), 32-38. More recent appraisals,
however, have emphasized the degree to which Puritans used typology to explain the significance of the American experience. See, for example, Sacvan
Bercovitch, *The Puritan Origins of the American Self* (New Haven: Yale University
Press, 1975); Rosenmeier, "The Teacher and the Witness," 422; and Harry S. Stout,
The New England Soul: Preaching and Religious Culture in Colonial New England
(New York: Oxford University Press, 1986), 45. The possible sources for Williams's

use of typology as part of his argument for religious liberty are explored in Richard Reinitz, "The Separatist Background of Roger Williams' Argument for Religious Toleration," in *Typology and Early American Literature*, ed. Sacvan Bercovitch (Amherst: University of Massachusetts Press, 1972), 107-37. For Williams's use of typology to disconnect colonial experience from biblical law, see Reinitz, "The Separatist Background of Roger Williams' Argument," 107-38; and W. Clark Gilpin, *The Millenarian Piety of Roger Williams* (Chicago: University of Chicago Press, 1979), 109.

11. Roger Williams, *The Bloudy Tenent, of Persecution*, in *The Complete Writings of Roger Williams*, 7 vols. (New York: Russell and Russell, 1963), 3:239.

12. Williams, *The Bloudy Tenent Yet More Bloudy*, 29. For the inapplicability of Israel as a model for contemporary governments, see Williams, *The Bloudy Tenent, of Persecution*, 3, 322-23, 347.

13. Williams, *Mr. Cottons Letter*, 356.

14. Ibid., 332; see also Williams, *The Bloudy Tenent, of Persecution*, 359; and Williams, *The Bloudy Tenent Yet More Bloudy*, 154.

15. Williams, *Mr. Cottons Letter*, 360-61; Williams, *The Bloudy Tenent, of Persecution*, 281, 317, 319-21.

16. Williams, *The Bloudy Tenent Yet More Bloudy*, 180.

17. Williams, *The Bloudy Tenent, of Persecution*, 160.

18. Williams, *The Bloudy Tenent Yet More Bloudy*, 181, 245, 322, 347, 485-86.

19. John Winthrop, "A Modell of Christian Charity," in *The Puritans: A Source-book of Their Writings*, 2 vols., ed. Perry Miller and Thomas H. Johnson (New York: Harper and Row, 1963), 1:198.

20. Williams, *The Bloudy Tenent Yet More Bloudy*, 397.

21. Ibid., 393.

22. For the Old Testament prescription against adultery and the use of capital punishment to punish violations, see Exodus 20:14 and Deuteronomy 22:22. For Williams's objections to the use of death to punish adultery, see Roger Williams to John Winthrop, Jr., Jan. 1649/50 and 16 Feb. 1649/50, in *The Correspondence of Roger Williams*, ed. LaFantasie, 1:307, 309; and Williams, *The Bloudy Tenent Yet More Bloudy*, 487, 489. See also "Answers about Death Penalty for Adultery," enclosure, possibly to Williams's letter to John Winthrop, Jr., (ca. 20 June 1650), in *The Correspondence of Roger Williams*, ed. LaFantasie, 1:320-21.

23. Williams, *The Bloudy Tenent, of Persecution*, 366-67.

24. *A Model of Church and Civil Power*, quoted in Williams, *The Bloudy Tenent, of Persecution*, 254.

25. Nathaniel Ward, *The Simple Cobler of Aggawam in America*, ed. P. M. Zall (Lincoln: University of Nebraska Press, 1969), 6.

26. Williams, *The Bloudy Tenent Yet More Bloudy*, 28-29, 187.

27. Roger Williams, *Queries of Highest Consideration*, in *The Complete Writings of Roger Williams*, 7 vols. (New York: Russell and Russell, 1963), 2:260.

28. Williams, *The Bloudy Tenent, of Persecution*, 121.

29. Roger Williams, *A Key to the Language of America*, in *The Complete Writings of Roger Williams*, 7 vols. (New York: Russell and Russell, 1963), 1:227.

30. Williams, *Mr. Cottons Letter*, 335.

31. Williams, *The Bloudy Tenent, of Persecution*, 108-10.

32. Ibid., 160-61.

33. Ibid., 163.

34. Roger Williams, *The Examiner Defended*, in *The Complete Writings of Roger Williams*, 7 vols. (New York: Russell and Russell, 1963), 7:243; see generally Edmund S. Morgan, *Roger Williams: The Church and the State* (New York: W. W. Norton, 1967), 126-29; Williams, *The Bloudy Tenent Yet More Bloudy*, 222.

35. Williams, *The Bloudy Tenent, of Persecution*, 247.

36. Ibid., 43.

37. Ibid., 53. The appeal to possible divine judgment as grounds for legislative actions survived the Puritans, although it receded to the ground of prohibiting immoral actions only (not erroneous opinions). Various legislation concerning "morals" continued even after the First Amendment became effective, in part because "the major non-Anglican Protestant sects remained impressed with the fate of Sodom and Gomorrah." Gerald Bradley, "The No Religious Test Clause and the Constitution of Religious Liberty: A Machine That Has Gone of Itself," *Case Western Reserve Law Review* 37 (1987): 685.
During the second half of the nineteenth century, when Congress waged legislative war against polygamy in the territories, the report of the Committee on the Judiciary, which reported the 1860 anti-polygamy bill to the House of Representatives, declared astonishment that "in the midst of the blaze of the light of the nineteenth century, clouds and darkness should overshadow one of the Territories of the American Union, and an effort should be made, in a remote and almost inaccessible part of the confederacy, to bring our holy religion into contempt, to defy the opinions of the civilized world, and to invoke the vengeance of Heaven by a new Sodom and a new Gomorrah to attract its lightnings and appease its wrath." H.R. Rep. No. 83, 36th Cong., 1st sess. 4 (1860). John Stuart Mill noted the similar prevalence of this argument in defenses of Sabbath laws. He described it as "the belief that God not only abominates the act of the misbeliever, but will not hold us guiltless if we leave him unmolested." John Stuart Mill, *On Liberty*, ed. Elizabeth Rapaport (Indianapolis: Hackett Publishing, 1978), 89.

38. Williams, *The Bloudy Tenent Yet More Bloudy*, 153.

39. Ibid., 175.

40. Ibid., 68

41. Williams, *The Bloudy Tenent, of Persecution*, 73.

42. Ibid., 77.

43. Ibid., 79.

44. Ibid., 80.

45. Ibid., 142, 246, 355, 399; Williams, *The Examiner Defended*, 209; Williams, *The Bloudy Tenent Yet More Bloudy*, 174-75, 242.

46. Williams, *The Bloudy Tenent, of Persecution,* 331.

47. Williams, *The Bloudy Tenent Yet More Bloudy,* 238, 242.

48. Williams, *The Examiner Defended,* 209-12; Williams, *The Bloudy Tenent, of Persecution,* 398-99. Williams hedged somewhat on the question of whether it was desirable, even though unnecessary, for magistrates to be Christians. He seemed to suggest that one might desire magistrates to be Christians and pray for, and peaceably endeavor to achieve, this result but that it was nevertheless not in any sense necessary to the health of the civil order. Ibid., 413.

49. Williams, *The Bloudy Tenent, of Persecution,* 224-25, 251; Williams, *The Bloudy Tenent Yet More Bloudy,* 71.

50. Williams, *The Bloudy Tenent Yet More Bloudy,* 365.

51. Williams, *Key,* 38. For a general account of Williams's dealings with Native Americans, see Jack L. Davis, "Roger Williams among the Narragansett Indians," *New England Quarterly* 43 (1970): 593-604.

52. Williams, *Key,* 110.

53. Ibid., 98-99.

54. On Williams's role in establishing a secular state, see Samuel Hugh Brockunier, *Irrepressible Democrat: Roger Williams* (New York: Ronald Press, 1940), 118, 151.

55. Mark DeWolfe Howe, *The Garden and the Wilderness: Religion and Government in American Constitutional History* (Chicago: University of Chicago Press, 1965), 6.

56. Williams, *Mr. Cottons Letter,* 392; see also Williams, *The Bloudy Tenent, of Persecution,* 184-85.

57. Williams, *The Bloudy Tenent, of Persecution,* 249.

58. Ibid., 178; see also Williams, *The Bloudy Tenent Yet More Bloudy,* 262, 270-71, 430.

59. Williams, *The Bloudy Tenent, of Persecution,* 374-75.

60. Williams, *The Bloudy Tenent Yet More Bloudy,* 197.

61. Williams, *The Bloudy Tenent, of Persecution,* 201, 415.

62. Williams, *Mr. Cottons Letter,* 328, 336.

63. Williams, *The Bloudy Tenent Yet More Bloudy,* 414.

64. Williams, *The Bloudy Tenent, of Persecution,* 163-64; Williams, *The Bloudy Tenent Yet More Bloudy,* 284-85.

65. Williams, *The Bloudy Tenent, of Persecution,* 389.

66. Roger Williams, *The Hireling Ministry None of Christs,* in *The Complete Writings of Roger Williams,* 7 vols. (New York: Russell and Russell, 1963), 7:180.

67. Williams, *The Bloudy Tenent, of Persecution,* 111.

68. Ibid., 125-26, 198.

69. Ibid., 149-50.

70. Williams, *The Examiner Defended,* 248-49; Williams, *The Bloudy Tenent Yet More Bloudy,* 179, 200. Williams also denied that a nation's adherence to righteousness guaranteed it material prosperity. He found this gospel of good times inconsistent with "the afflicted and persecuted estate of God's people now."

Williams, *The Bloudy Tenent, of Persecution*, 359; see also Williams, *The Bloudy Tenent Yet More Bloudy*, 403-4, 406-7.

71. See, for example, Williams, *The Bloudy Tenent Yet More Bloudy*, 71, 73, 170, 180. But Williams was not altogether consistent in enumerating the circumstances likely to provoke God's judgment. While he was a teacher at Salem, he "discovered eleven public sins" for which he believed "it pleased God to inflict, and further to threaten public calamities." Williams, *Mr. Cottons Letter*, 321.

72. Williams, *The Bloudy Tenent Yet More Bloudy*, 170, 179, 189, 238.

73. Williams, *Mr. Cottons Letter*, 340.

74. Williams, *The Bloudy Tenent, of Persecution*, 6.

75. Williams, *Queries of Highest Consideration*, 258.

76. Williams, *The Bloudy Tenent, of Persecution*, 112, 117.

77. Ibid., 182.

78. Williams, *The Examiner Defended*, 229.

79. Williams, *Queries of Highest Consideration*, 260.

80. Williams, *The Bloudy Tenent, of Persecution*, 58.

81. Williams, *Queries of Highest Consideration*, 274; see also Williams, *The Bloudy Tenent, of Persecution*, 178.

82. Williams, *The Bloudy Tenent, of Persecution*, 182. See also 60 (referring to the effects of persecution as "the deflowering of chaste souls"), and 259 (declaring that coercion of worship by the state was a "ten thousand fold" greater sin than for "a natural father [to] force his daughter, or the father of the commonweal [to] force all the maidens in a country to the marriage beds of such and such men whom they cannot love").

83. Williams, *The Bloudy Tenent Yet More Bloudy*, 325.

84. Roger Williams to John Endicott, ca. Aug.–Sept. 1651, in *The Correspondence of Roger Williams*, ed. LaFantasie, 1:340.

85. Williams, *The Bloudy Tenent, of Persecution*, 139.

86. Ibid., 354.

87. Ibid., 136; see also Williams, *The Bloudy Tenent Yet More Bloudy*, 209.

88. Roger Williams to Maj. John Mason and Gov. Thomas Prence, 22 June 1670, in *The Correspondence of Roger Williams*, ed. LaFantasie, 2:617.

89. Williams, *The Bloudy Tenent, of Persecution*, 12, 138, 258-59.

90. Ibid., 62.

91. Ibid., 225; see also Williams, *Queries of Highest Consideration*, 261, 266. Williams also argued that to punish heretics with death was to frustrate the possibility that God might yet grant them repentance. *The Bloudy Tenent, of Persecution*, 95, 209.

92. Williams, *The Bloudy Tenent, of Persecution*, 12.

93. Williams, *Key*, 220-21.

94. Ibid., 221.

95. Williams even suggested that most of those who had ever suffered for being heretics were in fact the disciples and followers of Christ. Williams, *The Bloudy Tenent Yet More Bloudy*, 99.

96. Williams, *Key*, 190, 202.

97. Williams, *The Bloudy Tenent, of Persecution*, 3.

98. For description of the incidents, see William G. McLoughlin, *New England Dissent, 1630-1883*, 2 vols. (Cambridge: Harvard University Press, 1971), 1:19-21; and Thomas Curry, *The First Freedoms: Church and State in America to the Passage of the First Amendment* (New York: Oxford University Press, 1986), 15. Roger Williams to John Endicott, ca. Aug.–Sept. 1651, in *The Correspondence of Roger Williams*, ed. LaFantasie, 1:344-45

99. Williams, *The Bloudy Tenent, of Persecution*, 82.

100. See David S. Lovejoy, "Roger Williams and George Fox: The Arrogance of Self-Righteousness," *William and Mary Quarterly*, 3d ser., 62 (1993): 224-25.

101. See, for example, Williams, *Queries of Highest Consideration*, 268.

102. Roger Williams to John Endicott, ca. Aug.–Sept. 1651, in *The Correspondence of Roger Williams*, ed. LaFantasie, 1:346.

103. Williams, *The Bloudy Tenent, of Persecution*, 206. See also 214 ("Since there is so much controversy in the world . . . concerning the true Church, the ministry and worship, and who are those that truly fear God; I ask who shall judge in this case, who be they that fear God?").

104. Williams, *The Bloudy Tenent Yet More Bloudy*, 29.

105. Williams, *The Bloudy Tenent, of Persecution*, 217.

106. Ibid., 71; see also 205.

107. Ibid., 213-14, 395, 402 (his frequent condemnation of the Puritans' "partiality"); Williams, *The Bloudy Tenent Yet More Bloudy*, 44, 74, 82, 85, 251, 290, 344, and 6, 27, 47, 255, 276 (the corresponding praise of religious freedom in terms of its equity and impartiality); Williams, *The Hireling Ministry*, 154-55, 174, 177.

108. Williams, *The Bloudy Tenent Yet More Bloudy*, 494.

109. Williams, *The Bloudy Tenent, of Persecution*, 188, 238, 243; Williams, *The Bloudy Tenent Yet More Bloudy*, 165; Williams, *The Examiner Defended*, 210-11.

110. Williams, *The Bloudy Tenent Yet More Bloudy*, 223.

111. Ibid., 223.

112. Williams, *Queries of Highest Consideration*, 275. For an example of the Puritans' appeal to Christ as a model supportive of their punishment of religious dissenters, see Thomas Cobbet's discussion of the gospel accounts of Jesus' cleansing of the temple in *The Civil Magistrates Power in Matters of Religion* (1653, repr. New York: Arno Press, 1972), 1-12.

113. Williams, *The Bloudy Tenent, of Persecution*, 11, 4.

114. Williams, *Mr. Cottons Letter*, 326; Williams, *The Bloudy Tenent, of Persecution*, 122.

115. Ibid., 421, 193, 425. Roger Williams's protest against persecution was echoed by occasional acknowledgments that persecution, although a bloody tenet, still accomplished some good. Persecution, he believed, was the "common and ordinary portion of the saints under the Gospel." Williams, *The Bloudy Tenent Yet More Bloudy*, 75. He believed that the church had never been so pure, never so keenly focused on God, than when it had endured the violent opposition of Roman emperors in its first three centuries. Ibid., 72. God's people, he suggested, were "most sweet when most hunted." Williams, *The Bloudy Tenent, of Persecution*, 245. Persecution reminded believers that they were citizens of a kingdom other than whichever one claimed them as temporary residents in this life. Persecution "forced them to hasten home to another country which they profess to seek." Ibid., 245.

116. Williams, *The Bloudy Tenent Yet More Bloudy*, 7.

117. Ibid., 85, 59, 414.

118. Williams, *The Bloudy Tenent, of Persecution*, 297-305, 366; Williams, *The Examiner Defended*, 178; Williams, *The Bloudy Tenent Yet More Bloudy*, 391; Roger Williams, *The Fourth Paper, Presented by Major Butler*, in *The Complete Writings of Roger Williams*, 7 vols. (New York: Russell and Russell, 1963), 7:135; Williams, *The Hireling Ministry*, 178, 180.

119. Williams, *The Bloudy Tenent, of Persecution*, 299.

120. Quoted in Brockunier, *Irrepressible Democrat*, 208.

121. See, for example, Williams, *The Bloudy Tenent, of Persecution*, 129, 280, 334, 341, 372; Williams, *The Bloudy Tenent Yet More Bloudy*, 192, 251; and Williams, *The Hireling Ministry*, 183. The Baptist John Clarke similarly encouraged the English Parliament "To countenance and encourage . . . such as are faithful, and upright in the land." Epistle dedicatory in Clarke, *Ill Newes from New-England* (London: Henry Hills, 1652).

122. Williams, *The Bloudy Tenent, of Persecution*, 402, 242, 419.

123. Ibid., 280, 129, 373, 334; Williams, *The Bloudy Tenent Yet More Bloudy*, 192.

124. Williams, *The Bloudy Tenent, of Persecution*, 129.

4

Order and "Civility"

Williams, who thought long and deeply about the odiousness of religious persecution, was more than a theoretician. His ideas were born and took root in the fire of his experience, and that experience consisted of nearly four decades of activities relating to the founding and development of the Providence Colony.[1] We are left to wonder what might have become of his ideas had the Puritans of Massachusetts Bay Colony permitted him to remain as a kind of prophet-in-residence. Because they did not, however, Williams was forced to create not only ideas but also a place to live. Thus, the exiled Roger Williams and a group of fellow refugees ultimately found their way to the head of Narragansett Bay and founded first a town and ultimately a colony in what is now Rhode Island.[2] In doing so, they were forced to explore the intersection between religious faith and civil government, not as critics but as craftsmen.

The Struggle for Order in Early Rhode Island

The colony established by Williams and others lacked from the start the orderly framework of governance possessed by other colonies that had received royal patents. Williams and his friends had no patent, and their first attempts at communal order consisted simply of meeting together "once a fort night" and resolving the various issues attending their "common peace, watch, and planting" by mutual consent with "speed and peace."[3] But the simple meetings at which the Providence settlers originally chartered their common destiny could not survive the arrival of newcomers who did not share the community's brief past but nevertheless desired a part in its future. Something more than an appeal to a common past was required to maintain agreement and its consequent order. With the coming of "some young men single persons" who desired a share in the governance of the colony, Williams began to contemplate the creation of a social compact, and the early Providence settlers ultimately signed one in 1638.[4] By this compact, each member of the settlement promised to submit "in active and passive obedience to all such orders or agreements as shall be made for the public good of the body in an orderly way, by the major consent of the present inhabitants . . . and others whom they shall admit unto them *only in civil things.* "[5]

Roger Williams and the other Providence settlers were mostly religious dissenters fleeing established orthodoxies. Of course, they were not the first to have done so. They followed a path already well trodden by the Massachusetts Puritans, who had themselves sought refuge in New England from an Anglican establishment made inhospitable to them by the likes of Archbishop Laud. But the founders of Providence were remarkable for their day, chiefly in the fact that although they had the wherewithal to dictate the terms of Providence orthodoxy and thus erect their own brand of religious establishment, they declined to do so. Instead, they established only the principle of disestablishment. No church—not even one of their own liking—would be granted state-backed preeminence among them. No authority was granted the infant government to supervise religion, for the Providence founders had explicitly tethered its jurisdiction to "civil things."

Providence colonists thus launched their fragile experiment in government without the benefit of either an inherited or an imposed religious uniformity. The provision in the 1638 compact reserving uses of civil authority for "civil things" was not the first signal that Providence would seek foundations for its civil establishment other than in religious consensus. From the start, according to John Winthrop's contemporary account, "Mr. Williams and the rest did make an order, that no man should be molested for his conscience."[6] Later, after the 1638 compact, Providence colonists enacted a new plantation covenant called "The Combination," whose second article continued Providence's experiment in religious liberty by providing "as formerly has been the liberties of the town, so still, to hold forth liberty of conscience."[7] Such order as Providence inhabitants were able to establish over the next half century was purchased without the execution of a single heretic or payment of the least tithe to an established church.[8]

It would not be soon evident whether this attempt to construct a social order without the foundation of religious uniformity would succeed.

Early observers predicted failure. Nathaniel Ward, the "Simple Cobler of Aggawam," was frankly baffled by the prospect of order among such a band of misbegottens. "How all religions should enjoy their liberty, justice its due regularity, civil 'cohabitation moral' honesty, in one and the same jurisdiction," was, he declared, "beyond the Arctic my comprehension."[9]

For observers such as Ward, who thought "poly-piety" was the foremost entry in the devil's dictionary, the various miscreants who proposed to dwell peaceably together in Providence were a motley lot.[10] Certainly, if contrariness were a chief qualification for would-be Rhode Island colonists, then the new settlements attracted some outstanding citizens. While Roger Williams and his fellow settlers worked at crafting a town out of the Narragansett wilderness, other spiritual misfits took up residence nearby. Anne Hutchinson, invited by Massachusetts to terminate her residence there, joined with other antinomians to establish a town— eventually called Portsmouth—on the island of Aquidneck. These settlers soon fragmented, however, spinning off a new town at Newport. Another Portsmouth settler, Samuel Gorton, caused such disturbance there that he was whipped and banished. He and a few followers stayed for a time in Providence but ultimately left to establish the town of Warwick.

Trouble had no difficulty finding Roger Williams and the other souls gathered in the four settlements planted about the Narragansett Bay. In the same year that the Providence compact was signed, Williams wrote John Winthrop for advice on how to deal with "one unruly person who openly in town meeting more than once professed to hope for and long for a better government than the country has yet."[11] And, within a few years, one townsman would complain that "there was brawling continually in Mr. Williams' meadow."[12] Even after the passage of the first decade of the colony's existence, Williams was forced to admit to Winthrop that "our poor colony is in civil dissention."[13] Winthrop observed wryly in his journal that "at Providence . . . the devil was not idle."[14] Initial signs suggested that the expected demise of Providence and the sister towns that ultimately became Rhode Island was in full motion. Stable government had to overcome the fierce independence of the early settlers, their generally radical religious and political ideas, the threat of Indian attacks, and the intense rivalry among the towns of Providence, Newport, Portsmouth, and Warwick.[15]

The internal turbulence of the early Rhode Island towns and the threat of violence from Indians coincided with continued attempts by the Massachusetts Bay Colony to exert control over, or at least disrupt, the congregations of dissidents on its borders. As a result, Williams embarked to England in 1643 to secure a charter for the colony. He succeeded in obtaining a patent from Parliament, but after the restoration of the English monarchy in 1660 the earlier patent was cast in doubt and Williams again traveled to England to secure a charter for Rhode Island. Working together with the Baptist John Clarke, he succeeded in obtaining a second charter in 1663. Significantly, the charter incorporated the terms of the experiment in religious liberty whose beginnings had been so tempestuous. It declared:

> No person within said colony, at any time hereafter, shall be any wise molested, punished, disquieted, or called in question, for any differences in opinion in matters of religion, and do not actually disturb the civil peace of our said colony; but that every person and persons may . . . freely and fully have and enjoy his and their own judgments and consciences, in matters of religious concernments . . . they behaving themselves peaceably and quietly, and not using this liberty to licentiousness and profaneness, nor to the civil injury or outward disturbance of others.[16]

Williams later described the origin of the religious liberty provision in the Rhode Island charter as constituting an experiment by the king "whether civil government could consist with such liberty of conscience."[17] The outcome of this experiment was for some time in doubt. In 1653 or 1654, news of disorder prompted Sir Henry Vane, a former governor of the Massachusetts Bay Colony and one of Providence's English supporters, to express exasperation over the colony's fractiousness, wondering whether there was any "fear and awe of God" among its citizens.[18]

Williams wrote to the town of Providence during this same period and lamented its disorderliness: "I am like a man in a great fog. I know not well how to steer. I fear to run upon the rocks at home, (having had trials store abroad). I fear to run quite backward (as men in a mist do) and undo all, that I have been this late long time undoing of my self to do, to wit to keep up the name of a people, a free people not enslaved to the bondages and iron yokes of the great (both soul and body) oppressions of the English and barbarians [Indians] about us: nor to the divisions and disorders within our selves."[19] When Williams, newly returned from his mission on behalf of the colony to England, finally managed to restore order to the tumult that had beset the colony, he composed the colony's reply to Vane: "Possibly a sweet cup has rendered many of us wanton and too active. . . . For we have long drunk of the cup of as great liberties, as any people that we can hear of under the whole Heaven."[20]

The branding of religious dissenters as unstable anarchists is, of course, a favorite past-time of the orthodox. No doubt the Massachusetts faithful tended to exaggerate the degree of instability in early Providence settlements.[21] Massachusetts order endured more than a few tremors of its own, and it shared some of its neighbor's maladies.[22] Yet if Providence was not so disorderly as Massachusetts thought, it was, nevertheless, troubling for advocates of religious liberty to see unruliness threaten to discredit their social endeavors. Roger Williams in particular, even while waging rhetorical war against Massachusetts persecution, also sought to secure civil order from the sometimes disruptive claims of religious conscience. He admitted candidly on occasion that he and his Providence neighbors had "some gusts among us as to our whole colony and civil order."[23] For Williams, the success of the colony lay in finding some mediation between the eternally warring principles of liberty and license: "We enjoy liberties of soul and body but it is licence we desire except the most holy help us."[24]

The Limits of Religious Liberty

As an aggressive advocate of religious liberty, Roger Williams sought to erect a citadel for conscience that the civil magistrate could not surmount. But as a citizen and a politician, he endeavored to obtain for civil authority the power to secure public order in the face of occasional religious rambunctiousness. He thought it possible to achieve these twin aspirations by rigorously policing the boundaries between two jurisdictions: the spiritual and the civil. Within the realm of spiritual matters, "the poorest peasant must disdain the service of the highest Prince."[25] The believer pressed between the conflicting claims of God and Caesar must obey God and refuse obedience to Caesar.[26]

Williams classed as persecutions all government intrusions into the spiritual jurisdiction, including molestation of believers for "either professing doctrine, or practicing worship merely religious or spiritual."[27] God had established the civil jurisdiction, on the other hand, "for the defense of persons, estates, families, liberties of a city or civil state, and the suppressing of uncivil or injurious persons or actions."[28] Within this realm of authority the civil magistrate had received a divine commission to preserve peace and civility. Moreover, within the jurisdiction of civil affairs, Williams specifically declared that the religious conscience was not exempt from the commands of law. If the church disturbed the peace, then

the civil magistrate was authorized to punish the church.[29] If a religious
leader committed a crime against the civil state, then God was honored
by civil punishment of such a leader.[30] An asserted claim of conscience
would not exempt a religious believer from the civil magistrate's power
to punish in cases "wherein civility is wronged, in the bodies and goods
of any."[31] The civil magistrate could therefore punish human sacrifice, or
immodesty and uncleanness, even though such practices were masked under "religious pretenses."[32]

Early Providence settlers valued religious liberty but refused to allow it
to become a kind of magical immunity from civil law. Joshua Verin was a
case in point. Joshua and his wife Jane had followed Williams from Salem
to Providence and built a home near that of Roger and Mary Williams.
Williams, at last, was free to conduct informal religious meetings in his
home without fear of civil reprisal, and Jane Verin—but not Joshua—soon
began attending these meetings regularly. So regular was her attendance
and so frequent the meetings that Joshua Verin decided that Jane was being unduly absent from home. He ordered her to give up the meetings.
When she refused, he beat her mercilessly. According to Williams, Joshua
Verin had "trodden her under foot tyrannically and brutishly: Which she
and we long bearing though with his furious blows she went in danger
of life."[33] Joshua's Providence neighbors eventually disenfranchised him
for violating her freedom of conscience.[34] They did not find convincing
the argument that Providence was violating his freedom of religion by
interfering with his biblically rooted right to have submission from his
wife. Rejecting this claim, the Providence settlers sent Verin packing, dis-
carding him, as Williams later wrote, "from our civil freedom."[35]

Some observers claimed to see inconsistency in Providence's elevation
of Jane Verin's conscience over that of her husband. John Winthrop, observing the issue from his perch in Massachusetts, appears to have taken
special delight in pointing out what seemed to him a contradiction. By
Winthrop's account, the conduct of Joshua Verin sparked a lively debate
in Providence. Citizen Arnold protested the sanction against Verin, arguing that he had never understood the colony's protection of religious liberty to extend to "the breach of any ordinance of God, such as the
subjection of wives to their husbands." Another citizen retorted that "if
they should restrain their wives, all the women in the country would cry
out of them." To this observation Arnold noted how strange it was that
the Providence colonists had left Massachusetts because "they would not
offend God to please men" but were now prepared to offend God (by violating the ordinance concerning subjection of wives to their husbands)

to please women. Arnold insisted, moreover, that Providence colonists anxious to punish Joshua Verin for denying religious liberty to his wife were actually betraying the principle of religious freedom themselves, because Verin did what he did "out of conscience."[36]

Winthrop's account leaves us with no Providence rejoinder to Arnold's final point: that Providence had trampled on Joshua Verin's conscience even as it purported to safeguard his wife's religious liberty. Perhaps the majority that censured Verin doubted that religious sensibilities played any part in his wife-beating; it would have been easy enough to characterize his actions as merely vicious rather than conscientious. Providence might have legitimately suspected that Verin's viciousness was not the product of any sincerely held religious scruples but rather an example of what Williams referred to as "religious pretenses": unadorned meanness masquerading as religious sensibility.

There are obvious dangers in such judgments, though. Williams's topography of the spiritual and civil realms sometimes seems to suffer a defect common to other attempts to distinguish the sacred from the profane: It appears to assume that these jurisdictions never overlap. When Williams argues that the civil magistrate must "cut off all incivilities though under religious pretenses masked and covered," he seems to doubt whether acts of incivility could ever be authentically religious.[37] But only a myopic familiarity with religious experience could fail to discover examples of religiously inspired viciousness. Verin may well have been one such example. Williams's willingness to subject "religious pretenses" to the general requirements of civil law may have betrayed an overly confident "I know it when I see it" attitude toward authentic religion. In this confidence he may have failed to ponder seriously the conflict between the faith of the dissident one and the civil desires of the orthodox many. Orthodoxy has a tendency to deny to the heterodox the virtue of conscientiousness, preferring to impute baser motives to dissent. Massachusetts Puritans, for example, punished religious deviants for having "sinned against their own consciences." Providence, and Roger Williams himself, may have been yet possessed by some vestige of this thinking. It cloaks difficult questions in a comforting simplicity. Shorn of any claim to conscientiousness, Joshua Verin is merely brutish and for that suffers justly the penalties of civil law. But if the brute is also devout, then those committed to soul liberty must decide whether civil concerns are sufficiently weighty to override a cherished principle of liberty. In the case of Verin, this calculation could have been made readily. But in other cases society's interest in preserving civility may appear less compelling than it did here.

At his best, Williams was sensitive to this issue. In theory, at least, he allowed the possibility that sincere faith might desire to inflict civil harm
on others. For example, he recognized that some religions practiced human sacrifice and was prepared to acknowledge that both religious belief
and incivility were at issue.[38] In these cases he believed that faith should
give way to law.[39] But he argued that not all seeming incivilities were actually incivil and maintained that the state was obligated to distinguish
between the appearance and the reality of incivility with "a more tender
and observant eye."[40] In a passage almost universally neglected by commentators, Williams piled one biblical example on top of another to
suggest that "incivility" was a standard capable of manipulation. Circumcision, he suggested, is a fairly bloody affair. Does that mean that government should be able to suppress religious circumcision as an act of
incivility? Was the virgin mother of Jesus to be punished for the apparent
uncivil offense of illegitimacy? Should the patriarch Abraham be stripped
of honor for having attempted the sacrifice of his son Isaac at the command of God?[41]

At least with respect to Williams's reference to the aborted sacrifice
of Isaac by Abraham (Gen. 22:1-19), his argument seems inconsistent
with his previous contention that human sacrifice amounts to incivility and may be restrained by the civil magistrate. Williams's marginal
note to the passage concerning Abraham refers to "Abraham's sacrificing of Isaac a seeming incivility."[42] By concluding that Abraham's
attempted sacrifice only *seemed* to be incivil, Williams seems to be smug-
gling into his argument the premise that God had commanded the sacrifice and supernaturally communicated this command to Abraham.
But other human sacrificers no doubt hold similar beliefs about the divine sanction of human sacrifice. Without taking a theological side and
choosing among gods, Williams posits no independent criterion for
distinguishing between acceptable human sacrifice and incivil human
sacrifice.

The examples of circumcision and Mary's virgin birth are less problematic. In each case, Williams sought to challenge the designation of
particular conduct as incivil and thus limit the power of the magistrate to
intrude upon religious practice. Incivility consisted for Williams in conduct that was either immoral or causes injury to the "bodies or goods" of
someone else. As to circumcision, Williams emphasized the lack of any
lasciviousness in the rite as a way of demonstrating that it was not immoral. With respect to the birth of Jesus, he suggested that it presented
"no violence of civility, no wrong to the bodies or goods of any."[43] More-

over, he noted that the event had been "gloriously free" from the kind of sexual promiscuity present in some religious practice.

Williams thus appears to have concluded that attempting to ban circumcision or to punish Mary for an illegitimate pregnancy would be beyond the scope of proper government authority because no incivility was involved. That conclusion envisions government as possessing a limited sphere of authority. Even when the civil magistrate was not attempting to burden a religious practice in particular, for Williams it was apparently possible that the magistrate might nevertheless oppress religious conscience without sufficient justification.[44]

Just as civil society required even believers to refrain from harming the bodies and goods of others, the very nature of civil government required, Williams contended, certain positive contributions from each citizen. From these contributions conscience could claim no exemption. He appears to have envisioned two positive duties of every citizen: paying taxes to support the common government and assisting in the defense of the community. In a letter written toward the end of his life, Williams set out his argument for the duty to pay taxes. Because it reflects Williams's general views regarding the relationship between the individual and the state, it is worth quoting at length.

Considerations presented, touching rates.
1. Government and order in families towns etc. is the Ordinance of the most High (Rom. 13) for the peace and good of mankind.
2. Six things are written in the hearts of all mankind yea even in pagans: First that there is a Deity, 2 that some actions are naught 3 that the Deity will punish 4 that there is another life 5 that marriage is honorable 6 that mankind can not keep together without some government.
3. There is no English man in his Majesty's dominions or elsewhere, who is not forced to submit to government.
4. There is not a man in the world (except robbers pirates, rebels) but does submit to government.
5. Even robbers, pirates and rebels themselves can not hold together but by some law among themselves and government.
6. One of these 2 great laws in the world must prevail, either that of judges and justices of peace, in courts of peace: or the law of arms, the sword and blood.
7. If it come from the courts of trials in peace, to the trial of the sword and blood, the conqueror is forced to settle law and government.
8. Till matters come to a settled government, no man is ordinarily sure of his house, goods lands cattle wife children or life.
9. Hence is that ancient maxim: It is better to live under a tyrant in peace, than under the sword, or where Every man is a tyrant.

. . .

13. Our charter excels all in N. Engl. or the world, as to the souls of men.

14. It pleases God (Rom. 13) to command tribute custom and consequently rates etc. not only for fear, but for conscience sake.[45]

The letter illustrates well Williams's tendency to rely on both biblical interpretation and sociological observation to buttress his general arguments. In this case, he appealed both to Paul's discussion of the ordinance of government in chapter 13 of the letter to the Romans and to the general argument for the necessity of government and, accordingly, the necessity of taxes to support the activity of government. The letter also emphasizes Williams's commitment to the idea of government. Whatever spiritual anarchy his ideas about liberty of conscience may have spawned, he was anything but an anarchist.

According to Williams, citizens also owed obligations of civil defense from which the religious conscience was entitled to no exemption. A letter he sent the town of Providence in 1654 or 1655 addressed in more general terms the relationship between civil duty and individual conscience. Roger William's analogy of the seagoing vessel has become perhaps the most famous excerpt of all his writings:

There goes many a ship to sea, with many a hundred souls in one ship, whose weal and woe is common; and is a true picture of a common-wealth, or a human combination, or society. It has fallen out sometimes, that both Papists and Protestants, Jews, and Turks, may be embarked into one ship. Upon which supposal, I do affirm, that all the liberty of conscience, that ever I pleaded for, turns upon these two hinges—that none of the Papists, Protestants, Jews, or Turks, be forced to come to the ship's prayers or worship; nor, secondly, compelled from their own particular prayers or worship, if they practice any. I further add, that I never denied, that notwithstanding this liberty, the commander of this ship ought to command the ship's course; yea, and also command to that justice, peace, and sobriety, be kept and practiced, both among the seamen and all the passengers. If any seamen refuse to perform their service, or passengers to pay their freight;—if any refuse to help in person or purse, towards the common charges, or defense;—if any refuse to obey the common laws and orders of the ship, concerning their common peace or preservation;—if any shall mutiny and rise up against their commanders, and officers;—if any shall preach or write, that there ought to be no commanders, nor officers, because all are equal in CHRIST, therefore no masters, nor officers, no laws, nor orders, no corrections nor punishments—I say, I never denied, but in such cases, whatever is pretended, the commander or commanders may judge, resist, compel, and punish such transgressors, according to their deserts and merits.[46]

Williams's "ship of state" letter appears to have arisen out of the attempt by the town of Providence in November 1654 to establish regular musters of, and appoint officers for, its militia.[47] Some townspeople objected to this requirement of compulsory military service at least partially on grounds of religious liberty. Several objectors circulated a paper arguing "That it is blood-guiltiness, and against the rule of the Gospel, to execute judgment upon transgressors against the private or public weal."[48]

This brief summary of the dissident position leaves uncertain whether the objectors were urging conscientious grounds for exemption from military service or whether they advocated a far more sweeping objection to any civil punishment—anarchy.[49] The latter interpretation of the objector's position would make Williams's response more understandable. The ship of state letter has troubled some scholars because it seems to depart from principles Williams enunciated in his longer works.[50] Perry Miller, for example, suggested that Williams's letter reflected disillusionment and weariness with democracy and a deepening sense of the great gulf between "the perfection of the antitypical church and the miserable reality of the wilderness."[51] Perhaps a more convincing explanation of the letter, though, is that Williams simply chose a metaphor which—although powerful—was an imperfect analogy with which to elaborate his broader views about civil duty and religious conscience, and that his letter failed to address a host of unanswered questions about the subject.[52]

In any event, the previous discussion of Williams's understanding of the legitimate scope of the civil government's power should be recalled to understand the implicit limit upon the government's authority over conscience. Williams did not simply define an inviolate area of conscience and then leave the government free to act in any manner outside this narrowly prescribed area. For him, both conscience and government had limits. The civil government was limited to its responsibility for preserving peace and civility. The conscience was limited by its obligation to submit itself to the government as God's ordinance for preserving peace and civility. Thus, neither Williams's letter to Providence concerning taxes nor his ship of state letter may be read as subjecting the claims of conscience to *any* generally applicable law so long as it does not deliberately infringe upon religious belief or act. Rather, in both cases Williams saw conscience subjected to particular laws, and he viewed these laws as within the specific scope of the government's ordained responsibilities.[53]

Williams was at once a representative of his age and a seer who looked beyond it. In his concern for order within the civil commonwealth, he spoke and acted for his age.[54] He placed an excessive premium on peace and due respect for authority. At one point, for example, he attempted an abortive prosecution of several Providence inhabitants, and the language of the pleadings against these individuals shows the measure of Williams's regard for authority and the consequent distance between his world and ours. One indictment charged a William Harris "for his open defiance under his hand against our charter, all our laws, and court[,] the Lord protector and all government."[55] Williams indicted a group of inhabitants as "common opposers of all authority," another individual as "strongly suspected of contempt of the order of the colony," and yet another "for tearing a protest."[56] A similar example of Williams's high regard for authority and the deference he believed owed to it was his attitude toward the Quaker habit of addressing civil officials with the familiar *thou,* a practice he regarded as disrespectful of authority. "A due and moderate restraint and punishing of these incivilities (though pretending conscience)" was not persecution, he urged.[57]

Williams was also a captive to his age with regard to his confidence in the universal recognition of certain fundamental moral precepts whose violation could be punished as "incivilities." He believed that there was "a moral virtue, a moral fidelity, ability and honesty" that all individuals, Christian and non-Christian, could recognize.[58] Four moral violations in particular were "inconsistent to the converse of man with man": murder, adultery, theft, and lying.[59] Native Americans, he maintained, recognized these categories.

> Adulteries, murders, robberies, thefts,
>   Wild Indians punish these!
> And hold the scales of justice so,
>   That no man farthing less.
> When Indians hear the horrid filths,
>   Of Irish, English men,
> The horrid oaths and murders late,
>   Thus say these Indians then.
> We wear no clothes, have many gods,
>   And yet our sins are less:
> You are barbarians, pagans wild,
>   Your land's the wilderness.[60]

But Williams's table of universally agreed upon moral precepts ranged beyond this list. Thus, he praised the suppression of Ovid's *De Art Amandi* because he thought it was "a spark to immodesty and uncleanness." He also viewed it a duty of the civil magistrate to cut off such incivilities of the time as "the monstrous hair of women, upon the heads of some men," a moral offense he attributed to a forgetting of nature.[61]

We should not attempt to locate Williams's principal contribution to the subject of religious liberty and social order in these examples. If scrutinized closely, he must inevitably appear dressed in the garb of seventeenth-century colonial America. He found grounds for government intervention in matters of conscience over a broad spectrum of issues because he perceived universal categories of good order and civility that justified such intervention. But on other critical issues, Williams looked beyond his age and recognized the potential for limiting religious freedom based upon overly generous characterizations of public interest in peace and civility.

Notes

1. Clinton Rossiter, "Roger Williams on the Anvil of Experience," *American Quarterly* 3 (1951): 14-15. For an engaging attempt to reconstruct a picture of Williams's daily life, see Glen W. LaFantasie, "A Day in the Life of Roger Williams," *Rhode Island History* 46 (1987): 95-111.

2. For discussions of the early Providence Colony, see generally Sydney V. James, *Colonial Rhode Island: A History* (New York: Charles Scribner's Sons, 1975), 1-32; and Patrick Conley, *Democracy in Decline: Rhode Island's Constitutional Development, 1776-1841* (Providence: Rhode Island Historical Society, 1977), 14-20.

3. Roger Williams to John Winthrop, before 25 Aug. 1636, in *The Correspondence of Roger Williams*, 2 vols., ed. Glen W. LaFantasie (Hanover: Brown University Press, 1988), 1:53.

4. Ibid. Williams's 25 August 1636 letter to John Winthrop contains a draft version of the compact ultimately signed in 1638.

5. John R. Bartlett, ed., *Records of the Colony of Rhode Island and Providence Plantations, in New England* (Providence: A. Crawford Greene and Brother, 1856), 1:14 (emphasis added).

6. John Winthrop, *The History of New England from 1630 to 1649*, 2 vols., ed. James Savage (Boston: Phelps and Farnham, 1825, repr. New York: Arno Press, 1972), 1:282-83.

7. Bartlett, ed., *Records of the Colony of Rhode Island*, 8.

8. Bradley Chapin, *Criminal Justice in Colonial America, 1606-1660* (Athens: University of Georgia Press, 1983), 58, 117.

9. Nathaniel Ward, *The Simple Cobler of Aggawam in America*, ed. P. M. Zall (Lincoln: University of Nebraska Press, 1969), 23.

10. Ward, *The Simple Cobler*, 8.

11. Roger Williams to John Winthrop, early May 1638?, in *The Correspondence of Roger Williams*, ed. LaFantasie, 1:154.

12. Editorial note in *The Correspondence of Roger Williams*, ed. LaFantasie, 1:211.

13. Roger Williams to John Winthrop, before 29 Jan. 1648/49, in *The Correspondence of Roger Williams*, ed. LaFantasie, 1:268.

14. Winthrop, *History*, ed. Savage, 1:282.

15. Dwight Bozeman, "Religious Liberty and the Problem of Order in Early Rhode Island," *New England Quarterly* 45 (1972): 44.

16. Richard L. Perry and John C. Cooper, eds., *Sources of Our Liberties: Documentary Origins of Individual Liberties in the United States Constitution and Bill of Rights*, rev. ed. (Chicago: American Bar Foundation, 1978), 170. This provision influenced a number of other colonial documents relating to religious freedom. It was copied in 1665 in the Charter of Carolina, and it influenced the wording of the Concession of 1664 of New Jersey and the Concessions of the Proprietors of Carolina of 1665. Ibid., 166.
The Rhode Island charter, although not the first colonial document guaranteeing religious freedom, was the first such document in which the guarantee stood side by side with the framing of the government. Maryland's Act Concerning Religion (1649) contained an earlier, although more limited, guarantee of religious liberty. According to the act, no person "professing to believe in Jesus Christ" could be "troubled, molested or discountenanced for or in respect of his or her religion nor in the free exercise therefore." Ibid., 166.

17. Roger Williams to Maj. John Mason and Gov. Thomas Prence, 22 June 1670, in *The Correspondence of Roger Williams*, ed. LaFantasie, 2:616-17.

18. Sir Henry Vane to the Town of Providence, 8 Feb. 1653/54, in *The Correspondence of Roger Williams*, ed. LaFantasie, 2:389.

19. Roger Williams to the Town of Providence, ca. Aug. 1654, in *The Correspondence of Roger Williams*, ed. LaFantasie, 2:399-400.

20. Town of Providence to Sir Henry Vane [letter in Williams's handwriting], 27 Aug. 1654, in *The Correspondence of Roger Williams*, ed. LaFantasie, 2:397; Samuel Hugh Brockunier, *The Irrepressible Democrat: Roger Williams* (New York: Ronald Press, 1940), 220.

21. Bruce C. Daniels, *Dissent and Conformity on Narragansett Bay: The Colonial Rhode Island Town* (Middletown: Wesleyan University Press, 1983), 111-12; Carl Bridenbaugh, *Fat Mutton and Liberty of Conscience: Society in Rhode Island, 1636-1690* (Providence: Brown University Press, 1974), 7.

22. Daniels, *Dissent and Conformity*, 21.

23. Roger Williams to John Winthrop, Jr., ca. 15 Feb. 1654/55, in *The Correspondence of Roger Williams*, ed. LaFantasie, 2:427.

24. Ibid., 2:429.

25. Roger Williams, *The Bloudy Tenent, of Persecution*, in *The Complete Writings of Roger Williams*, 7 vols. (New York: Russell and Russell, 1963), 3:12-13.

26. Williams, *The Bloudy Tenent, of Persecution,* 375, 379; Roger Williams, *The Bloudy Tenent Yet More Bloudy,* in *The Complete Writings of Roger Williams,* 7 vols. (New York: Russell and Russell, 1963), 4:267.

27. Williams, *The Bloudy Tenent, of Persecution,* 63. Williams clearly believed that religious liberty extended beyond matters of belief to "what is merely point of worship, as prayer, and other services and administrations." *The Bloudy Tenent Yet More Bloudy,* 144.

28. Williams, *The Bloudy Tenent, of Persecution,* 160-61.

29. Ibid., 232, see also 229. Although Williams does not appear to have justified civil punishment for the Quaker practice of appearing naked in public as a religious sign, he vehemently opposed the practice and may have counted it as an example of either a breach of the peace or a violation of civility under the guise of religious conscience. For Williams's opposition to the practice, see Roger Williams, *George Fox Digg'd out of His Burrowes,* in *The Complete Writings of Roger Williams,* 7 vols. (New York: Russell and Russell, 1963), 5:59-62; and Roger Williams to John Throckmorton, 18 July, ca. 23 July, and 30 July 1672, in *The Correspondence of Roger Williams,* ed. LaFantasie, 2:657, 662, 672. A celebrated instance of this Quaker practice occurred in England while Williams was there in 1652, when, during a sermon on the Resurrection, a Quaker woman ran nude through a church congregation, shouting "welcome the Resurrection." Brockunier, *Irrepressible Democrat,* 212-13.

30. Williams, *The Bloudy Tenent, of Persecution,* 410.

31. Roger Williams, *The Examiner Defended,* in *The Complete Writings of Roger Williams,* 7 vols. (New York: Russell and Russell, 1963), 7:243.

32. Williams, *The Examiner Defended,* 243. The example of human sacrifice as a challenge to the scope of religious liberty has been a fixture in arguments concerning freedom of conscience. John Locke also used it in *A Letter Concerning Toleration,* ed. James Tully (Indianapolis: Hackett Publishing, 1983), 46. When the Supreme Court first addressed the scope of the free-exercise clause, it returned to the same example to justify in part its determination that the religious beliefs of a Mormon did not entitle him to an exemption from a statute making polygamy illegal in the territories. See *Reynolds v. United States,* 98 U.S. 145, 166 (1878). For a fictional case in the spirit of Lon Fuller, "The Case of the Speluncean Explorers," *Harvard Law Review* 62 (1949): 616, involving the application of the free-exercise clause to an instance of human sacrifice, see Stephen Pepper, "The Case of Human Sacrifice," *Arizona Law Review* 23 (1981): 897.

33. Roger Williams to John Winthrop, 22 May 1638, in *The Correspondence of Roger Williams,* ed. LaFantasie, 1:156.

34. Bartlett, ed., *Records of the Colony of Rhode Island,* 1:16.

35. Roger Williams to John Winthrop, 22 May 1638, in *The Correspondence of Roger Williams,* ed. LaFantasie, 1:156.

36. Winthrop, *History,* ed. Savage, 1:282-83.

37. Williams, *The Examiner Defended,* 243 (margin note).

38. Ibid., 243.

39. Ibid.

40. Ibid., 244.

41. Ibid., 243-45.

42. Williams, *The Examiner Defended*, 245.

43. Ibid., 244-45.

44. Relying only on Williams's ship of state letter, Gerard V. Bradley has argued that Williams was "politically an authoritarian" and would have nothing to do with the idea of constitutional exemptions for religious believers from laws of general applicability, nor for the general "solicitation of conscience" embraced by cases some of the Supreme Court's decisions under the free-exercise clause. Gerald V. Bradley, "Beguiled: Free Exercise Exemptions and the Siren Song of Liberalism," *Hofstra Law Review* 20 (1991): 266. The passage quoted in the text illustrates that Williams was less authoritarian than Bradley has imagined and far more solicitous of conscience than Bradley is prepared to be.

45. Roger Williams to the Town of Providence, 15 Jan. 1681/82, in *The Correspondence of Roger Williams,* ed. LaFantasie, 2:774.

46. Roger Williams to the Town of Providence, ca. Jan. 1654/55, in *The Correspondence of Roger Williams,* ed. LaFantasie, 2:423-24. For a similar use of the ship metaphor, see Williams, *The Examiner Defended,* 209.

47. Brockunier, *Irrepressible Democrat,* 225.

48. Ibid. Williams reproduced the quoted language in the opening lines of the ship of state letter, see *The Correspondence of Roger Williams,* ed. LaFantasie, 2:423.

49. Brockunier, *Irrepressible Democrat,* 225.

50. LaFantasie, ed., *The Correspondence of Roger Williams,* 2:423.

51. Perry Miller, *Roger Williams: His Contribution to the American Tradition* (Indianapolis: Bobbs-Merrill, 1953), 225.

52. LaFantasie, ed., *The Correspondence of Roger Williams,* 2:423. On the obligation to defend the state, in addition to the ship of state letter, see Williams, *The Examiner Defended,* 203.

53. For an attempt to marshal Williams in support of a position against any religious exemption from an otherwise valid law, see Elias West, "The Case against a Right to Religion-Based Exemptions," *Notre Dame Journal of Law, Ethics and Public Policy* 4 (1990): 630-31. West does not take sufficient notice of either Williams's enunciation of specific categories of laws as to which the religious believer could claim no exemption or his recognition of the extent to which even facially neutral categories of legitimate government action could be manipulated to limit religious freedom impermissibly.

54. Robert D. Brunkow, "Love and Order in Roger Williams' Writings," *Rhode Island History* 35 (1976): 115-20. For a discussion of the reverence for order demonstrated by both Anglican and Puritan writers in the early 1600s, see T. H. Breen, *The Character of the Good Ruler: A Study of Puritan Political Ideas in New England, 1630-1730* (New Haven: Yale University Press, 1970), 4-6.

55. LaFantasie, ed., *The Correspondence of Roger Williams*, 2:468.

56. Ibid.

57. Williams, *George Fox Digg'd out of His Burrowes*, 307. For Williams's general view of the Quakers as uncivil barbarians, see John Canup, *Out of the Wilderness: The Emergence of an American Identity in Colonial New England* (Middletown: Wesleyan University Press, 1990), 129-33.

58. Williams, *The Bloudy Tenent Yet More Bloudy*, 365.

59. Williams, *The Examiner Defended*, 263.

60. Roger Williams, *A Key to the Language of America*, in *The Complete Writings of Roger Williams*, 7 vols. (New York: Russell and Russell, 1963), 1:227. For Roger Williams's favorable comparison of Native American civility with English morality, see Canup, *Out of the Wilderness*, 144-48.

61. Williams, *The Examiner Defended*, 243; Williams, *Key*, 136.

5

Roger Williams and the Theoretical Foundations of the First Amendment

In 1683, death finally quenched Roger Williams's insatiable thirst for debate. New England found itself free at last from the sound of his polemic and, in honor of the event, promptly forgot him. The rush of events that culminated in state and federal guarantees of religious liberty by the end of the next century proceeded with almost no apparent influence from the Massachusetts renegade. Williams essentially dropped out of sight, and the colony whose "lively experiment" in religious liberty he had helped inaugurate became a despised outcast, playing no significant role in the next century's development toward religious freedom.[1] In fact, most colonial and revolutionary Americans viewed Rhode Island not as a model but as a kind of social outhouse. They pronounced its experiment with religious liberty a dismal failure.[2] During the revolutionary period, one Massachusetts Antifederalist reminded his readers that Rhode Islanders "do whatever they please without any compunction. . . . they have no principles of restraint but laws of their own making. . . . From such laws," he added, "may heaven defend us."[3]

As for Williams himself, "almost no one in colonial New England ever praised his experiment, sought his advice, quoted his books, or tried to imitate his practices."[4] No library catalog in colonial America listed his works.[5] Toward the end of the seventeenth century, shortly after Williams's death, the American colonies began to moderate the harshest elements of their religious intolerance. They did so, however, not in homage to Williams but in response to pressure from England to comply with the Toleration Act of 1689, for which John Locke, rather than Williams, was the intellectual father.[6] Not until the 1770s was Williams's thought reintroduced to the American discourse concerning religious

liberty through the work of the Baptist historian Isaac Backus.[7] Even
then, influential theorists such as Locke, Madison, and Jefferson proceeded without apparent influence from Williams's ideas.[8]

Roger Williams is nevertheless important to First Amendment history chiefly because he exemplifies a voice within that history often
drowned out by the Enlightenment resonance of Jefferson and Madison. It is now well established that the First Amendment religion
clauses had their origins in conflicting traditions: the one variously described as Enlightenment or humanistic rationalism, the other as evangelical or Protestant dissent.[9] A common opposition to Anglican and
Congregationalist establishments joined such divergent perspectives as
those of Thomas Jefferson, on the one hand, and Isaac Backus, on the
other, in a struggle to untangle government from its close alliance with
religious institutions. Subsequently, however, a theoretical posture derived principally from Jefferson, the archetypical American representative of Enlightenment thought, came to dominate First Amendment
jurisprudence. In *Reynolds v. United States,* the Supreme Court accepted Jefferson's letter to the Danbury Baptists "almost as an authoritative declaration of the scope and effect" of the First Amendment's
religion clauses.[10]

This Jeffersonian dominance of First Amendment theory is historically
untenable. There are persuasive grounds for believing that, if anything, the
First Amendment owes more to evangelical passion than to Enlightenment skepticism.[11] As William Lee Miller has observed, dissenting Protestantism "had more to do, over all, over time, pound for pound, head for
head, with the shaping of the American tradition of religious liberty than
did the rational Enlightenment."[12] We therefore cannot pretend to give
historical content to the religion clauses without taking seriously their
origin, at least in part, in a believing parentage, and Williams is a key theoretician of this parentage.

Roger Williams, then, may serve as a useful counterpoint to the Enlightenment luminaries whose thought has tended to captivate investiga-
tors of First Amendment underpinnings. Jefferson and Madison have long
been credited with critical roles in the formation of the background out
of which the First Amendment religious clauses had their genesis.[13] I
therefore propose to compare Williams's thought concerning religious
liberty with each of these figures. In addition, because John Locke played
an important role in the development of the ideas of Jefferson and
Backus and in the creation of the general climate out of which the First
Amendment religion clauses had their origin, the following discussion

will begin by comparing Locke's views of religious liberty with those of Williams.[14]

John Locke

Six years after Williams died, John Locke published *A Letter Concerning Toleration,* a tract whose main arguments were strikingly similar to those of the Rhode Island firebrand.[15] The arguments of both men were overwhelmingly religious in tenor. Of course, the biblical references that drench Williams's writings occur less frequently in *A Letter Concerning Toleration,* but Locke nevertheless remained firmly situated within a specifically Christian discourse.[16] Many of the *Letter's* arguments are reasoned extrapolations from commitments Locke expected Christians of a variety of stripes to share. For example, he maintained that persecution was inconsistent with the character of Christ and that persecutors had selected weapons ill-fit for spiritual warfare. Christ, according to Locke, sent out his followers "not armed with the sword, or other instruments of force, but prepared with the gospel of peace, and with the exemplary holiness of their conversation."[17] Toleration, he added, was "agreeable to the gospel of Jesus Christ."[18]

Both Locke and Williams attempted also to defend religious liberty by circumscribing the scope of civil government. A key aim of each man's rhetorical strategy was to demarcate the boundaries between civil and spiritual concerns so that government would not trample upon the consciences of believers nor believers exempt themselves from the necessary obligations of the social order. Locke and Williams structured critical arguments in favor of religious liberty around a definition of the proper sphere of the civil magistrate's power. "I esteem it above all things necessary," Locke stated, "to distinguish exactly the business of civil government from that of religion, and to settle the just bounds that lie between the one and the other."[19]

For Williams, the civil government had charge over the bodies and goods of individuals insofar as necessary to assure peace and civility. For Locke, the government was responsible for assuring that each citizen was free to possess life, liberty, health, "indolence of body," money, and physical possessions.[20] Of course, the attempt to secure religious liberty through the act of categorization stated a conclusion, not an argument. Why was government limited to this range of concerns? Why did its jurisdiction not extend to matters of religion? To answer that question, both Williams and Locke set forth a multiple-pronged argument. First, both specifically rejected any claimed authority of the civil magistrate over religious con-science by denying that God had ever granted such authority or that citi-zens could surrender freedom of conscience to the civil magistrate.[21] The rights of conscience were thus for Locke "inalienable," not only because they could not be taken by force from an individual but also, even more fundamentally, because an individual could not surrender these rights, which belonged to God.[22] Second, both Williams and Locke maintained that the exercise of civil authority over religious affairs could yield no more than coerced worship and hypocrisy because real belief could never be compelled.[23] "True and saving religion," Locke wrote, "consists in the inward persuasion of the mind, without which nothing can be acceptable to God. . . . I may grow rich by an art that I take not delight in; I may be cured of some disease by remedies that I have not faith in; but I cannot be saved by a religion that I distrust, and by a worship that I abhor."[24] Locke's argument on this point was a reprise of Williams's curt declara-tion that "forced worship stinks in God's nostrils."[25] Third, Williams and Locke, in discussing the proper bounds of civil government, made use of comparisons with the governments of non-Christian cultures. Surely, they argued, it cannot be the business of civil governments to support their favored religion by the sword, or else the majority of the world would be compelled to remain non-Christian. Thus, they both concluded that the essence of civil government was "the same in every place" and could not include oversight of spiritual affairs.[26] Fourth, both Locke and Williams saw clearly that the denial of freedom of conscience, rather than securing the public peace, was the scourge that had robbed the world of peace and ignited a thousand fires of discord.[27]

Notwithstanding their agreement on the fundamentals of an argument for religious liberty, Locke and Williams proceeded from somewhat dif-ferent points of reference. On the issue of the applicability of general laws to believers, Locke articulated a position that moved him in a direction away from that taken by Williams. Williams never faced quite squarely the question of whether religious belief was subject to what now would be termed the neutral laws of general applicability. If government enacts a law not intended to burden religious practice but that nevertheless has that effect, should believers be exempted from the law's requirement? Williams clearly believed that they were not entitled to blanket exemp-tions from every law to which they had conscientious objection. He ar-gued that believers were subject to general laws designed to maintain public peace, avoid injury by one citizen against another, and provide the essentials needed to maintain government, such as taxes and military defense. But Williams also perceived the possibility that government, as aggressive guardian of the public good, might trample upon religious conscience. He could envision some overly zealous magistrate punishing the Virgin Mary for her illegitimate pregnancy. But that pregnancy, no matter how unusual, had posed no "violence of civility, no wrong to the bodies or goods of any."[28] Thus, an attempt to punish Mary would have amounted to overstepping the bounds of appropriate civil authority. Williams seems to have contemplated that government could exceed its proper bounds even in cases not involving a deliberate attempt to burden religious conscience.

Locke, on the other hand, stated a simple rule to govern conflicts between religious conscience and general law, and his rule resolved all conflicts in favor of government authority. He maintained that the government should neither prohibit within the church that which it allowed within the commonwealth in general nor allow within the church that which it generally prohibited.[29] "Is it permitted to speak *Latin* in the market-place?" he asked. "Let those that have a mind to it, be permitted to do it also in the Church. Is it lawful for any man in his own house, to kneel, stand, sit, or use any other posture; and to clothe himself in white or black, in short or in long garments? Let it not be made unlawful to eat bread, drink wine, or wash with water, in the Church. In a word: Whatsoever things are left free by law in the common occasions of life, let them remain free unto every church in Divine worship." According to this principle, the civil magistrate was free to prevent any citizens—including those who purported to act under the constraints of conscience—from sacrificing infants or "lustfully pollute themselves in promiscuous uncleanness."[30] If some disease had ravaged the community's livestock and the magistrate deemed it prudent to forbid the slaughter of any calf, then the prohibition would be equally applicable to religious individuals, who would be entitled to no exemption allowing them to kill a calf for religious reasons.[31] Locke recognized that the domains of the outward civil state and the inward religious conscience could not always be surveyed with precision and that legitimate conflicts between laws of general applicability and conscience might consequently arise.[32] He believed, however, that such conflicts would be rare.[33] When they occurred, Locke maintained that the believer should follow his conscience but nevertheless suffer the punishment, "which it is not unlawful for him to bear."[34]

Locke's discussion of the relationship between religious conscience and general law is ultimately less penetrating than the arguments Roger Williams presented, because Locke failed to acknowledge sufficiently the extent to which notions of "public peace" and "harm to others" could be manipulated to limit religious freedom. A deconstruction of these concepts was Williams's central contribution to the discussion of religious liberty, and one not replicated in Locke's *Letter.* To be sure, Locke denied that one citizen's religious belief could harm another. "If any man err from the right way," he said, "it is his own misfortune, no injury to thee."[35] Moreover, he cautioned the civil magistrate against employing allegedly neutral legislation "to the oppression of any church, under pretense of public good."[36] But by failing to scrutinize sufficiently the state's interest in "order," Locke ultimately adopted a more limited guarantee of religious liberty than did Williams.

Locke, for example, denied freedom of religion to Catholics and atheists.[37] He did so with respect to atheists because he believed that promises and oaths were critical to the stability and order of society and were ineffectual to bind atheists, who professed no belief in the God in whose name the oath was sworn. He denied religious liberty to Catholics because he viewed their allegiance to a foreign potentate inconsistent with the demands of loyalty to their own commonwealth and believed their intolerance toward other religious beliefs was grounds for denying them a corresponding tolerance.[38] In both cases, Locke advanced uncritically a vision of the minimum prerequisites of orderly society. By that vision, to preserve order the state could legitimately deny freedom of conscience to certain citizens. Williams, on the other hand, was able to envision a social order that did not demand the sanctity of oaths, and thus he could tolerate the presence of atheists.[39] He was further able to envision a commonwealth in which Catholics, even though loyal to the pope, could live as useful citizens so long as the civil magistrate took elementary precautions, such as disarming them or requiring them to wear distinctive clothing.[40] To force a Catholic to a Protestant worship was a "soul-rape," and they were entitled to the same freedom of conscience as should be granted to all believers.[41]

In at least one other important respect Locke represented a shift away from Williams's vision of church and state. Locke, along with Williams, addressed the question of religious liberty in part by defining the legitimate sphere of existence of the state. But unlike Williams, Locke also began to articulate a proper sphere for the existence of the church.[42] He narrowly circumscribed that sphere to include inward conviction, traditional acts of public worship, and virtuous living. Locke thrust the essential core of religion into the privacy of the religious mind and out of the public space, where it might encounter conflicts with law. "All the life and power of true religion consist in the inward and full persuasion of the mind," he wrote. He added to this inner essence of religion simple acts of public worship, unadorned by expensive finery, and of such a traditional nature as to not pose substantial possibility of conflict with the jurisdiction of the state. "The end of a religious society . . . is the public worship of God, and by means thereof the acquisition of eternal life. Nothing ought, nor can be transacted in this society, relating to the possession of civil and worldly goods." Finally, Locke did not hesitate to specify the precise contours of the "business of true religion," which was to inspire lives of pious virtue.[43]

Religion, then, in Locke's view, was not very much about doctrine or creed. He was far more skeptical about the possibility of religious knowledge than Williams and inclined to view questions of morality as significantly more important than those relating to religious doctrine and exercise.[44] Thus, although his view of religious liberty would have protected matters of doctrine and worship, that protection—one senses—was achieved by marginalizing such aspects of religion. Locke characterized as "frivolous" the subjects of most religious disputes, and the matters so characterized were all related to religious acts and external observances.[45] In the overall scheme, such matters were not worthy of coercion because they were not important.

Locke's descriptions of religion and religious societies were not simply neutral comments derived from objective observation. For a fair portion of humanity, true religion is neither essentially an "inward" matter nor one characterized chiefly by "persuasion of mind." In many religious traditions, act is as important as belief and emotional experience as critical as mental assurance. It is not surprising that Locke should have preferred religions flavored heavily with rationality and adorned with simply and traditional acts of worship. But we have cause to be skeptical of a theory of tolerance that offers shelter to the favored religions of its author but not to others. This is precisely the case with Locke's account of toleration. The account favors religions of the mind over religions of the heart and body, yielding a stunted concept of religious liberty inhospitable to the real diversity that characterized religious experience in Locke's day and even more now.

In one other central respect, Locke's defense of religious liberty appears relatively meager when set against Roger Williams's more vigorous attempt to free religious conscience from government interference. Locke comes off the poorer in this comparison not so much because he betrayed his stated principles but because those principles were themselves not sufficiently developed. Locke relied chiefly on one argument—and Thomas Jefferson followed him in this regard—to defend religious freedom. He urged repeatedly that true faith could not be created at the tip of the magistrate's sword and that attempts to coerce belief were therefore doomed to produced nothing but hypocrisy. This argument asserts simply that government coercion in matters of religion is ineffective and ought to be abandoned because it does not work. If someone is dedicated to religious liberty solely out of a belief that coercion is ineffectual, though, a rebuttal of that argument would jeopardize the commitment to religious liberty.

The notion that coercion in matters of religious belief is ineffectual, although persuasive at some level, is vulnerable to substantial challenge on at least two counts. First, what I will call the "ineffectiveness" argument does not explain why indirect exercises of government power could not effectively influence religious belief in some circumstances. Saying that true religious conversions do not take place at the sharp end of a sword is not the same as saying that government cannot use less extreme measures to induce people to alter their religious convictions. Perhaps unbelievers would become believers if only they had some exposure to particular sermons or books or made-for-television movies. Why couldn't government arrange such exposure through relatively mild exercises of coercion, such as compelled attendance at government-sanctioned speeches that would attempt to persuade the crowd of at-tenders to convert to a particular religious faith? Many parents, for example, require their children to attend religious services, no doubt hoping that such compelled attendance will ultimately produce either conversion of their children or a desirable pattern of religious observance. Of course, many children rebel against the religious upbringing their parents force upon them. But parents continue to exert these kinds of coercions because they believe them more likely to be effective than doing nothing. Perhaps similar undertakings by government would also be effective, at least in some cases. On the other hand, orthodox believers are likely secure in their orthodoxy so long as they avoid certain heretical influences—books or theater or MTV. Why would it be ineffective for government to exercise its power to suppress these influences and thus secure continued orthodoxy?[46] Of course, there are other reasons for not attempting to shield citizens from corrupting influences, but these reasons do not turn very much on any categorical notion that government power can never be harnessed successfully to influence religious beliefs.[47]

Second, a further weakness of Locke's justification of religious liberty in terms of the ineffectualness of coercion is that this account of religious liberty has little to say once a would-be persecutor asserts that infringements of religious liberty serve ends other than conversion. What does it matter whether a heretic is converted if persecution protects the civil community from God's wrath by dispensing retributive justice upon spiritual wrongdoers or if civil punishments such as banishment or death purge a community of infectious error? Roger Williams addressed these claims head on, but Locke seems not to have either recognized or addressed these justifications of persecution and religious establishment.

As well as being at least partially unconvincing, Locke's principal argument for religious liberty also yields a stunted concept of that liberty. His argument concerning the ineffectiveness of persecution never forcefully replicates Roger Williams's metaphor of persecution as rape. In Locke's defense of religious liberty, persecution was more a mistake than a moral wrong.[48] One might finish reading *A Letter Concerning Toleration* still convinced that persecution was not such a bad idea itself, but one that simply does not work. Moreover, Locke made no attempt to secure liberty for believers to worship God according to the dictates of their conscience. Rather, he advocated freedom from religiously inspired government interference with worship and practice.[49] Government, under Locke's view, was free to pursue secular policy without any sensitivity to the consequences of such policy on the religious conscience. He would have thus outlawed the Inquisition but not indifference toward consciences trapped between the conflicting claims of Caesar and God.

Thomas Jefferson

We have no sustained exposition by Thomas Jefferson concerning religious liberty, certainly none that encompasses the scope of Williams's writings. Although Jefferson had much to say on the subjects of religious liberty and religious disestablishment, his comments were more occasional than systematic. For example, Jefferson's metaphor of the "wall of separation" between church and state—his most famous contribution to the language of church-state relations in the United States—appears not in a treatise but a letter.[50] Moreover, his key attempt to articulate the grounds and contours of religious liberty—the Virginia Bill for Establishing Religious Freedom, which he wrote—spans fewer than a thousand words.[51] In spite of its brevity, though, the Virginia Bill is a useful point of departure for summarizing Jefferson's views concerning religious liberty.

In its main elements, the Virginia Bill repeats arguments that Williams had urged a century before and that Locke had expressed in *A Letter Concerning Toleration*. Jefferson would routinely summon these arguments to combat religious establishments throughout his life. Attempts to coerce religious belief, he insisted, are inconsistent with the nature of belief, which arises solely out of the evidence presented to the mind's attention.[52] The mind "cannot be restrained," and attempts to do so "tend only to begat habits of hypocrisy and meanness." Coercion in matters of religion, Jefferson had written earlier in *Notes on the State of Virginia*, had made "half the world fools, and the other half hypocrites"; state support of religion inevitably corrupts religion.[53] Moreover, the opinions of citizens are not within the jurisdiction of civil government and cannot be restrained on the basis of their supposed "ill tendency." Only when religious principles "break out into overt acts against peace and good order" should the government intervene to prevent such acts.[54]

Both Williams and Jefferson argued that religious assessments and other forms of religious establishments illicitly infringed on the rights of conscience. The Virginia Bill for Establishing Religious Freedom declared that "no man shall be compelled to frequent or support any religious worship, place, or ministry whatsoever."[55] Jefferson, along with Williams, extended religious liberty to atheists and Catholics, two of the categories Locke excluded from his general rule of toleration.[56] Nevertheless, Williams and Jefferson differed unmistakably in their approaches to the subject of religious liberty on several critical issues.

Religion: Belief and Act

Williams summarized the essence of persecution as either a restraint of individuals from the worship deemed proper by their conscience, on the one hand, or the compulsion of individuals to practice or accept forms of worship their conscience forbids, on the other hand.[57] He understood religious liberty not only as freedom to believe but also as freedom—at least with respect to worship—either to act or not to act according to the dictates of belief. Jefferson, however, tended to shift the theoretical ground of religious freedom to the field of opinion rather than action. One has to look hard in the Virginia Bill for Establishing Religious Freedom to discover that religion consists of anything other than opinion. The bill regularly describes religious liberty in terms of belief or opinion.[58] It declares that "the opinions and belief of men" do not depend upon their own will, "but follow involuntarily the

evidence proposed to their minds." It also condemns as "impious presumption" the attempt of legislators and governments of imposing on
others "their own opinions and modes of thinking" and declares "the
opinions of men" and the "field of opinion" to be beyond the jurisdiction of civil government.[59]

The only religious activities in which the bill specifically grants freedom to engage are those of professing and arguing on behalf of religious
opinions or belief.[60] The bill contains no explicit guarantee protecting the
right of Catholics to partake of wine in the Mass, of Jews to circumcise,
or of Baptists to baptize. The bill guarantees only the freedom not to be
required to worship. There is liberty in the Virginia Bill to believe and to
opine and to profess beliefs and opinions. But if the religious conscience
desires liberty to act in accordance with that conscience or freedom from
compelled action contrary to conscience, the liberty so desired must either be sought between the lines of the Virginia Bill or in some other
place altogether. The document will not make such a right explicit. Belief and opinion are placed beyond the government's ability to coerce, but
its arm may reach to actions, even if motivated by or resisted because of
religious belief.

Jefferson's subsequent comments about the bill illustrate the same focus. In December 1786 he wrote to Madison from France, describing
the approbation with which the Virginia Bill had been received in Europe and declaring his pleasure that "the standard of reason had be at
least erected, after so many ages during which the human mind has been
held in vassalage by kings, priests and nobles." Virginians could claim
first rank in having "the courage to declare that the reason of man may
be trusted with the formation of his own opinions." Jefferson later
indicated in his *Autobiography* that "[the Virginia Bill's] protection of
opinion was meant to be universal."[61] Nor was the Virginia Bill for Establishing Religious Freedom an exception within Jefferson's overall
thought on this point, which treated religious freedom simply a subset
of a larger freedom of the mind generally.[62] Three years before he drafted
the bill, Jefferson had prepared a proposed revolutionary constitution
for Virginia in which the guarantee of religious freedom was worded as
"full and free liberty of religious opinion."[63] Moreover, while he was
president, Jefferson returned to the same distinction between belief and
action in his famous letter to the Danbury Baptists, insisting that religion was "a matter which lies solely between man and his God" and
that the "legislative powers of the government reach actions only, and
not opinions."[64]

Nevertheless, although Jefferson habitually spoke of religious liberty in terms of freedom as to matters of "opinion," he occasionally suggested that religious freedom embraced not simply matters of belief and opinion but acts as well. "The restoration of the rights of conscience," Jefferson wrote in his *Autobiography*, "relieved the people from taxation for the support of a religion not theirs." It was the *act* of supporting a religion not one's own, an act justified as necessary for the public good because fostering religion was viewed as essential to that good, which conscience found objectionable.[65]

The argument in favor of religious assessments was based on precisely the kind of simplistic distinction between belief and act that Jefferson was too inclined to make. Conscience was not violated by the requirement that all citizens pay assessments, it was said, because conscience was not compelled to change its religious opinions. One supporter of assessments declared that "there was nothing of conscience in the matter; it was only a contending about paying a little money."[66] The same argument was used in seventeenth-century New England to punish Baptists for holding private meetings. To which argument John Clarke, a Baptist who became Rhode Island's agent in England, replied that there was no such thing as freedom of conscience without freedom to act.[67] Similarly, compelled attendance at religious services—an act, not an opinion—was deemed odious to religious liberty.[68] Jefferson, of course, viewed such compelled acts as violations of religious liberty. He also recognized a penumbra of religious acts, centered around religious opinions, which lay beyond the cognizance of civil government. Jefferson's vow of "eternal hostility against every form of tyranny over the mind of man" extended to any government attempt to intrude itself in religious exercises such as fasting and prayer.[69] Similarly, censorship of the publication of books on religious issues was, for Jefferson, an affront to religious liberty.[70] He thus made not only religious beliefs but also certain religious acts categorically off-limits to the state's regulatory power.

Jefferson, therefore, demonstrated that the distinction between belief and action is far too blunt a tool for use in safeguarding religious liberty.[71] It fails to justify objections to compelled religious observance and financial support of religious organizations as violative of religious liberty. Furthermore, it offers no protection from deliberate attempts of the state to restrict or regulate religion as religion. The distinction comes closest to being useful when reduced simply to the maxim that government has absolutely no jurisdiction over religious beliefs. Even here, however, anything but direct attempts at mind control must inevitably act upon or coerce some kind of action. Thus, to say that government may not coerce beliefs is to say very little.[72]

Religious Liberty and Harm to the Individual Conscience

Jefferson's tendency to define the scope of government power in terms of a distinction between belief and act illustrates a further difference between his thought and that of Williams. Williams's arguments for religious liberty may be summarized broadly under two headings: the argument that religious liberty is necessary to avoid the "rape" of the individual conscience and the argument that religious liberty is justified by the civil government's lack of jurisdiction over matters of religion. The two arguments need not rest on the same foundations. The jurisdictional argument, for example, may be supported by considerations that have nothing to do with any sensitivity to the conscience being "raped." It may be based upon the pragmatic judgment that attempts to coerce religious beliefs are simply not effective and that the government has no business undertaking projects for which it has no likely chance of success. Or, the argument may proceed from recognition that state attempts to control religious belief inevitably plunge the state into discord. Yet again, depriving government of jurisdiction over religious affairs may be rooted in dislike of religion itself and a desire to insulate the public arena from its contaminating influence.

Jefferson emphasized the jurisdictional argument but made almost no use of the argument against harming the individual conscience. Once this omission is understood, his articulation of the distinction between belief and act as a basis for defining the contours of religious liberty becomes more comprehensible. The state, Jefferson maintained, lacks any jurisdiction over religious beliefs or opinions; its jurisdiction is invoked only when beliefs or opinions "break out into overt acts against peace and good order."[73] In this context, it makes some sense to distinguish between opinions, which are absolutely protected, and actions, which may be subject to government regulation to preserved "peace and good order." But the distinction is critically insufficient to define the limits on the government's intended or inadvertent injury to the religious conscience of an individual believer. Such injury may be occasioned as readily by an attempt to coerce or restrain acts as it may by efforts to control belief or opinion.[74] And a test that focuses on general legislative competence to enact laws that restrict religious activities or coerce performance of acts violative of the individual conscience will never ad-

dress the specific injury to an individual's conscience and the reasonableness of such injury.

Jefferson's failure to consider the harm to the individual conscience occasioned by legislative activity made it unlikely that he would exempt believers from laws of general applicability. One of Williams's central
arguments for the inviolability of the rights of conscience was that the
people, who were the source of any legitimate powers of government,
could not delegate authority over conscience to the state because God
had not entrusted power to the people themselves to rule the church.
Locke repeated the same argument. Freedom of religion thus constituted
for both Williams and Locke not simply individual freedom to make
choices among diverse religious opinions but the freedom to obey God.[75]
Moreover, both Williams and Locke recognized that the demands of conscience might conflict with laws of general applicability. Williams believed
that laws intended to maintain civility and order took precedence over
conscientious scruples but nevertheless recognized the possibility that the
government's purported interest in maintaining civility and order could
be manipulated to oppress believers. Locke denied believers an exemption from general laws intended to protect the public but recognized that
conscience and law would sometimes clash and thought that in such cases
believers should follow conscience and suffer due punishment.

Jefferson appeared to follow Williams and Locke at least part of the way
down this argumentative path. He declared in Notes on the State of Virginia
that the rights of conscience could not be surrendered to civil authority.
"The rights of conscience we never submitted, we could not submit. We
are answerable for them to our God."[76] But Jefferson does not appear to
have recognized any possibility that the government, acting within its
proper sphere, might conflict with an individual following the demands
of conscience. He came close to admitting this outright in his letter to the
Danbury Baptists, where he acknowledged his conviction that man "has
no natural right in opposition to his social duties." It is possible to read this
statement as simply an echo of Locke's rule that denies to believers any exemption from a law of general applicability. But it is hard not to suspect
that Jefferson denied that there were occasions when duties to God might
conflict with "social duties." Jefferson, unlike Locke, never suggested that
believers, faced with a general law that conflicted with the demands of
conscience, should engage in civil disobedience. It is more than a little
likely that he did not countenance such acts of civil disobedience because
he believed that duties to God never clashed with duties to Caesar.[77]

Jefferson intimated as much in a letter to James Madison when he observed that "the declaration that religious faith shall be unpunished, does not give impunity to criminal acts dictated by religious error."[78] Jefferson seems here again to suggest that religious error, rather than religious truth, occasions the only conflicts between the demands of law and claims of conscience. If this suggestion is correct, then Jefferson's concept of religious liberty is critically flawed because it smuggles a theological premise—that God and Caesar never issue conflicting commands—into a legal doctrine.

Freedom from Religion and Freedom for Religion

Jefferson's ideas concerning religious liberty were unmistakably flavored with a concern more for freedom from religion than concern for freedom of the individual to be religious or freedom for religion.[79] He is a principal father of the establishment clause, but little in his thought suggests any concern for the separate interest represented by the free-exercise clause. For Jefferson, a fairly rigorous separation between government and religious affairs fit conveniently with his ideas of what was important in the social order. Religion, being of little importance, should be quarantined so that the public sphere would not be contaminated by it. But beyond that quarantine, Jefferson showed little interest in protecting religion for its own sake.[80] Admirers of his views concerning church and state have frequently emulated Jefferson's perspective. For example, Leonard Levy, who seeks to expose Jefferson's "darker side" with respect to civil liberties other than those relating to religion, argues that his "record on religious liberty was really quite exceptional." What Levy appears to mean is that Jefferson consistently maintained the separation of church and state—establishment as opposed to free-exercise concerns.[81]

Jefferson's personal religious beliefs have been the subject of comment almost since the first moment he declared, somewhat cavalierly and to the great consternation of some believers, that "it does me no injury for my neighbor to say that there are twenty gods, or no gods. It neither picks my pocket nor breaks my leg."[82] This, of course, is no more than Williams acknowledged in a different way. But it is hard not to detect a shift from Williams's reluctant acknowledgment of this fact to Jefferson's far more casual dismissal of the idea that religious beliefs might affect anyone other than the individual. The difference between the two arises out of Jefferson's relegation of religion to a status of social insignificance. He reduced religious experience to little more than a matter of morality. He labeled himself a Christian, but his Christianity was of a quite different sort than that of Calvin or Athanasius, whom he named "impious dogmatists."[83]

Jefferson claimed to be a Christian "in the only sense [Christ] wished any one to be; sincerely attached to his doctrines, in preference to all others; ascribing to himself every *human* excellence and believing he never claimed any other."[84] True Christianity was for Jefferson "the most benevolent and sublime" system of morality that ever shone upon the world.[85] Orthodox doctrine—other than a belief in a "future state," which Jefferson found "an important incentive, supplementary to other motives to moral conduct"—was a perverse combination of "foggy mindedness" borrowed from Plato and the scheming of clergy intent upon creating a religion complicated enough so that their services would always be in demand.[86] It was therefore necessary to "strip off" the "artificial vestments in which they have been muffled by priests, who have travestied them into various forms, as instruments of riches and power to them."[87] Jefferson performed this operation literally upon the New Testament gospels "by cutting verse by verse out of the printed book, and arranging, the matter which is evidently [Jesus'], and which is as easily distinguishable as diamonds in a dunghill."[88]

But even if Christianity, rightly understood, was for Jefferson a sublime moral system, it was, in a sense, still irrelevant to the social world because the Creator had sense enough to incorporate within each individual a moral sense.[89] Individuals did not need, therefore, religious belief as a source from which moral demands could be derived.[90] These demands were given in the nature of humanity and were "totally unconnected" to religious dogma. Hence, one suspects that Jefferson protected religious belief partially because it was a matter of indifference to him. It was largely irrelevant to morality, the thing that Jefferson considered most important for society's well-being.[91]

I make no attempt to join the dispute of whether Jefferson was religious or anti-religious, Deist or Christian.[92] Nevertheless, one can fairly observe that his views concerning religious liberty were remarkably hospitable to his own brand of religious experience and far less protective of the religious experiences of others. Jefferson, like Locke, relegated religion to the interior domain of mind and opinion, divorced from the world of conduct and act. He then crafted a concept of religious liberty that would safeguard interior religious opinions but not external religious acts, thus protecting what he considered the essence of religion and leaving undefended most external manifestations of religious faith, which he found of little social value. It is difficult not to suspect that the main differences between Williams and Jefferson arise out of Jefferson's notions about the nature of true religion, from his impatience—even intolerance—of religious views different than his own, and from his apparent willingness to let his religious ideas define the scope of other individuals' religious liberty. Williams also possessed quite definite ideas about the measure of true religion, but he demonstrated a far greater sensitivity than Jefferson to consciences that differed from his own.

James Madison

In 1773, at the age of twenty-two, James Madison exhibited what would become a life-long devotion to religious freedom and opposition to most forms of religious establishment. "Is an Ecclesiastical Establishment absolutely necessary to support civil society in a supreme Government?" he asked William Bradford, then also a student at Princeton, "and how far is it hurtful to a dependent State?"[93] In a letter to Bradford shortly thereafter, Madison complained at length.

> That diabolical Hell conceived principle of persecution rages among some and to their eternal Infamy the Clergy can furnish their quota of Imps for such business. This vexes me the most of any thing whatever. There are at this [time?] in the adjacent County not less that 5 or 6 well meaning men in close Gaol for publishing their religious Sentiments which in the main are very orthodox. I have neither patience to hear talk or think any thing relative to this matter, for I have squabbled and scolded abused and ridiculed so long about it, [to so lit]tle purposes that I am without common patience. So I [leave you] to pity me and pray for Liberty of Conscience [to revive among us].[94]

Although Madison would ally himself closely with Jefferson over the coming years in matters relating to religious liberty, one already sees in the two quotations from his early adult thinking a focus distinct from that which preoccupied Jefferson. The young Madison's first question to William Bradford shows that he understood the principal concern of establishment proponents. With historical authority stretching back through the middle ages, they asserted that stable civil government could not exist unless erected on the foundation of religious uniformity. To Bradford, Madison expressed doubt about this venerable proposition. By fastening on this issue, he entered the heart of the debate about religious establishment. Jefferson, on the other hand, never seems to have squarely considered this central claim of establishment advocates. Like John Locke, he argued that attempts to coerce religious belief were doomed to failure because religious opinions could not be swayed by the tip of a sword. But establishment advocates would have replied to Jefferson that they were not so much interested in converting heretics as they were in preserving a religious uniformity that would sustain the weight of civil society. Madison, at least, seems to have grasped this essential issue.

Madison's complaint about the jailed dissenters shows a concern for oppressed religious conscience that one sometimes wonders if Jefferson shared to any substantial degree. Jefferson's focus seems largely to have been upon securing freedom from religious compulsion. His interest in the cause of conscience seems to have paralleled his distaste for organized religion and his fervent desire to be free from any civil entanglements with such religion. But the plight of believers caught between the claims of Caesar and God seems not to have greatly troubled him. For Jefferson, restraint on religious liberty and support of religious establishment were occasions for moral outrage, but he shows no indication of having grasped that, for some believers, government attempts to superintend religion were occasions of real suffering. Madison, however, seems to have preserved something of Roger Williams's horror at the spectacle of the "raped" conscience.

Madison's most important contribution to the cause of religious liberty was his well-known "A Memorial and Remonstrance," written as a form of petition in opposition to the proposed Virginia Bill Establishing a Provision for Teachers of the Christian Religion.[95] The petition was ultimately signed and presented to the Virginia legislature and became an important, although not by any means exclusive, factor in the ultimate defeat of the proposed bill and the enactment of Jefferson's Bill for Establishing Religious Freedom.[96]

There is a good deal of similarity between Madison's "Memorial and Remonstrance" and Roger Williams's arguments for religious liberty. Madison's work, for example, repeats one of Williams's favorite arguments in a slightly less pietistic form. Williams had charged that God had not delegated to men in general the task of governing the church and that this task could not be transferred to the civil government. Madison argued in a more Lockean style, but to similar effect, that men—because they could not—had not surrendered their rights to conscience upon entry into the social compact.[97] Madison suggested two reasons why individuals could not surrender the rights of conscience: because their opinions depend upon evidence presented to their minds and cannot be dictated by others and because the rights of conscience involve duties to a divine sovereign prior in time and degree to the duties owed the civil state.

The second justification will have critical relevance to whether religious liberty is defined to embrace opinions alone or whether it extends to worship and other religiously motivated conduct. The first justification would allow a distinction between belief and action. Although it may be impossible to coerce opinions (and modern experience with mind control may lend some doubt to Madison's conviction on this point), it is certainly not impossible to coerce actions. Thus, if the inalienable right to religious liberty is grounded only in the futility of attempts to coerce opinions, then that right would offer no protection from attempts to coerce an individual's conduct for purposes other than effecting a conversion of religious opinion. If, however, the inalienability of the right to conscience is rooted in Madison's second point—prior obligation to God—then it becomes difficult to articulate any justification for limiting this inalienable right to opinions only. Perceived religious duties have often involved engaging in or abstaining from particular actions. Therefore, if the nature of the duty to the Divine Sovereign defines the scope of the inalienability of the right to freedom of religion, there is no reason to distinguish arbitrarily between religious belief and religious act. God may require both right belief and right conduct; consequently, an individual is not at liberty to surrender either in formation of the social contract. Although Madison framed part of the argument against the assessment bill by appealing to general notions of equality, this was only one strand of his overall argument, and it occupied a secondary position in the "Memorial and Remonstrance." An understanding of religious freedom based exclusively upon a right of believers not to be singled out by government for unequal burdens would neglect the more pivotal elements of Madison's argument: that religious freedom arises out of the recognition of prior and weightier obligations owed the Divine Sovereign and that the state may not, absent serious justification, deprive any individual of freedom to respond to these obligations.

Both Madison and Williams emphasized that civil magistrates had not demonstrated themselves to be dependable in spiritual matters but had varied from place to place and from period to period in their prescribed orthodoxies. They also argued that Christianity neither needed nor was helped by government support and, conversely, that the civil government did not require the aid of a religious establishment to perform its functions.[98] Moreover, Madison and Williams both urged that religious establishments tended to disrupt the public peace rather than preserve it. Finally, Madison and Williams both recognized that religious establishments frustrated the cause of Christian evangelism by their intolerance

The agreement between Madison and Williams on these points does not, however, adequately comprehend the measure of their intellectual alliance and their mutual distance from Jefferson's thought. Although Madison's writings lack the evangelical fervor and profoundly biblical orientation of Williams's tracts, they nevertheless share a common framework in which religion is protected because it is itself worth protecting and not simply isolated from the public sphere to the satisfaction of those like Jefferson who were bothered by any religion other than a mute and unseen one.[99]

The religious freedom Madison envisioned was, like Williams's, a freedom at least in significant part *for* religion rather than a Jeffersonian freedom *from* religion. Moreover, Madison consistently recognized that freedom of religion had to embrace more than mere opinion and even more than acts of worship. It was the right of every man, Madison wrote in the "Memorial and Remonstrance," to "exercise" his religion according to the dictate of his conscience, and Madison thus advocated freedom "to embrace, to profess and to observe" whatever religion an individual believed to be of divine origin.[100] He echoed the same idea in an article published in the *National Gazette* on 27 March 1792, when he described various categories of "property" rights and included man's "property of peculiar value in his religious opinions, *and in the profession and practice dictated by them.*"[101]

Together with Williams, Madison believed that freedom to practice religion must have some limits, and he frequently stated them. In fact, early in his political career Madison appeared to have been willing to grant religion an even broader protection than contemplated by Williams, by giving the government power to abridge religious liberty only when "the preservation of equal liberty and the existence of the state are manifestly endangered."[102] Madison proposed this language for incorporation into the Virginia Declaration of Rights, adopted by the state in the wake of the Revolutionary War. Although the Virginia convention did not adopt Madison's expansive language and it does not appear again in his later writings, he never abandoned the idea of a religious liberty limited solely by certain specified government interests.[103]

An expansive concept of religious liberty was combined in Madison's thought with an understanding of religious establishment issues that called for a relatively strict separation between government and religious affairs. Madison opposed the practice of appointing congressional chaplains, especially when they were paid out of public funds. Likewise, he opposed the appointment of military chaplains at public expense. Furthermore, he objected to the incorporation of churches and of grants of land to churches.[104] Finally, Madison's rhetoric encouraged the drawing of a sharp demarcation between church and state. He thought it important that there be examples of "a perfect separation between ecclesiastical and civil matters."[105]

Madison's record on establishment issues is, however, a somewhat uncertain ground for supplying information as to the "intent" of the Framers for purposes of construing the establishment clause. His actions did not always coincide with his professed opinions, particularly with those he professed late in life. For example, it has been noted that on the same day Madison introduced Jefferson's Bill for Establishing Religious Freedom in the Virginia legislature, he also introduced a bill for the punishment of Sabbath-breakers.[106] Earlier, during the Revolution, Madison showed impatience with ministers who declined to observe a day of fasting proclaimed by the Virginia House of Burgesses.[107] Moreover, unlike Jefferson, Madison, while he was president, followed the example of his predecessors by issuing proclamations recommending public humiliation and prayer and a proclamation recommending a day of thanksgiving to the Almighty, although later in life he questioned that practice.[108]

In terms of personal faith, Roger Williams, evangelical Separatist, had little in common with James Madison, son of the eighteenth-century Enlightenment. Nevertheless, from near the opposite poles of religious understanding, they brought a concept of religious toleration of uncanny resemblance. Each could imagine a society in which religious disorder did not inevitably destroy public order. Each saw the world under the dominion of competing sovereigns and sought to fashion bounds by which individuals would not be called upon to betray either. Each took religion seriously, seriously enough to deem it worthy of the most vigilant protection.

Notes

1. Thomas Curry, *The First Freedoms: Church and State in America to the Passage of the First Amendment* (New York: Oxford University Press, 1986), 91.

2. For the description of Rhode Island as the "latrine of New England," see Johannes Megapolensis and Samuel Drisius to the Classis at Amsterdam, 14 Aug. 1657, in *Ecclesiastical Records of the State of New York,* 7 vols., ed. E. T. Corwin (Albany: J. B. Lyon, 1901-16), 1:400, quoted in Patricia U. Bonomi, *Under the Cope of Heaven: Religion, Society, and Politics in Colonial America* (New York: Oxford University Press, 1986), 20.

3. Herbert J. Storing, ed., *The Complete Anti-Federalist,* 7 vols. (Chicago: University of Chicago Press, 1981), 4:242, quoted in Edwin S. Gaustad, "Religion and Ratification," in *The First Freedom: Religion and the Bill of Rights,* ed. James E. Wood, Jr. (Waco: J. M. Dawson Institute of Church-State Studies, 1990).

4. William G. McLoughlin, *New England Dissent,* 1630-1883, 2 vols. (Cambridge: Harvard University Press, 1971), 1:8. For a similar assessment of Roger Williams's influence, see LeRoy Moore, "Roger Williams and the Historians," *Church History* 32 (1976): 432-33.

5. Curry, *The First Freedoms,* 91.

6. David A. J. Richards, *Toleration and the Constitution* (New York: Oxford University Press, 1986), 105.

7. Isaac Backus, *A History of New England with Particular Reference to the Denomination of Christians Called Baptists* (Providence: Providence Press, 1871, repr. New York: Arno Press, 1969). For a discussion of Backus, see William G. McLoughlin, *Isaac Backus and the American Pietistic Tradition,* ed. Oscar Handlin (Boston: Little, Brown, 1967).

8. LeRoy Moore, "Religious Liberty, Roger Williams, and the Revolutionary Era," *Church History* 34 (1965): 57. Some scholars have suggested, on the basis of similarities between Williams's and Locke's arguments for religious freedom, that Locke merely restated Williams's arguments. See Winthrop S. Hudson, "Locke: Heir of Puritan Political Theorists," in *Calvinism and Political Order,* ed. George L. Hunt (Philadelphia: Westminster Press, 1965), 117-18; and David Little, "Roger Williams and the Separation of Church and State," in *Religion and the State: Essays in Honor of Leo Pfeffer,* ed. James E. Wood, Jr. (Waco: Baylor University Press, 1985), 7. William Lee Miller has also suggested that Locke had "what seem at least to be many echoes of Roger Williams." *The First Liberty: Religion and the American Republic* (New York: Alfred A. Knopf, 1987), 64. There does not appear to be any direct evidence, however, that Locke relied on Williams's works.

9. Donald Giannella, "Religious Liberty, Nonestablishment, and Doctrinal Development: Part 1. The Religious Liberty Guarantee," *Harvard Law Review* 80 (1967): 1386; Mark DeWolfe Howe, *The Garden and the Wilderness: Religion and Government in American Constitutional History* (Chicago: University of Chicago Press, 1965), 5-15; Stephen Pepper, "Taking the Free Exercise Clause Seriously," *Brigham Young University Law Review* (1989): 301; Martin Marty, "On Medial Moraine: Religious Dimensions of American Constitutionalism," *Emory Law Journal* 39 (1990): 10.

10. *Reynolds v. United States,* 98 U.S. 145, 164 (1878).

11. Howe, *The Garden and the Wilderness,* 19. For the proposition that religious belief was ascendant during the eighteenth century, see Bonomi, *Under the Cope of Heaven,* 6-9.

12. Miller, *The First Liberty,* 153.

13. *Reynolds v. United States,* 98 U.S. 145, 162-64 (1878).

14. S. Gerald Sandler, "Lockean Ideas in Thomas Jefferson's 'Bill for Establishing Religious Freedom,'" *Journal of the History of Ideas* 21 (1960): 110-16; Sanford Kessler, "Locke's Influence on Jefferson's 'Bill for Establishing Religious Freedom,'" *Journal of Church and State* 24 (1983): 231-52; McLoughlin, *Isaac Backus and the American Pietistic Tradition*, 122; Richards, *Toleration*, 104-10; Michael McConnell, "The Origins and Historical Understanding of Free Exercise of Religion," *Harvard Law Review* 103 (1990): 1430-31.

15. John Locke, *A Letter Concerning Toleration*, ed. James H. Tully (Indianapolis: Hackett Publishing, 1983), 21.

16. For the importance of religious commitments in Locke's overall thought, see E. Clinton Gardner, "John Locke: Justice and the Social Compact," *Journal of Law and Religion* 9 (1992): 347.

17. Locke, *A Letter Concerning Toleration*, ed. Tully, 25.

18. Ibid.

19. Ibid., 26.

20. Ibid.

21. Ibid. Locke, like Roger Williams, also countenanced attempts by civil magistrates to exhort and encourage citizens in matters of religious truth so long as the magistrate did not use force to supplement exhortation and encouragement. "Magistracy does not oblige him to put off either humanity or Christianity; but it is one thing to persuade, another to command; one thing to press with arguments, another with penalties." Ibid.

22. Richards, *Toleration*, 85n81.

23. Locke, *A Letter Concerning Toleration*, ed. Tully, 26-28.

24. Ibid., 27, 38.

25. Roger Williams to Maj. John Mason and Gov. Thomas Prence, 22 June 1670, in *The Correspondence of Roger Williams*, 2 vols., ed. Glen W. LaFantasie (Hanover: Brown University Press, 1988), 2:617.

26. Locke, *A Letter Concerning Toleration*, ed. Tully, 32.

27. Ibid., 34, 63.

28. Roger Williams, *The Examiner Defended*, in *The Complete Writings of Roger Williams*, 7 vols. (New York: Russell and Russell, 1963), 7:244-45.

29. Locke, *A Letter Concerning Toleration*, ed. Tully, 41-42, 53-54.

30. Ibid., 53, 41-42. David Richards argues that for Locke the right to conscience was inextricably linked to the necessity of ethical independence, so that the individual is free to experience "the uncompromising demands of an ethical God." Because Locke could not readily imagine a conscience that could motivate immorality, he left no room for conscientious objection to laws intended to prevent immoral acts. Richards, *Toleration*, 97.

31. Locke, *A Letter Concerning Toleration*, ed. Tully, 42.

32. Ibid., 48.

33. Ibid.

34. Ibid. Michael McConnell has argued that Locke's resolution of conflicts between religious conscience and positive law in favor of law arose partially out of a failure to envision the modern notion of judicial review. For Locke, there was no one to arbitrate disputes between the magistrate and the believer in cases of conflict between law and religious conscience. *A Letter Concerning Toleration,* ed. Tully, 49. But, McConnell insists, "Locke's key assumption of legislative supremacy no longer holds under a written constitution with judicial review. The revolutionary American contribution to political theory was that the people themselves are sovereign and therefore possess inherent power to limit the power of the magistrate, though a written constitution enforced by judges independent of the legislature and executive.'"The Origins and Historical Understanding," 1444.

35. Ibid., 32.

36. Ibid., 42.

37. Ibid., 49-51. He also denied religious freedom to those who were intolerant of the religious liberty of others. Ibid., 50.

38. Richards, *Toleration,* 95-96.

39. Ibid., 90n108. Williams's normal litany of the categories of non-Christians to whom he would extend freedom of conscience—Jews, Turks, Pagans, and "Antichristians"—did not include atheists, nor is it certain that he would have even recognized the existence of such a category. See Roger Williams, *The Bloudy Tenent, of Persecution,* in *The Complete Writings of Roger Williams,* 7 vols. (New York: Russell and Russell, 1963), 4:171, 272. Nevertheless, there is nothing in the content of his argument for religious freedom that would have excluded atheists from the ambit of protection.

40. Roger Williams, *The Bloudy Tenent Yet More Bloudy,* in *The Complete Writings of Roger Williams,* 7 vols. (New York: Russell and Russell, 1963), 4:313-14; Williams, *The Bloudy Tenent, of Persecution,* 204, 252.

41. Williams, *The Bloudy Tenent Yet More Bloudy,* 327, 47.

42. For the suggestion that Locke addressed the problem of intolerance in part through a modification of the nature and claims of religion, see McConnell, "Origins and Historical Understanding," 1431-33.

43. Locke, *A Letter Concerning Toleration,* ed. Tully, 26, 30, 23.

44. Ibid., 23-24.

45. Ibid., 38.

46. Locke believed that government ought to exercise coercive power to compel citizens—insofar as was possible—to lead sober and upright lives, and he believed that citizens thus compelled were more likely to be receptive to religious truth. Peter Nicholson, "John Locke's Later Letters on Toleration," in *John Locke: A Letter Concerning Toleration in Focus,* ed. John Horton and Susan Medus (London: Routledge, 1992), 180.

47. For a recent development of this response to Locke's argument, see Jeremy Waldron, "Locke: Toleration and the Rationality of Persecution," in

Justifying Toleration: Conceptual and Historical Perspectives, ed. Susan Mendus (New York: Cambridge University Press, 1988), 81-82. For similar responses at the time Locke originally published his *Letter*, see Mark Goldie, "The Theory of Religious Intolerance in Restoration England," in *From Persecution to Toleration: The Glorious Revolution and Religion in England*, ed. Ole Peter Grell, Jonathan I. Israel, and Nicholas Tyacke (New York: Oxford University Press, 1991), 346-48; and Nicholson, "John Locke's Letters on Toleration," in *John Locke*, ed. Horton and Medus, 165-71.

48. Waldron, "Locke: Toleration and the Rationality of Persecution," 85.

49. Susan Mendus suggests that Locke "does not think that there is a right to freedom of worship as such, but only a right not to have one's worship interfered with for religious ends." Medus, "Locke: Toleration, Morality and Rationality," in *John Locke: A Letter Concerning Toleration in Focus*, ed. John Horton and Susan Mendus (London: Routledge, 1991), 157.

50. Thomas Jefferson to Messrs. Nehemiah Dodge and Others, a Committee of the Danbury Baptist Association, in the State of Connecticut, 1 Jan. 1802, in *Thomas Jefferson: Writings*, ed. Merrill D. Peterson (New York: Library of America, 1984), 510.

51. Thomas Jefferson, "A Bill for Establishing Religious Freedom" (12 June 1779), in *Thomas Jefferson: Writings*, ed. Peterson, 346-48 (hereafter cited as the Virginia Bill). For a useful collection of essays concerning the bill, see Merrill D. Peterson and Robert C. Vaughan, eds., *The Virginia Statute for Religious Freedom: Its Evolution and Consequences in American History* (New York: Cambridge University Press, 1988). Query XVII of Jefferson's *Notes on the State of Virginia* contains his other principal discussion of the issue of religious freedom. *Thomas Jefferson: Writings*, ed. Peterson, 283-87.

52. The Virginia Bill, 346.

53. *Thomas Jefferson: Writings*, ed. Peterson, 286. Jefferson attributed the increase in number of religious dissenters in Virginia before the Revolutionary War to the "indolency" of the Anglican clergy arising out of the state's establishment of that religion. Ibid., 283.

54. The Virginia Bill, 347.

55. Ibid.

56. Jefferson's grant of religious liberty to atheists may not have been absolute. In an almost offhand observation after his famous declaration in the *Notes on the State of Virginia* that the belief of a polytheist or an atheist neither "picks my pocket nor breaks my leg," Jefferson addressed the contention that such beliefs rendered a man untrustworthy under oath in a court of law. "If it be said, his testimony in a court of justice cannot be relied upon, reject it then, and be the stigma on him." *Thomas Jefferson: Writings*, ed. Peterson, 285. Jefferson appears to have been arguing that atheists should be generally tolerated, but that their testimony in court could be rejected. Kessler, "Locke's Influence on Jefferson's 'Bill for Establishing Religious Freedom,'" 241. Jefferson seems

also to have agreed with Locke that only those religious groups prepared to swear an oath that they would tolerate others should be tolerated themselves. Ibid., 243.

57. Williams, *The Bloudy Tenent Yet More Bloudy,* 7.

58. Even after the passage of the bill, Jefferson remained concerned that the protection for opinions on religious matters was still not complete because heresy was still punishable under the common law in Virginia. "The error seems not sufficiently eradicated," he maintained, "that the operations of the mind, as well as the acts of the body, are subject to the coercion of the laws." Jefferson, *Notes on the State of Virginia,* in *Thomas Jefferson: Writings,* ed. Peterson, 284-85, quotation on 285.

59. The Virginia Bill, 346-47.

60. Ibid., 347.

61. Thomas Jefferson to James Madison, 16 Dec. 1786, in *James Madison on Religious Liberty,* ed. Robert S. Alley (Buffalo: Prometheus Books, 1985), 69; *Thomas Jefferson: Writings,* ed. Peterson, 40. Likewise, in his June 1776 draft constitution for Virginia, a guarantee of religious freedom is worded as "full and free liberty of religious opinion." Ibid., 344.

62. Miller, *The First Liberty,* 61.

63. *Thomas Jefferson: Writings,* ed. Peterson, 40.

64. Thomas Jefferson, Letter to the Danbury Baptists, in *Thomas Jefferson: Writings,* ed. Peterson, 164.

65. Ibid., 44, 140.

66. Philip Kurland and Ralph Lerner, eds., *The Founders' Constitution,* 5 vols. (Chicago: University of Chicago Press, 1987), 5:65.

67. Curry, *The First Freedoms,* 15.

68. Jefferson's 1776 draft constitution for Virginia, after guaranteeing "full and free liberty of religious opinion," proceeded immediately to declare that no one shall be compelled "to frequent or maintain any religious institution." *Thomas Jefferson: Writings,* ed. Peterson, 344. The Virginia Bill Establishing Religious Freedom reiterated a similar prohibition against compelled attendance or maintenance of religious institutions and stated that no one shall be "enforced, restrained, molested, or burthened in his body or goods, nor shall otherwise suffer, on account of his religious opinions or belief." Ibid., 347.

69. Thomas Jefferson to Dr. Benjamin Rush, 23 Sept. 1800, and to Rev. Samuel Miller, 23 Jan. 1808, both in *Thomas Jefferson: Writings,* ed. Peterson, 1082, 1186-87.

70. Thomas Jefferson to N. G. Dufief, 19 April 1814, in *Thomas Jefferson: Writings,* ed. Peterson, 1334.

71. The distinction has been widely criticized. See Lawrence Tribe, *American Constitutional Law,* 2d ed. (Mineola: Foundation Press, 1988), 1184; Philip Kurland, "Of Church and State and the Supreme Court," *University of Chicago Law Review* 29 (1961): 96; and Ira Lupu, "Where Rights Begin: The Problem of Burdens on the Free Exercise of Religion," *Harvard Law Review* 102 (1989): 937-38.

72. For a discussion of the Supreme Court's use of the belief/action distinction and the meager protection of religious liberty to which this distinction has contributed, see Marci A. Hamilton, "The Belief/Conduct Paradigm in the Supreme Court's Free Exercise Jurisprudence: A Theological Account of the Failure to Protect Religious Conduct," *Ohio State Law Journal* 54 (1993): 713-96.

73. The Virginia Bill, 347. Jefferson on more than one occasion stated limits to the state's power to regulate. For example, in his *Notes on the State of Virginia,* the resounding declaration that "the rights of conscience we never submitted" is immediately followed by an observation of the proper scope of government activity: "The legitimate powers of government extend to such acts only as are injurious to others." In *Thomas Jefferson: Writings,* ed. Peterson, 285.

74. The jurisprudence of the First Amendment has been critically confused by the failure to recognize these two separate grounds for urging religious liberty. Upon the Supreme Court's first occasion to consider the construction of the free-exercise clause, for example, in *Reynolds v. United States,* 96 U.S. 144 (1876), the Court resolved the case solely on the basis of the jurisdictional issue—that is, whether Congress was competent to pass legislation concerning polygamy even though it impacted a religious practice.

75. For an elaboration of this distinction, see generally Michael Sandel, "Freedom of Conscience or Freedom of Choice?" in *Articles of Faith, Articles of Peace: The Religious Liberty Clauses and the American Public Philosophy,* ed. James Davison Hunter and Os Guiness (Washington, D.C.: The Brookings Institution, 1990), 74.

76. *Thomas Jefferson: Writings,* ed. Peterson, 285.

77. If so, then Jefferson demonstrates less "concern for the predicament of persons claimed by dictates of conscience they are not at liberty to choose" than Sandel suggests. See "Freedom of Conscience," 90.

78. Thomas Jefferson to James Madison, 31 July 1988, in *The Papers of Thomas Jefferson,* ed. Julian P. Boyd (Princeton: Princeton University Press, 1950-95), 13:442-43.

79. McConnell, "Origins and Historical Understanding," 1452. Consider also William Miller's description of Jefferson's view of religious freedom as "negative liberty—absence of external coercion" in *The First Liberty,* 71.

80. Jefferson, therefore, contrary to Michael Malbin's assertion, was anything but in the vanguard of the drive for free exercise of religion (as opposed to disestablishment). Malbin, *Religion and Politics: The Intentions of the Authors of the First Amendment* (Washington, D.C.: American Enterprise Institute, 1978), 25. His advocacy of the belief/action distinction "placed him at least a century behind the argument for full freedom of religious exercise in America." McConnell, "Origins and Historical Understanding," 1451.

81. Leonard W. Levy, *Jefferson and Civil Liberties: The Darker Side* (Cambridge: Harvard University Press, 1963, repr. Chicago: Ivan R. Dee, 1989), 21, 7-8. Concerning whether Jefferson's record on even establishment issues was "excep-

tional," see the catalog of Jefferson's departures from a strict separation between church and state in Kessler, "Locke's Influence on Jefferson's 'Bill for Establishing Religious Freedom,' " 241.

82. *Thomas Jefferson: Writings,* ed. Peterson, 285.

83. Thomas Jefferson to Dr. Benjamin Waterhouse, 26 June 1822. Jefferson called the doctrine of the Trinity "unintelligible Athanasian jargon" (Thomas Jefferson to Wells and Lilly, 1 April 1818), labeled Calvin an "Atheist," and declared that "if ever a man worshiped a false god, he did" (Thomas Jefferson to John Adams, 11 April 1823). All in *Thomas Jefferson: Writings,* ed. Peterson, 1458, 1414, 1466.

84. Thomas Jefferson to Dr. Benjamin Rush, 21 April 1983, in *Thomas Jefferson: Writings,* ed. Peterson, 1122 (emphasis in the original). Consider also Jefferson's description of himself as "a *real Christian.*" Thomas Jefferson to Charles Thomson, 9 Jan. 1816, ibid., 1373.

85. Thomas Jefferson to Dr. Joseph Priestly, 9 April 1803, to Samuel Kercheval, 19 Jan. 1810 (Jesus' principles "the purest system of morals ever before preached to man"), to John Brazier, 24 Aug. 1819 (Jesus the founder of "this most benign and pure of all systems of morality"), and to William Short, 31 Oct. 1819, (the result of abstracting the gospels is to discover "the outlines of a system of the most sublime morality which has ever fallen from the lips of man"). All in *Thomas Jefferson: Writings,* ed. Peterson, 1121, 1214, 1424, 1431.

86. Thomas Jefferson to Dr. Benjamin Rush, 21 April 1803, in *Thomas Jefferson: Writings,* ed. Peterson, 1126. Jefferson claimed that the Socratic dialogues consisted of the "whimsies of Plato's own foggy brain." He lamented to Adams that their advanced ages prevented them from preparing the necessary "euthanasia for Platonic Christianity." Thomas Jefferson to John Adams, 5 July 1813, William Short, 4 Aug. 1820, and John Adams, 12 Oct. 1813. All in *Thomas Jefferson: Writings,* ed. Peterson, 1342, 1436, 1302. Jefferson to John Adams, 5 July 1814, to Elbridge Gerry, 29 March 1801, to Samuel Kercheval, 19 Jan. 1810, and to Mrs. Samuel H. Smith, 6 Aug. 1816. Ibid., 1342, 1090, 1213-14, 1404.

87. Thomas Jefferson to John Adams, 12 Oct. 1813, in *Thomas Jefferson: Writings,* ed. Peterson, 1301.

88. Ibid. Jefferson's compilation of extracts from the New Testament are contained in two works: *The Philosophy of Jesus* and *The Life and Morals of Jesus.* Both works are reprinted in *Jefferson's Extracts from the Gospels,* ed. Dickinson W. Adams (Princeton: Princeton University Press, 1983).

89. Thomas Jefferson to James Fishback, 27 Sept. 1809, quoted in Daniel Boorstin, *The Lost World of Thomas Jefferson* (Boston: Beacon Press, 1948), 162.

90. Kessler, "Locke's Influence on Jefferson's 'Bill for Establishing Religious Freedom,'" 240.

91. David Little, "Thomas Jefferson's Religious Views and Their Influence on the Supreme Court's Interpretation of the First Amendment," *Catholic University Law Review* 26 (1976): 58-64. Jefferson appears to have acknowledged a limited

role for religion in reinforcing the moral instinct with the prospect of future judgment. Kessler, "Locke's Influence on Jefferson's 'Bill for Establishing Religious Freedom,' " 240.

92. For the general contours of the debates of Jefferson's religious beliefs, see William B. Huntley, "Jefferson's Public and Private Religion," *South Atlantic Quarterly* 79 (1980): 286-87; for a discussion of Jefferson's religious beliefs, see generally Charles B. Sanford, *The Religious Life of Thomas Jefferson* (Charlottesville: University Press of Virginia, 1984).

93. James Madison to William Bradford, 3 Dec. 1773, in *James Madison on Religious Liberty*, ed. Alley, 46.

94. James Madison to William Bradford, 24 Jan. 1774, in *James Madison on Religious Liberty*, ed. Alley, 48.

95. James Madison, "A Memorial and Remonstrance," in *The Mind of the Founder: Sources of the Political Thought of James Madison*, rev. ed. (Hanover: University Press of New England for Brandeis University Press, 1981), 6-13.

96. Curry, *The First Freedoms*, 71-143, describes the events surrounding Madison's drafting of the "Memorial." See also Lance Banning, "Madison, the Statute, and Republican Convictions," in *The Virginia Statute for Religious Freedom*, ed. Peterson and Vaughan, 115-23. Of somewhat less importance for this discussion is his "Detached Memoranda," which discusses a number of specific church-state issues that arose during Madison's career as a public official. "Detached Memoranda," in *James Madison on Religious Liberty*, ed. Alley, 89. The existence of the "Detached Memoranda" was first noted by the Supreme Court in 1947. See *Everson v. Board of Education*, 330 U.S. 1, 12 (1947) and at 37n21 (Rutledge, J., dissenting). Justice William J. Brennan referred occasionally to the "Detached Memoranda" in the years after 1947. See *Marsh v. Chambers*, 463 U.S. 783, 807-8 (1983) (Brennan, J., dissenting); and *Walz v. Tax Commission*, 397 U.S. 664, 684n5 (1970) (Brennan, J., concurring). The portion of the "Detached Memoranda" relevant to the construction of the First Amendment religion clauses addresses the issues of ecclesiastical monopolies, church incorporation, grants of public lands to churches, tax exemption of churches and other religious organizations, congressional chaplains, military chaplains, and religious proclamations by government officials. Leo Pfeffer, "Madison's 'Detached Memoranda': Then and Now," in *The Virginia Statute for Religious Freedom: Its Evolution and Consequences in American History*, ed. Merrill D. Peterson and Robert C. Vaughan (New York: Cambridge University Press, 1988), 283.

97. Madison made a similar argument in his "Essay in *National Gazette*," 27 March 1792, in *James Madison on Religious Liberty*, ed. Alley, 77: "To guard a man's house as his castle, to pay public and enforce private debts with the most exact faith, can give no title to invade a man's conscience which is more sacred than his castle, or to withhold from it that debt of protection, for which the public faith is pledged, by the very nature and original conditions of the social pact."

98. Madison, like Williams, rejected the idea of the United States having one national religion. "Detached Memoranda," in *James Madison on Religious Liberty*, ed. Alley, 93.

99. McConnell, "Origins and Historical Understanding," 1452-53.

100. Madison, "A Memorial and Remonstrance," 7, 8.

101. Reprinted in *James Madison on Religious Liberty*, ed. Alley, 76 (emphasis added). It is surely reading too much into the language of the "Memorial and Remonstrance" to suggest, as does Michael Malbin, that Madison, by the time he wrote the work, no longer believed religious activity other than worship should be protected in the name of religious liberty. Malbin, *Religion and Politics*, 26-27. In fact, Madison feared precisely the limitation of the rights of conscience that would occur if they were "submitted to public definition." James Madison to Thomas Jefferson, 17 Oct. 1788, in *James Madison on Religious Liberty*, ed. Alley, 72.

102. He wrote, for example, to Edward Livingston in 1822: "I observe with particular pleasure the view you have taken of the immunity of Religion from civil jurisdiction, in every case where it does not trespass on private rights or the public peace." *James Madison on Religious Liberty*, ed. Alley, 52.

103. James Madison to Edward Livingston, 10 July 1822, in *James Madison on Religious Liberty*, ed. Alley, 82.

104. Madison, "Detached Memoranda," in *James Madison on Religious Liberty*, ed. Alley, 92, 93, 91; Veto Message from James Madison to Congress, 28 Feb. 1811, in *James Madison on Religious Liberty*, ed. Alley, 79-80.

105. James Madison to Edward Livingston, 10 July 1822, in *James Madison on Religious Liberty*, ed. Alley, 83.

106. Steven D. Smith, "Separation and the 'Secular': Reconstructing the Disestablishment Decision," *Texas Law Review* 67 (1989): 970.

107. William T. Hutchinson et al., eds., *The Papers of James Madison*, 17 vols. (Chicago: University of Chicago Press, 1962-69), 1:161, quoted in Donald L. Drakeman, "Religion and the Republic: James Madison and the First Amendment," *Journal of Church and State* 25 (1983): 441.

108. "Detached Memoranda," in *James Madison on Religious Liberty*, ed. Alley, 93-94. Arlin M. Adams and Charles Emmerich, *A Nation Dedicated to Religious Liberty: The Constitutional Heritage of the Religion Clauses* (Philadelphia: University of Pennsylvania Press, 1990), 25. Jefferson's reasons for declining to follow this practice are stated in Thomas Jefferson to Rev. Samuel Miller, 23 June 1808, in *Thomas Jefferson: Writings*, ed. Peterson, 1186-87. Although the argument in the "Detached Memoranda" runs not only to *prescribed* religious observances by the nation but also to the mere *recommendation* of such services, Madison, perhaps because he had undertaken the latter, took pains to distinguish between prescribed and merely suggested observances. Ibid., 94; see also Madison to Edward Livingston, 10 July 1822, 82-83.

6

The Significance of Roger Williams

A book about Roger Williams must ultimately ask what a Puritan renegade of the seventeenth century has to do with the cause of religious liberty three hundred years later. The driving winter into which Williams
fled from Massachusetts in 1636 seems very long ago and very far away;
the Congregationalist establishment that engineered his exile has been
long since abandoned; and the conflict in which Williams raged against a
civil government happy to crop the ears of religious dissenters and hang
obdurate Quakers is, we sigh, mercifully over. While he complained about
the public scourging of Baptists who ventured into the Bay Colony, our
establishment battles are more likely to be about publicly sponsored na-
tivity scenes or bland invocations uttered during high school graduations.
What has Williams to offer these?

Of course, seventeenth-century threats to religious liberty were far
more grave than any posed at present or likely to be posed in the near
future. Moreover, some current establishment issues, such as the appropriateness of allowing religious institutions to share in the largesse of the
modern welfare state, pose issues perhaps different from any Williams
contemplated. Nevertheless, it is possible to exaggerate the remoteness
of Williams's context from our own. Contemporary debates about religious liberty and religious establishment frequently overlay more enduring questions. Does faith have anything to fear from government
sponsorship? Must government rely upon religious belief to inculcate the
virtues necessary to sustain a stable polity? Williams has much to say on
such issues.

Roger Williams and the Politics of Religious Liberty

Contemporary defenders of religious liberty have reason to maintain a vigilant guard on two fronts. Like Williams, they must be prepared to turn back attempts by religious adherents to capture the state as an ally against heresy or unbelief. But unlike Williams, present advocates of religious liberty have good reason to fear encroachment from the purely secular front by secularists who are either hostile or indifferent toward religious practice or belief.[1] These separate threats to religious liberty must be met at least partially through public debate and may well require separate rhetorical arsenals. No doubt there are people with intellectual vocabularies broad enough to respond to both secular and religious rhetorics. But there are other citizens—and these may include many of those from whom religious liberty has most to fear—whose fundamental vision of life can only be communicated within religious terms on the one hand or secular terms on the other.

Roger Williams, for example, was an apostle of religious freedom to the religiously devout. To whatever radicalism he ultimately inclined, Williams nevertheless remained steadfastly within the world of faith, prophesying liberty to inhabitants of that world. He argued in religious syllables to people who understood these syllables and would have received blankly any argument for religious liberty coached in wholly secular terms. Williams had a daunting task in attempting to persuade Massachusetts Puritans to abandon their experiment in holy commonwealth. That task would have become altogether impossible had Williams elected to assault the Puritans with Enlightenment-style arguments purged of religious references. A defense of religious liberty that depends upon skeptical premises is a poor shield against militant certitude. Arguments that will justify toleration to a Jefferson will frequently fail to move a Winthrop. What, then, if Winthrop's faith still commands substantial assent in a post-Enlightenment society? If it does, then an overlapping consensus in support of religious liberty must take into account the believing premises of people who share a religious vision closer to Williams and the New England Puritans than to Enlightenment skeptics. For the task of building such a consensus, the religiously clad discourse to which Roger Williams invites us is indispensable.

There are, of course, subdialects of religious language. These variations within a larger religious vocabulary mean that believers will often find it difficult to communicate meaningfully with one another. Williams clearly spoke in such a subdialect—that of Protestant Separatism. Protestant dissenters who followed him, such as the colonial Baptists, shared something of the same vocabulary, and it was frankly one that followers of establishment faiths such as Congregationalism and Anglicanism found almost incomprehensible at times. Therefore, I make no extravagant claims about the usefulness of various religious dialects in assembling a consensus favoring religious liberty. Nevertheless, meaningful discourse is hard to come by in the best of circumstances, and its possibility is critically diminished when the language of religious faith or its various dialects are excluded from political conversation.

Some legal scholars, however, have proposed models of public discourse that would exclude some or all religious rhetoric from the public square.[2] These proposals tend to find their roots in the asserted desirability of preserving an inclusive political discourse. To preserve such inclusiveness, it is said, citizens ought not to clutter the public square with words that other citizens find unintelligible. These scholars have generally displayed too much optimism about the possibility of an all-inclusive public discourse and a blinkered view of the manifold ends served by this discourse. At least one of these ends is the ongoing construction of a political consensus in support of religious liberty. The parchment existence of the First Amendment's religion clauses does not guarantee the security of religious freedom.[3] A political culture hostile to the value of religious liberty is not likely to be altered from political actions reflecting this hostility by the words of the First Amendment. Moreover, an erosion of a consensus in favor of religious liberty may well preside over the enactment of constitutional amendments that weaken the commitment to religious freedom presently enshrined in the First Amendment.

A political consensus in favor of religious liberty requires a formative political discourse. Because the issue of religious freedom touches the deepest intuitions of citizens regarding the value of liberty and the nature of the political community, a consensus-building discourse must communicate with these intuitions. The threat to religious liberty proceeds at least partially from religious quarters. Any political discourse likely to include believers within a liberty-supporting consensus must speak to their deepest intuitions—and these, being religious, must be spoken to in religious syllables.[4] In fact, the principal overseers of the original overlapping consensus in favor of religious liberty were well familiar with this political reality. John Locke, Thomas Jefferson, and James Madison each argued in favor of religious liberty at least partially in religious terms.[5] Locke and Madison, especially, were bilingual: They moved readily between secular and religious arguments in favor of religious freedom and disestablishment. Moreover, at least some Protestant dissenters who allied themselves in this cause with the likes of Madison were also bilingual. They learned to speak of natural rights and the consent of the government even as they proclaimed religious establishments an offense against "the gospel of Jesus Christ." This kind of bilingualism is becoming increasingly rare, though. And we have cause to wonder how long a consensus in favor of religious liberty may endure when its constituents can no longer speak meaningfully to one another.

Roger Williams's writings are an important resource for the work of sustaining a commitment among believers to religious liberty. His arguments for religious liberty—although frequently based on appeals to history or sociological observation—nevertheless partake of a profoundly religious worldview, in fact a specifically Christian one. Of course, Williams's membership in the Christian rhetorical community that existed in seventeenth-century New England did not ensure that he would persuade Massachusetts Puritans. But that membership at least created the possibility of a common discourse about the nature and value of religious liberty. The particular vocabulary Williams used to champion the cause of religious liberty is still coherent to some believers and offers a possible resource for engaging them in a liberty-supporting consensus.

The Special Place of Religion in the Constitution

The key manifestation of a believing parentage within the First Amendment was the understanding shared by Protestant dissenters, such as Williams, as well as Enlightenment heirs, such as Madison, that religious freedom was rooted—at least in substantial part—in the right of the individual to respond to the divine command.[6] The liberty of conscience for which Williams maintained his relentless advocacy across four decades was not simply a freedom of the mind to consider matters of ultimate concern. It was the freedom to be captive to the divine will, the freedom to be subject to a power other than Caesar's. Liberty of conscience protected the individual from the dilemma of having to choose between sovereigns, under temporal penalties for failure to heed the one but suffering eternal consequences for failure to obey the other.[7]

A constant refrain in theoretical defense of religious liberty was the necessity of leaving the individual free to obey the divine command and the odiousness of the harm that individuals prevented from so obeying suffered. Among the varied strands of the case for liberty of conscience, a core theoretical argument centered on the perversity of subjecting individuals to conflicting claims of sovereignty by God, on one hand, and civil government, on the other. As a jurisdictional matter, civil intrusion into the sphere of religion was an invasion of God's prerogatives. During the colonial period, evangelicals such as Roger Williams and William Penn emphasized that persecution trod upon the Almighty's sovereignty. Williams argued that God had not entrusted to civil government the supervision of the church or the preservation of its purity.[8] Penn referred in similar fashion to God's "incommunicable right of government over conscience" and urged that "imposition, restraint, and persecution, for matters relating to conscience, directly invade the Divine prerogative, and divest the Almighty of a due, proper to none besides himself."[9] Although John Locke tended to argue in favor of religious liberty by emphasizing the futility of attempts to coerce religious belief and the danger to civil peace that such attempts posed, he also joined with the evangelicals in denying that God had committed to the civil magistrate "the care of souls."[10]

During the revolutionary period, a similar concern with conflicting sovereignties was a prominent feature in the debate concerning religious liberty. Again, evangelicals such as the Baptists Isaac Backus and John Leland argued the case for freedom of conscience in a manner that emphasized the divine prerogative over conscience. "He who is the only worthy object of worship has always claimed it as his sole prerogative to determine by express laws what his worship shall be, who shall minister in it, and how they shall be supported," Backus argued. Leland charged more bluntly that "it would be sinful for a man to surrender that to man, which is to be kept sacred for God."[11]

The evangelicals were not alone in stating the case for religious liberty in terms of the necessity of preserving the individual's ability to obey God. Expounding on the nature of religious liberty as an inalienable right, Madison asserted in "A Memorial and Remonstrance" that religious duties were those owed to God and could not be surrendered as a condition for entry into the social contract.[12] Jefferson's argument spoke more in terms of freedom from religious coercion than freedom for the performance of religious duties. But in *Notes on the State of Virginia* he also placed religious liberty in the context of the individual's right to respond to divinely imposed obligations: "The rights of conscience we never submitted, we could not submit. We are answerable for them to our God."[13] The struggle for freedom of conscience, then, was not viewed as a bilateral contest between the individual believer and the civil government. The revolutionary generation widely perceived it as a trilateral affair in which God was the additional contestant. This view made the concept of toleration suspect, because it implied that religious liberty was the a mere product of the state's beneficence.

Religious obligations were different from other conscientious obligations because of their divine orientation, and the frustration of these obligations inflicted a peculiar harm on believers. For the state, armed with its claim of civil sovereignty, to force individuals to disobey their consciences was to perpetrate upon them "soul or spiritual rape," according to Roger Williams; for William Penn, it was to cause them to sin; and, according to John Locke, it would cause them to offend God.[14] "To impose such things [concerning the worship of God], upon any people, contrary to their own judgment," Locke wrote, "is in effect to command them to offend God, which, considering that the end of all religion is to please Him and that liberty is essential to that end, appears to be absurd beyond expression."[15] So long as the state could not hold the individual harmless at the bar of God for violating duties owed to God, it was an "intolerable hard measure" to coerce such violations.[16] "Must [believers] be persecuted here if they do not go against their consciences, and punished hereafter if they do?" Penn asked.[17]

An understanding of religious freedom as embracing the freedom to render to the Creator those obligations due him explains, at least in part, the special place of religious freedom in the constitutional scheme.[18] Religion was not simply a generic example of personal preference or even a subset of a broader class of conscientious moral or philosophical beliefs.[19] Nor was it, for Williams and the later generation that enacted the First Amendment, merely a category of speech.[20] It entailed a special class of right, proceeding out of obligations to a divine sovereign arising prior to and in degree to those undertaken in the social compact.[21] Of course, other considerations also prompted enactment of the First Amendment religion clauses. The desire to preserve social peace by forbidding government establishments of religion undoubtedly contributed to the passage of the establishment clause.[22] Moreover, the free-exercise clause has roots in a civic republicanism that saw religion as worthy of protection because it was necessary to inculcate values thought essential to the commonwealth.[23]

But a desire to preserve public peace and protect religious associations as mediating structures critical to the long-term survival of the Republic does not alone explain why the Framers singled out religion in the First Amendment. For that unique position, Madison's appeal to religion as the duty we owe to the Creator, Jefferson's declaration that the rights of conscience were inalienable because we are answerable for them to God, and Williams's belief that God had not committed the rule of his church to any civil society are more likely explanations.

What the Framers found obvious—that religious duties were categorically different than other kinds of duties—is not so unanimously agreed upon now. Believers, it is said, "do not hold a monopoly on conscience," and the crisis of conflicting duties is not unique to religion.[24] It is hard to contest either observation on the general level. There are religious as well as nonreligious duties of varying significance in the lives of individuals. The duty of an Episcopalian to celebrate the Eucharist with wine instead of grape juice may be perceived as of lessor significance than the duty of refraining from killing other persons, even as a part of military service. There are also different intensities of conviction about the necessity of performing certain duties. Again, the crisis of conflicting duties for an individual with profound moral objections to killing in war may be of a far greater intensity than the crisis experienced by a believer who discovers that a Prohibition-like statute has foreclosed the use of wine during the communion service. But it has always been possible to produce counterexamples to the proposition that religious duties are somehow unique. Marginal believers for whom religious duties claim no excessive hold and skeptics for whom matters of conscience are duties of the highest order are not unique to this century. Religious liberty must have achieved special protection in the Constitution in spite of such counterexamples because the Framers nevertheless believed that religion in general warranted a protection not to be shared by other nonreligious conscientious beliefs or acts.

Disestablishment and the Separatist Impulse

Roger Williams was a Separatist and driven by a theological impulse with deep roots in the American experience. In addition to Williams, the chief exemplars of the Separatist vision in seventeenth-century America were the Plymouth Pilgrims.[25] They and Williams were united in their commitment to one overriding principle: The appropriate response to spiritual impurity was separation, the severance of communion. Both the Pilgrims and Williams felt compelled to separate from religious associations they believed to be corrupted.[26] Unlike most of their Puritan contemporaries, these Separatists, as their theological opponents named them, believed that the Church of England was a spiritual wreck that no amount of reform could salvage. In contrast, most Puritans of the early seventeenth century saw a good deal wrong with the Anglican establishment but were not ready to abandon it.They believed that England's Reformation in the sixteenth century had not gone nearly far enough.They saw lingering vestiges of Catholicism on every hand and were frustrated by a succession of English monarchs who failed to purge the Anglican Church of its remaining ties to the papacy.Yet for all their criticism of the Church of England, these Puritans—both those who traveled to the New World and those who remained in England—were not ready to leave it entirely. Those who stayed in England tried to reform the church from the inside; those who traveled to the Massachusetts Bay Colony claimed continuing loyalty to the Church of England.

Some individuals concerned with the spiritual bankruptcy of the Anglican establishment saw no hope for its reform, however. Their consciences could not tolerate continued association with the pollution they saw swirling about the church. Association, they believed, was sinful, and they elected to separate entirely from the Anglican Church.They risked, and often suffered, civil penalties for this betrayal of England's official ecclesiastical establishment, and many ultimately fled risks and penalties by escaping to the Netherlands to form Separatist congregations there.Those who became dissatisfied with their lives in the Netherlands chose a further pilgrimage that would cast them on the shores of Plymouth and name them Pilgrims. In Plymouth they found relief from the spiritual impurity they perceived in the Old World.[27] Williams, although a fierce advocate of religious liberty in the public sphere, was also as fiercely dedicated to severing ecclesiastical ties with those he believed to be engaged in false or sinful worship. He was convinced that the Church of England was spiritually polluted and managed to put an ocean between himself and that church by migrating to the Massachusetts Bay Colony, where he quickly took the position that the churches there should sever all ties with the impure Church of England.

Colonial Baptists also illustrate the Separatist impulse. In seventeenth- and eighteenth-century America, a number of Protestant believers concluded that the ceremony of baptism was a rite that should not be administered to infants.[28] They believed that baptism was an ordinance reserved for individuals who were visible followers of Christ. In spite of objections to infant baptism, however, these early Baptists (as they came ultimately to be called) were generally required by law to attend church

services where the rite was performed.[29] Moreover, many were not immediately inclined to break all ties with the churches with which they
were associated yet believed themselves implicated in an erroneous practice unless they made some gesture of withdrawal from association with
infant baptism. Thus, Baptists would frequently leave the service during
infant baptisms or choose to remain and turn their backs, cover their ears,
or simply remain seated during the rite.[30] Ultimately, many chose to sever
all association with the churches.[31]

Colonial authorities viewed these Separatist scruples with less than
benevolent regard. At first they continued to require Baptists to attend the
services of whatever church (generally Congregational or Anglican) was
established by law. Civil authorities punished failure to attend these services or failure to display the appropriate respect for the ordinance of infant baptism with fines or whippings. Eventually, authorities let the
dissenters depart from established churches to form churches of their own
but continued to tax them to support state churches.[32]

The Separatists, vexed by their treatment at the hands of civil authorities, provided critical momentum for the movement toward religious disestablishment.[33] That movement must be understood in terms of the
harms that religious minorities had long endured under state religious establishments and from which they sought escape. Of course, disestablishment might not have occurred had not other social forces also been set
in motion. The movement toward disestablishment harnessed Enlightenment fears that alliances between government and religion corrupted
politics and religious fears that such alliances corrupted religion. But behind these relatively abstract concerns lay the far more tangible injuries
that religious dissenters were eager to escape and that sympathetic observers were anxious to see ended. Therefore, a key source for giving
content to the First Amendment's establishment prohibition is an understanding of these injuries. What, then, were the harms religious dissenters
experienced under state religious establishments?

Certainly the most tangible harms were the variety of civil penalties inflicted either to punish dissenters' deviance or compel them to support
established churches. Baptists who failed to display proper reverence for
baptismal rites in established churches were fined, whipped if they could
not pay the fine, and imprisoned indefinitely if they refused to pay the
fine.[34] After the Great Awakening, when many members of established
churches separated from those churches to form "New Light" congregations, those congregations suffered similar punishments. Local authorities
fined and jailed New Light ministers, New Light believers could be

placed in stocks for declining to attend established church services, New Light students were expelled from Yale and Harvard, New Light judges were removed from the bench, and New Light legislators refused their seats.[35] Dissenters of all stripes, at least during the early years of their Separatist existence, had to pay taxes to support established churches and suffer levy of their property for failure to pay.[36]

But these civil penalties and burdens do not exhaust the injuries religious dissenters suffered. Consider again Baptist scruples concerning the rite of infant baptism. What injuries were suffered by Baptists compelled to attend religious services where infant baptism was practiced and defended in sermons? They were made to sit through experiences of government-backed proselytization or indoctrination, which perhaps harmed some Baptists by causing them to abandon deeply held beliefs. But that seems not to have happened generally. Religious minorities do not appear to have complained that government-backed indoctrination threatened to alter their religious opinions. Nor did government-backed indoctrination of religious dissenters succeed in keeping them in the established fold.[37]

The Supreme Court has on occasion given the impression that government-sponsored indoctrination is likely to alter individual religious opinions and is a principal evil against which the establishment clause serves as a bulwark. Most of its rhetoric in this vein has occurred in the context of elementary or secondary education. In *Grand Rapids School District v. Ball,* for example, the Court declared that the prohibition against government-supported religious indoctrination was one of the few absolutes of establishment clause jurisprudence. "Such indoctrination," the Court emphasized, "if permitted to occur, would have devastating effects on the right of each individual voluntarily to determine what to believe (and what not to believe) free of any coercive pressures from the State, while at the same time tainting the resulting religious beliefs with a corrosive secularism."[38]

Certainly, if indoctrination is likely to be successful it will be when it is directed at children. But by making successful indoctrination a principle evil against which the establishment clause is aimed, the Court has sometimes concluded too readily that no real establishment clause issue is present where there is no risk of successful indoctrination. In *Marsh v. Chambers,* for example, the Court determined that "the individual claiming injury by the practice [of legislative prayer] is an adult" and therefore presumed to be not readily susceptible to indoctrination or peer pressure.[39] The Court assumed without discussion that no real injury had taken place because the objector was never in serious danger of having his mind bent. By focusing on the potential of government indoctrination, however, the Court at most identified one possible harm that may have generated support for disestablishment.

In reality, fear of indoctrination seems to have played an insignificant part in the drive to abolish state establishments of religion. In the case of the Baptist forced to attend services in an established church, one might also characterize the relevant harm as that of being forced to observe religious exercises that offended deeply held religious beliefs. Certainly, exposure to practices they considered objectionable would have been offensive to religious minorities, but offense seems a rickety basis for understanding the drive for disestablishment. One might reasonably conclude that life in a liberal democracy necessitates that citizens put up with a fair amount of offense.[40]

Because church and civil leaders branded Baptists as ignorant and dangerous and frequently treated them as second-class citizens, one might locate the essence of the harm Baptists suffered as one of social stigma or alienation. William McLoughlin has argued that "the discontent of dissenters in colonial New England sprang less from any civil disabilities they suffered under the ecclesiastical laws than from feelings of social inferiority and ostracism."[41] Although there is some cause to identify stigma as a harm inflicted by religious establishments, it does certainly not exhaust them. A focus on stigma sometimes conflicts with the self-identify of religious dissenters. Religious minorities often find a source of strength rather than a badge of weakness in their position as outsiders.[42]

Consider again Baptists with conscientious objections to infant baptism who felt compelled to turn their backs to the rite or cover their ears during it. These acts of disassociation were motivated not simply by the desire to avoid proselytization or offense or stigma; rather, they were reactions to the perception of spiritual stain. For Baptist dissenters, the occasion of infant baptism presented the risk of a contaminating communion with impurity. For at least some of them, respectful silence was not possible because they viewed such silence as making them partakers of a perceived evil.[43] They believed that only a visible denial of communion could preserve them from stain. Thus, they turned their backs or clapped their hands over their ears or left the baptismal service.

Liberalism's absorption with the unencumbered self makes it difficult to understand religious dissent such as that of the Baptists.[44] Liberalism conceives of the world mostly in terms of competing ideas and of these ideas mostly through the metaphor of a marketplace; it assumes that no one is harmed merely by exposure to an offending idea.[45] But Baptists believed that their ties with certain individuals and ideas were far more tangible than liberalism maintains, and they believed that some ties were themselves sinful and to be avoided.[46] To have treated infant baptism with a kind of benevolent, but disagreeing, respect would have been to embrace communion with it, at least in their eyes.

The Separatist scruples of the Baptists mirrored Roger Williams's preoccupation with spiritual stain. By the important role they and other Protestant dissenters played in disestablishment, the concepts of stain and religious separation should have earned a more prominent place in the theory of religious liberty. Unfortunately, however, although scholars of the First Amendment's religion clauses have begun to acknowledge the importance of Separatists to religious liberty in America, they have not attended to Separatism's peculiar voice within the American tradition.

As a way of conceptualizing the Separatist impulse in a modern context, consider the establishment concerns posed by the practice of civic prayers. The Supreme Court's 1992 decision relating to this practice held that graduation prayers offered by a rabbi at a public middle school graduation ceremony violated the establishment clause.[47] Justice Anthony M. Kennedy's opinion for the majority emphasized the coercive effect of the graduation prayers on dissenting believers and unbelievers whose "attendance and participation in the state-sponsored religious activity [was] in a fair and real sense obligatory."[48] Yet understanding civic prayer in terms of an impermissible mingling of civil and spiritual communions more accurately identifies the core problem of public religious exercises than a focus on coercion. A focus on the subtle coerciveness of civic prayers casts religious dissenters and nonbelievers into an unflattering role of weakness, as though the establishment clause were a necessary guardian for timid souls likely to be overawed by relatively mild exercises of government power on behalf of competing religious visions.[49] But colonial and revolutionary history flatly contradicts the common legal tendency to exaggerate the potential for government coercion to stamp out religious dissent.[50] If anything, the opposite appears to have been true. Dissenting groups such as the Baptists and the Quakers were whipped and hanged and taxed and levied upon and made to sit through indoctrinating sermons. But the chief result of these government exercises in coercive power seems to have been explosive growth on the part of these groups.

I do not mean to suggest that coercion never works. The successful war waged on the nineteenth-century Mormon practice of polygamy is at least one example where coercion had the desired effect.[51] But this success seems not to have been the rule. In general, religious dissenters have not been afraid that the whip would cause them to betray their religious beliefs. Rather, they objected to being cut off from common civil partnership. Thus, although coercion ought to be an important concept in understanding the religion clauses, especially when children are involved, attention to the actual experiences of religious minorities suggests that judges and legal scholars may have misperceived the harms government coercion caused in religious matters.

Viewed through Separatist eyes, the harm inflicted by government-sponsored religious exercises is twofold. First, civic religious exercises force religious minorities to sever civil communion to avoid spiritual pollution. Such exercises have the tendency, in Madison's words, "to banish our Citizens."[52] It is not so much that they are denied citizenship as that they are compelled to renounce it. They may feel excluded by a civic communion created on a religious foundation, but this is not the essence of the Separatist objection to government-sponsored religious exercises. Rather, the Separatist insight focuses on whether religious minorities are forced to exclude themselves from a mixed civil and spiritual communion. One might understand this harm in terms of coercion. The coercion is not merely pressure to betray or otherwise act contrary to deeply held beliefs, although this kind of coercion may well be present, especially in the case of children. Rather, the real danger of civic prayer is that citizens will be coerced to deny their citizenship rather than submit to what they perceive to be an unholy spiritual fellowship.[53]

The second harm is that civic religious exercises wound the civil community by compelling the severance of religious minorities and thus fracturing community.[54] However valuable insular religious communities may be to political health, the civil community suffers when it fortifies insularity by forcing religious minorities to exclude themselves from the public square.[55] When believers banish themselves to avoid spiritual stain, their voices are removed from the republican discourse concerning the common good and may be less inclined to sacrifice for it.[56] They may be more likely to doubt the legitimacy of law itself.[57] Moreover, the abdication of religious minorities from public space increases the danger, feared especially by Madison, that a religious faction embracing a majority will jeopardize individual rights and the health of the political community.[58]

Separatism and Tolerance

A possible objection to the perspective so far articulated is that it displays an inappropriate respect for Separatists. Why should government be concerned with people so religiously "intolerant" that they cannot endure someone else's prayer, even if they disagree with its content? Why should the state bother itself to protect the sensibilities of those who feel compelled to separate "for trifles"?[59] This disapproving view of Separatism lies close to the surface of Justice Antonin M. Scalia's dissenting opinion in *Lee v. Weisman*.[60] The justice dissented vigorously from the majority's holding, which declared unconstitutional the prayers delivered by a rabbi at a public middle school graduation ceremony. He justified his dissent partially by reference to the place of civic prayers in American history generally.[61] But he concluded his argument with a bold effort to capture the label of tolerance for the position he had staked out. Justice Scalia suggested that the occasion of civic prayer in the middle school graduation ceremony trained citizens to respect the religious beliefs of others. "Maintaining respect for the religious observances of others is a fundamental civic virtue that government (including the public schools) can and should cultivate," he argued.[62] The concluding paragraph of Justice Scalia's dissent returned to the same theme.

> The founders of our republic knew the fearsome potential of sectarian religious belief to generate civil dissension and civil strife. And they also knew that nothing, absolutely nothing, is so inclined to foster among religious believers of various faiths a toleration—no, an affection—for one another than voluntarily joining in prayer together, to the God whom they all worship and seek. Needless to say, no one should be compelled to do that, but it is a shame to deprive our public culture of the opportunity, and indeed the encouragement, for people to do it voluntarily. The Baptist or Catholic who heard and joined in the simple and inspiring prayers of Rabbi Gutterman on this official and patriotic occasion was inoculated from religious bigotry and prejudice in a manner that can not be replicated. To deprive our society of that important unifying mechanism, in order to spare the nonbeliever what seems to me the minimal inconvenience of standing or even sitting in respectful nonparticipation, is as senseless in policy as it is unsupported in law.[63]

Justice Scalia's conception of religious toleration is rooted in the happy confidence that we all "worship and seek" the same God. Civic prayer is thus a "unifying mechanism" that reminds citizens of common religious beliefs. In doing so, civic prayer abates the potential of "sectarian religious belief" to disturb the civil peace and inoculates citizens against "religious bigotry and prejudice." The assumption implicit here is that anyone who cannot not endure an innocuous civic prayer is simply a bigot. In making this assumption, Justice Scalia aligns himself with no less a notable than Samuel Adams. When John Jay and John Rutledge opposed the motion to begin the first session of the Continental Congress with prayer, Adams apparently responded that "he was no bigot, and could hear a prayer from a gentleman of piety and virtue, who was at the same time a friend to his country."[64] In an age where religious beliefs are still capable of fueling bloody violence, we cannot neglect the possible value of an "inoculation against bigotry" such as Justice Scalia proposes. Nevertheless, before rushing too quickly to rally around the banner of toleration unfurled by the Justice, perhaps we should study its emblem more carefully.

At the heart of Justice Scalia's argument is the assertion that the prayers offered by the rabbi served as an acknowledgment to his hearers of "the God whom they all worship and seek." The impulse behind the justice's assertion is an ecumenical one; he sees the household of faith as relatively spacious and its residents as having much in common.[65] Of course, one might conclude that Justice Scalia's ecumenism is fairly meager, but that conclusion does not threaten the essential character of his position. Scalia's "ecumenical toleration" has two principal characteristics: It arises chiefly out of a focus on the similarities that unite various religious traditions rather than the differences that separate them, and it produces a particular kind of social feeling—"affection"—by one believer for another.

In contrast with Justice Scalia's proposed inoculation against bigotry, however, a very different view of toleration is wrapped fairly securely around the roots of the American political tradition, and Roger Williams is its most famous exemplar. We might attempt to capture Williams's curious dialectic of religious dogmatism and toleration by naming it Separatist toleration. And we may distinguish Separatist toleration from ecumenical toleration in two respects. First, Separatist toleration is preoccupied with a keen consciousness of the differences separating various religious traditions rather than similarities that may unite them. The world Roger Williams surveyed was one fractured by religious difference, crisscrossed with barriers of religious dogmatism. He saw no possibility of either finding ecumenical unity out of these differences or of surmounting the divisive barriers of religious dogmatism. Second, Separatist toleration does not necessarily engender affection among believers of different stripes, but simply civil cooperation. Williams harbored no affection for

Quakers and was willing to cross rhetorical swords with them to the end of his days, but he saw no reason not to carry on the business of citizenship with them. In a way, Williams succeeded in establishing a kind of fractured soul fit for the fractured world in which he perceived himself to live. He could exhibit civil pleasantness for individuals whose religious views filled him with grave alarm, as though his soul could display both affection and distrust toward the same individual at the same moment.

Williams and the Separatists who arose following the Great Awakening remind us that we must deny to ecumenical impulses any right to a smug place of preeminence in the history of religious freedom in America. Separatists have frequently been on what we would now designate the side of the angels in important disputes, and the more ecumenically spirited have championed causes that now smack of intolerance. In addition to the dispute between Separatist Roger Williams and the non-separating Puritans of Massachusetts Bay, one might recall the conflict over disestablishment in Virginia during the 1780s. There, a coalition of forces concerned with the necessity of a virtuous citizenry championed the proposed Bill Establishing a Provision for Teachers of the Christian Religion. But Protestant dissenters, chiefly Separatist Baptists, aligned with Madison and Jefferson to defeat the bill and enact Jefferson's Bill for Establishing Religious Freedom.[66] At least during the colonial and revolutionary periods, religious liberty found more allies among those animated by Separatist impulses than by ecumenical ones.

In fact, the advocates of Separatist toleration during the seventeenth and eighteenth centuries tended to be fiercely dogmatic about their religious beliefs. One eighteenth-century Virginia Anglican complained that you couldn't meet Separate Baptists in the road without their trying to ram a passage of scripture down your throat.[67] But, again, it was vociferous dissenters like these who provided critical support for disestablishment in Virginia. Religious dogmatism has been much maligned within some quarters of legal scholarship; the standard line labels it as incompatible with liberal democratic discourse. Thus, one hears that only dialogic or ecumenical religious beliefs should be used to justify political choices or that legislation motivated by "inerrant" religious beliefs violates the establishment clause.[68] Such proposals are curious in light of the important place of dogmatic Separatists in the American tradition of religious liberty. Of course, religion has a dark side, or at least some religious beliefs are not on the friendliest terms with liberal democracy.[69] But religion, as this century has abundantly illustrated, holds no monopoly on dark sides or antidemocratic sentiments. If anything, we should have learned from the events of the twentieth century to be on the watch for the "dark side of secularism."[70] The Separatist tradition should help people recognize that dogmatism alone does not threaten democracy. At least some kinds of religious dogmatism have been critical allies of liberal democracy and enemies of intolerance.

The curious irony of the vision of religious harmony expressed by Justice Scalia in his dissent to the majority's opinion in *Lee v. Weisman* is that it becomes the tool for an essentially intolerant project: the structuring of a civic occasion to include a religious component from which some believers and nonbelievers will be excluded because of conscience.[71] In truth, the lesson in toleration Justice Scalia so values is directed primarily to religious minorities and to unbelievers. In more candid moments, proponents of school prayer have sometimes acknowledged the pedagogical value of civic prayers for religious minorities. Erwin Griswold argued to this effect in opposition to the Supreme Court's decision in *Engel v. Vitale*, which held unconstitutional the prayer written and sponsored by the New York Board of Regents for New York public schools.

> Let us consider the Jewish child, or the Catholic child, or the nonbeliever, or the Congregationalist, or the Quaker. . . . When the prayer is recited, if this child or his parents feel that he cannot participate, he may stand or sit, in respectful attention, while the other children take part in the ceremony. Or he may leave the room. It is said this is bad, because it sets him apart from other children. It is even said that there is an element of compulsion in this. . . . But is this the way it should be looked at? The child of a nonconforming or minority group is, to be sure, different in his beliefs. That is what it means to be a member of a minority. Is it not desirable for him to learn and observe this . . . not so much that he is different, as that other children are different from him? And is it not desirable that, at the same time, he experiences and learns the fact that his difference is tolerated and accepted? No compulsion is put upon him. He need not participate. But he, too, has the opportunity to be tolerant. He allows the majority of the group to follow their own tradition, perhaps coming to understand and to respect what they feel is significant to them.[72]

Griswold artfully painted the Regents' Prayer as an occasion for mutual education in tolerance, but it is not easy to see how a nonconforming child "experiences and learns the fact that his difference is tolerated and accepted." The only difference the majority learns to respect in a nonconforming child is the difference of nonparticipation.[73] The majority is not schooled in toleration for listening to non-majority prayers or reading from non-biblical religious texts—the Bhagavad Gita, for instance.

But that is the kind of toleration demanded of religious minorities. They are expected to learn respect for prayers and Bible readings contrary to their faith. In the end, the schooling in toleration carried out under the aegis of the Regents' Prayer was a very one-sided kind of education. Religious minorities were expected to imbibe the stoutest dose. Toleration, of course, is not just the virtue of majorities. Nevertheless, it is odd to construe the establishment clause in a manner that requires religious minorities to provide its chief place of abode.

In reality, the irony of Justice Scalia's intolerant tolerance is as old as the Puritans of the Massachusetts Bay Colony. The fundamental premise in their willingness to persecute religious dissidents was a conviction that certain fundamental religious truths were so clear as to deny the possible of reasonable disagreement concerning them. Those who failed to hew to the line of orthodoxy on these fundamental matters were deemed unworthy of toleration. The voice of Scalia, trivializing the meritoriousness of objections to tainted worship, is the voice of John Winthrop, pronouncing the sentence of banishment on Roger Williams for his Separatist objections to unholy prayers.

Justice Scalia's vision of tolerance-in-sameness makes a civic virtue of the religious vision commonly referred to as ecumenism.[74] This, of course, is a religious vision with respectable credentials. It is, nevertheless, a particular religious vision. Religious ecumenism is the implacable foe of religious sectarianism. Ecumenism celebrates the many rooms within the common house of faith, sectarianism admits of only one room and guards the entrance to that room with vigor. Ecumenism hails commonality, and sectarianism highlights difference. Once again, this disjunction in religious vision is as old as the generally ecumenical Puritans who harried sectarian Roger Williams out of the Massachusetts Bay Colony. The only thing novel about Justice Scalia's dissent is his suggestion that government may enter the lists on the side of ecumenism. Sectarian citizens who question this partisanship become tainted with the brand of bigotry. Who, after all, would object to the government's generous "inoculation" against "religious bigotry and prejudice" but those already infected with these social contagions?[75]

The "respect" that Justice Scalia elevates to the status of civic virtue is thus a controversial one. It is a respect only possible for those ready to join Justice Scalia in asserting that citizens "serve and worship" the same God. For those armed with this perspective, the prayer of a rabbi in Providence, Rhode Island, will resonate with grounds for agreement rather than difference. But Justice Scalia's ecumenical partisanship treats believers in more sectarian religious visions as deformed citizens. Because their religious consciences do not permit them to join in the embrace of "respect . . . even affection" with followers of a different—and perhaps even offensive—religious tradition, they become casualties of Justice Scalia's intolerant program of inculcating tolerance. What Justice Scalia calls tolerance is in reality forced homogenization, and it is starkly at odds with the philosophy at the root of the American tradition of religious liberty, which is animated principally by a concern to preserve rather than subdue religious difference.[76]

The alternative to a toleration rooted in commonality is a tolerance based on the acknowledgment of difference. Difference-regarding toleration does not require a believer in one sacred vision to respect, much less feel affection for, differing sacred visions. It requires simply that the holders of these different visions refrain from attempting to make their own orthodoxy into a measure of civil standing. The Baptist remains free to judge that the Catholic is on the path to spiritual destruction and vice versa. Each, however, is precluded from making these supposed spiritual prospects a matter of civil disability, including a basis for exclusion from civil communion.

The curious alliance between Separatist pietism and enlightenment that wrested religious liberty from the grasp of religious establishment has deteriorated with age. Three developments have proved especially corrosive to the original alliance. First, the pietistic sects that found an unlikely friend in statesmen such as Madison and Jefferson have followed H. Richard Niebuhr's classic progression from sect to denominational church.[77] This progression has weakened the Separatist impulse within historically Separatist traditions. Sects that once perceived themselves as aliens and pilgrims have, as it were, purchased tract houses and joined the PTA. More at home with the world about them, they have concentrated less on separation and more on fashioning a social environment consistent with their religious beliefs. Second, the creation and expansion of the regulatory state has critically undermined the perceived barrier between public and private that made Separatist toleration possible. Room for private dogmatism in religious matters has been displaced by an ever-widening public sector. Religious dogmatism has faced the alternative of either disappearing or else learning to walk about in public. Because there is every evidence that religious dogmatism has not, nor will it, ever disappear, this means that it must inevitably become an ever more settled inhabitant of public life. Third, and finally, the original alliance between pietism and enlightenment was forged at least partially out of the willingness of each partner in that alliance to speak in a language that addressed the fundamental concerns of the other. Isaac Backus learned to talk at least partially in the language of Locke and social contract. James Madison erected the arguments of "Memorial and Remonstrance" over premises that were, at numerous points, frankly religious. But the heirs of Backus and Madison have grown impatient with the tiresome work of creating a consensus from alternately sacred and profane starting points. Barbed references to the dangers of "fundamentalism" and "secular humanism" are easier to hurl. They make for better sound-bites or, in the case of academics, better text-bites.[78]

These observations lead to the sober conclusion that the intellectual and theological possibilities represented in the Separatist thought of Roger Williams may be increasingly inaccessible to the American political debate about religious liberty because Separatism itself is on the wain. That may explain why the face worn by politically active religious groups today frequently seems to bear a family resemblance more to the Puritan John Winthrop than to Roger Williams. It remains to be seem whether the consensus in favor of religious liberty and disestablishment can survive the passing or temporary dormancy of Separatism—a once central ally of religious freedom.

Conclusion

Roger Williams redefined the nature of order and peace to embrace the beginnings of a fractured society, whose ever-multiplying religious sects pulled and tugged and jostled the world in which they were increasingly strangers. To name this violent conflagration of ideas peace was to speak a language that would not be heard again for a century. The territory Williams claimed for the individual conscience was captured from the broad notion of the public good shared by his opponents. He created a space for religious liberty by denying, in part, the degree to which individual members of the state are interconnected. His definition of the public good rejected, in an important sense, John Donne's tribute to human solidarity: "No man is an *island,* entire of it self; every man is a piece of the *continent,* a part of the *main;* if a *clod* be washed away by the *sea, Europe* is the less, as well as if a *promontory* were, as well as if a *manor* of thy *friends,* or of *thine own* were; any man's *death* diminishes *me,* because I am involved in *mankind;* And therefore never send to know for whom the *bell* tolls; It tolls for *thee.*"[79] The social world that Williams envisioned, at least with respect to matters of religion—and, for him, such matters were the most important of all—was a world of islands, each cut off from the unified promontories of meaning that his religious contemporaries thought essential to the maintenance of human society. The search for "lost Zion" upon which he was embarked would become a search conducted in increasing isolation.[80]

The price Williams paid for freedom of conscience was the de-Christianization of Christian America. To him, at least, this was not an exorbitant price, because he believed that Christian America had never existed and never would. He cared too deeply about God and the church to trivialize them with public professions of religiousness. Nevertheless, because his contemporaries could not accept that price, they labeled Williams a fanatic and forgot about him. He has few knowledgeable supporters in the present day for the same reason. He alienates Jeffersonian skeptics by the fervency of his faith and believers by the secularism of his political vision.[81]

Notes

1. For discussions of this phenomenon, see Stephen L. Carter, *The Culture of Disbelief: How American Law and Politics Trivialize Religious Devotion* (New York: Basic Books, 1993); Frederick Mark Gedicks, "Public Life and Hostility to Religion," *Virginia Law Review* 78 (1992): 671-96; and Edward McGlynn Gaffney, Jr., "Hostility to Religion, American Style," *DePaul Law Review* 42 (1992): 263.

2. See, for example, Bruce A. Ackerman, *Social Justice in the Liberal State* (New Haven: Yale University Press, 1980), 3-30; Robert Audi, "The Separation of Church and State and the Obligations of Citizenship," *Philosophy and Public Affairs* 18 (1989): 269-96; Kent Greenawalt, *Religious Convictions and Political Choice* (New York: Oxford University Press, 1988); and Abner S. Greene, "The Political Balance of the Religion Clauses," *Yale Law Journal* 102 (1993): 1614.

3. Consider James Madison's poor regard for "parchment barriers" against infringement of individual liberties. James Madison to Thomas Jefferson, 17 Oct. 1788, in *James Madison on Religious Liberty,* ed. Robert S. Alley (Buffalo: Prometheus Books, 1985), 72.

4. This speaking, and the consensus-building at which it is aimed, is made difficult by the reality and intensity of religious difference. Perhaps the common religious vocabulary available to a Muslim or a Southern Baptist is not substantially more extensive than that available to either of these and a devout secularist. This reality may mean that consensus-building among believers will be most successful in religious traditions that share common vocabularies. For example, the

consensus-building possibilities among Christians will perhaps be greater than those possible between Christians and Hindus.

5. For a discussion of the prevalence of religious arguments for religious liberty during the colonial and revolutionary periods, see Steven D. Smith, "The Rise and Fall of Religious Freedom in Constitutional Discourse," *University of Pennsylvania Law Review* 140 (1991): 154-66.

6. As Stanley Ingber has suggested, "The religion clauses represent an acknowledgment of pre-Enlightenment beliefs and a realization that for many there are duties or obligations that precede those made by human beings." Ingber, "Religion or Ideology: A Needed Clarification of the Religion Clauses," *Stanford Law Review* 41 (1989): 285.

7. Michael McConnell, "The Origins and Historical Understanding of Free Exercise of Religion," *Harvard Law Review* 103 (1990): 1496; Perry Dane, "Religious Exemptions under the Free Exercise Clause: A Model of Competing Authorities," student note, *Yale Law Journal* 90 (1980): 350. Choper identified this aspect of religious experience as a characteristic element and used it as the basis for a constitutional definition of religion. Jesse Choper, "Defining 'Religion' in the First Amendment," *University of Illinois Law Review* (1982): 599.

8. Roger Williams, *The Bloudy Tenent Yet More Bloudy,* in *The Complete Writings of Roger Williams,* 7 vols. (New York: Russell and Russell, 1963), 4:29, 187.

9. William Penn, *The Great Case for Liberty of Conscience* (London, 1670), in *A Collection of the Works of William Penn,* 2 vols. (London: Printed by the Assigns of J. Sowle, 1726, repr. New York: AMS Press, 1974), 1:443, 447-48.

10. John Locke, *A Letter Concerning Toleration,* ed. James H. Tully (Indianapolis: Hackett Publishing, 1983), 25.

11. Isaac Backus, "An Appeal to the Public for Religious Liberty," in *Isaac Backus on Church, State, and Calvinism,* ed. William McLoughlin (Cambridge: Harvard University Press, 1968), 313; John Leland, "The Rights of Conscience Inalienable," in *The Writings of the Late Elder John Leland,* ed. L. F. Greene (New York: G. W. Wood, 1845, repr. New York: Arno Press, 1969), 181.

12. James Madison, "A Memorial and Remonstrance," in *The Mind of the Founder: Sources of the Political Thought of James Madison* (Hanover: University Press of New England for Brandeis University Press, 1981), 7. The sense of inalienability focused on by Madison in "A Memorial and Remonstrance," that an individual could not relinquish the right to fulfill obligations owed to God, is distinct from other arguments in favor of inalienable rights. For examples of other arguments, see Diana T. Meyers, *Inalienable Rights: A Defense* (New York: Columbia University Press, 1985), 16.

13. Thomas Jefferson, *Notes on the State of Virginia,* in *Thomas Jefferson: Writings,* ed. Merrill D. Peterson (New York: Library of America, 1984), 285.

14. Penn, *The Great Case for Liberty of Conscience,* 443, 445.

15. Locke, *A Letter Concerning Toleration,* ed. Tully, 43.

16. "For not to be able to give us faith, or save our consciences harmless, and yet to persecute us for refusing conformity," Penn wrote, "is intolerable hard measure." *The Great Case for Liberty of Conscience,* 456. John Leland made a similar point. "Every man must give an account of himself to God, and therefore every man ought to be at liberty to serve God in a way that he can best reconcile to his conscience. If government can answer for individuals at the day of judgment, let men be controlled by it in religious matters; otherwise, let men be free." Leland, "A Plea for Liberty of Conscience Inalienable," in *The Writings of the Late Elder John Leland,* ed. L. F. Greene (New York: G. W. Wood, 1845, repr. New York: Arno Press, 1969), 181.

17. Penn, *The Great Case for Liberty of Conscience,* 452. Compare *West Virginia Bd. of Educ. v. Barnette,* 319 U.S. 624, 644 (1943) (Black, J., concurring) (referring to "fear of spiritual condemnation" experienced by children compelled to repeat pledge of allegiance); and *Braunfeld v. Brown,* 366 U.S. 599, 616 (1961) (Stewart, J., dissenting) (noting the "cruel choice" to which Orthodox Jews were put by Sunday closing law).

18. For general attempts to discuss the place of religion in the Constitution, see Michael Smith, "The Special Place of Religion in the Constitution," *Supreme Court Review* (1983): 83-123; and John Garvey, "Free Exercise and the Values of Religious Liberty," *Connecticut Law Review* 18 (1986): 779-802. Garvey is probably correct in stating (794) that the attempt to locate one ultimate principle supporting constitutional freedoms is futile and that these freedoms, including religious freedom, may be supported by a cluster of values. The focus upon the special nature of religious duties in the text is not intended to suggest that the free-exercise clause is not supported by other values. For example, as a student I suggested that a distinguishing characteristic of religion in many sociological studies is its perception of reality in the twin categories of sacred and profane. See Timothy L. Hall, "The Sacred and the Profane: A First Amendment Definition of Religion," *Texas Law Review* 61 (1982): 139. Because participation in the political process is affected, at least to some extent, by one's overall worldview, and religious belief is characterized by a perception of sacred categories of reality, it may be that the inability to express these perceptions of transcendent realities in the political process makes believers uniquely powerless when their minority worldviews conflict with a majority's, thus justifying special protection of their religious exercise. For a discussion of the sacred/profane distinction as a means of defining religion in the First Amendment, see Ingber, "Religion or Ideology," 285-86.

19. *Goldman v. Weinberger,* 475 U.S. 503, 525 (1986) (Blackmun, J., dissenting). For discussions suggesting that the free-exercise clause should be construed to protect conscientious beliefs even when such beliefs are not religious, see Milton Konvitz, *Religious Liberty and Conscience* (New York: Viking Press, 1968), 105; Philip Kurland, "The Supreme Court, Compulsory Education, and the First Amendment's Religion Clauses," *West Virginia Law Review* 75 (1973): 237-41; and

Note, "Toward a Constitutional Definition of Religion," 91 *Harvard Law Review* 91 (1978): 1066-67. Notwithstanding scholarly argument to the contrary, the Supreme Court, during the period in which First Amendment doctrine recognized that believers could, under some circumstances, obtain exemptions from facially neutral laws, maintained that the free-exercise clause applied only to beliefs rooted in religion. *Frazee v. Illinois Dept. of Empl. Security,* 489 U.S. 829, 832 (1989); *Thomas v. Review Bd.,* 450 U.S. 707, 713 (1981); and *Wisconsin v. Yoder,* 406 U.S. 205 (1972). The Court's decision in *Employment Div. v. Smith,* 494 U.S. 872 (1990), however, renders the question of whether religious acts are entitled to greater protection than conscientiously motivated but nonreligious acts essentially moot in many or even most cases.

20. For an attempt to describe free exercise in these terms, see William Marshall, "Solving the Free Exercise Dilemma: Free Exercise as Expression," *Minnesota Law Review* 67 (1983): 545. Marshall, although recognizing that his argument captured no scholarly adherents, has restated this position in "The Case against the Constitutionally Compelled Free Exercise Exemption," *Case Western Reserve Law Review* 40 (1989-90): 361-72.

21. *United States v. Macintosh,* 283 U.S. 605, 633-34 (1931) (Hughes, C. J., dissenting): "The essence of religion is belief in a relation to God involving duties superior to those arising from any human relation"; *McGowan v. Maryland,* 366 U.S. 420, 562 (1961) (Douglas, J., dissenting): "The institutions of our society are founded on the belief that there is an authority higher than the authority of the State; that there is a moral law which the State is powerless to alter; that the individual possesses rights, conferred by the Creator, which government must respect."

22. *Walz v. Tax Comm'n,* 397 U.S. 664, 694 (1970) (Harlan, J., concurring): "Government involvement in religious life . . . is apt to lead to strife and frequently strain a political system to the breaking point"; *Board of Educ. v. Allen,* 392 U.S. 236, 254 (1968) (Black, J., dissenting): "The First Amendment's prohibition against governmental establishment of religion was written on the assumption that state aid to religion and religious schools generates discord, disharmony, hatred, and strife among our people." But see *Meek v. Pittenger,* 421 U.S. 349, 386 (1975) (opinion by Chief Justice Warren Burger): "I see at least as much potential for divisive political debate in opposition to the crabbed attitude the Court shows in this case"; and Smith, "The Special Place of Religion," 97, questioning whether issues such as industrial unionization, McCarthyism, the campaign for racial equality, the prolonged nature of the Vietnam War, and perhaps the Watergate scandal, abortion, and sexual issues have been as divisive as religion.

23. I have explored the connection between concern for civil virtue and a theory of religious liberty elsewhere; see Timothy L. Hall, "Religion and Civic Virtue: A Justification of Free Exercise," *Tulane Law Review* 67 (1992): 87-134. For additional suggestions that the free-exercise and establishment clauses had origins partially in a regard for religion's role in creating the circumstances in which

civic virtue might flourish, see Michael W. McConnell, "Accommodation of Religion," *Supreme Court Review* (1985): 17-18; Charles Taylor, "Religion in a Free Society," in *Articles of Faith, Articles of Peace: The Religious Liberty Clauses and the American Public Philosophy,* ed. James Davison Hunter and Os Guinness (Washington, D.C.: The Brookings Institution, 1990), 93; and Mark Tushnet, "The Emerging Principle of Accommodation of Religion (Dubitante)," *Georgetown Law Journal* 76 (1988): 1696.

24. Konvitz, *Religious Liberty and Conscience, 99.* For a similar but more recent suggestion that it is impermissible to favor protection of religious beliefs over other contentious beliefs, except in circumstances where religious belief is especially vulnerable to suppression, see Christopher L. Eisgruber and Lawrence G. Sager, "The Vulnerability of Conscience: The Constitutional Basis for Protecting Religious Conduct," *University of Chicago Law Review* 61 (1994): 1245-315. Marshall, "Case against the Constitutionally Compelled Free Exercise Exemption," 383.

25. Sidney Ahlstrom, *A Religious History of the American People* (New Haven: Yale University Press, 1972), 137-38.

26. Sometimes Separatists have forged ecumenical alliances with other outgroups. John Winthrop noted, for example, Roger Williams's progress from a radical Separatist who refused communion with almost everyone to a seeker who eventually welcomed worship with "all comers." Winthrop, *History of New England from 1630 to 1649,* 2 vols., ed. James Savage (Boston: Phelps and Farnham, 1824, repr. New York: Arno Press, 1972), 1:307. Compare George Whitfield's insistence that converts during the Great Awakening separate themselves from churches led by Old Light leaders: "Don't tell me you are a Baptist, an Independent, a Presbyterian, a Dissenter; tell me you are a Christian, that is all I want." Stephen A. Marini, *Radical Sects of Revolutionary New England* (Cambridge: Harvard University Press, 1982), 13-14.

27. Francis J. Bremer, *The Puritan Experiment: New England Society from Bradford to Edwards* (New York: St. Martin's Press, 1976), 43-53.

28. Philip F. Gura, *A Glimpse of Zion's Glory: Puritan Radicalism in New England, 1620-1660* (Middletown: Wesleyan University Press), 93-125; William G. McLoughlin, *New England Dissent, 1630-1883,* 2 vols. (Cambridge: Harvard University Press, 1971), 1:3-25.

29. The argument in the text does not require a more precise genealogy of Baptist origins, although they were far more complicated. The first American Baptists can trace a lineage running back to the middle of the seventeenth century. These "Old Baptists" distinguished themselves from other Protestants principally over the issue of infant baptism. After the Great Awakening in the eighteenth century, a number of "New Lights" separated themselves from established Congregational churches to pursue a more pietistic religious vision. Many of these separators ultimately came to oppose the practice of infant baptism, but their separation from established churches had not originally been over

that issue. These eighteenth-century renegades from established religion are generally referred to as "Separate Baptists." Even after Old Baptists had gained a measure of religious liberty by the middle of the eighteenth century, the Separate Baptists, who had only recently broken with established religion, continued to be subject to a wide variety of civil penalties. For a general account of the distinction between Old Baptists and Separate Baptists, see Martin E. Marty, *Pilgrims in Their Own Land: Five Hundred Years of Religion in America* (Boston: Little, Brown, 1984), 150-54; and McLoughlin, *New England Dissent*, 1:277, 421-39.

30. McLoughlin, *New England Dissent*, 1:53. Compare Roger Williams's characterization of spiritual communion: "Communion is twofold, first, open and professed among church members: secondly, secret and implicit in all such as give their presence to such worships without witnessing against them." Williams, *The Bloudy Tenent Yet More Bloudy*, 417.

31. After the founding of the Boston-Charleston Baptist Church, a number of Congregationalist ministers undertook to debate the organizers of this congregation. The ministers challenged the Baptists to show some scriptural authority for their separation from Congregational churches. One of the Baptists pointed to 2 Corinthians 6:17 in response: "Wherefore come out from among them and touch no unclean thing and I will be your God." David D. Hall, *Worlds of Wonder, Days of Judgment: Popular Religious Belief in Early New England* (New York: Alfred A. Knopf, 1989), 63.

32. Hall, *Worlds of Wonder*, 3-91, 360-85; Rhys Isaac, *The Transformation of Virginia, 1740-1790* (New York: W. W. Norton, 1982), 161-63, 172-77, 192-93, 200-203, 299-300.

33. Cushing Strout, "Jeffersonian Religious Liberty and American Pluralism," in *The Virginia Statute for Religious Freedom: Its Evolution and Consequences in American History*, ed. Merrill D. Peterson and Robert C. Vaughan (New York: Cambridge University Press, 1988), 208-9; Anson Phelps Stokes and Leo Pfeffer, *Church and State in the United States*, rev. ed. (New York: Harper and Row, 1964), 3, 65, 151; Elwyn A. Smith, *Religious Liberty in the United States* (Philadelphia: Fortress Press, 1972), 7-26.

34. McLoughlin, *New England Dissent*, 1:15.

35. Ibid., 1:362-63.

36. Ibid., 1:421-87.

37. Roger Williams argued that religious dissenters rarely fear being "leavened" (indoctrinated to betray their beliefs) by being compelled to attend worship services contrary to their beliefs: "Among both Papists and Protestants about coming to church, and that not out of fear of being leavened (for what religion is ordinarily so distrustful of its own strength?) as of countenancing what they believe false, by their presence and appearance." Williams, *The Bloudy Tenent Yet More Bloudy*, 417.

38. *Grand Rapids School District v. Ball*, 473 U.S. 373, 385 (1985). See also *Levitt v. Committee for Public Educ. and Religious Liberty*, 413 U.S. 472, 480 (1973): "The

state is constitutionally compelled to assure that the state-supported activity is not being used for religious indoctrination."

39. *Marsh v. Chambers*, 463 U.S. 783, 792 (1983). See also *Wallace v. Jaffree*, 472 U.S. 38, 81 (1985) (O'Connor, J., concurring): "At the very least, Presidential Proclamations are distinguishable from school prayer in that they are received in a noncoercive setting and are primarily directed at adults, who presumably are not readily susceptible to unwilling religious indoctrination."

40. William P. Marshall, "The Concept of Offensiveness in Establishment and Free Exercise Jurisprudence," *Indiana Law Journal* 66 (1991): 353; Arlin M. Adams and Charles Emmerich, *A Nation Dedicated to Religious Liberty: The Constitutional Heritage of the Religion Clauses* (Philadelphia: University of Pennsylvania Press, 1990), 85.

41. McLoughlin, *New England Dissent,* 1:xviii. For the argument that the " 'hearts and minds' of children of minority faiths [in public schools which conduct religious exercises] are as vulnerable to enforced ostracism and being assigned a subordinate status as are the 'hearts and minds' of the children of racial minorities," see Alan E. Brownstein, "Harmonizing the Heavenly and Earthly Spheres: The Fragmentation and Synthesis of Religion, Equality, and Speech in the Constitution," *Ohio State Law Journal* 51 (1990): 136. Kenneth Karst has referred to this kind of injury as "status harm." Karst, "The First Amendment, the Politics of Religion and the Symbols of Government," *Harvard Civil Rights-Civil Liberties Law Review* 27 (1992): 505. He has argued that government endorsement of particular religious symbols creates the possibility of deep political division. This kind of division is not simply a matter of a dominant religious tradition squaring off against a minority tradition. Membership in the majority religious group becomes a surrogate for membership in the ranks of political, not just religious, insiders. "If government-sponsored symbols of religion produce strong reaction, the most important reason is that they touch the sense of identity, symbolizing the status of individual citizens as members of dominant or subordinate political groups" (508).

42. Erving Goffman, *Stigma: Notes on the Management of Spoiled Identity* (Englewood Cliffs: Prentice-Hall, 1963), 6: "It seems possible for an individual to fail to live up to what we effectively demand of him, and yet be relatively untouched by this failure; insulated by his alienation, protected by identity beliefs of his own, he feels that he is a full-fledged normal human being, and that we are the ones who are not quite human. He bears a stigma but does not seem to be impressed or repentant about doing so."

R. Lawrence Moore similarly describes how religious minorities transform their status as "outsiders" in a positive sense of self-identify. Moore, *Religious Outsiders and the Making of Americans* (New York: Oxford University Press, 1986). Compare Mark Tushnet's comments concerning the Supreme Court's decision in *Lynch v. Donnelly,* 465 U.S. 668 (1984): "Jews have always known that they were strangers in the land and have taken some succor from that fact. *Lynch* just reminds us of that status, and, distressing though it may be to have it brought to light, we may profit from learning the lesson again." Tushnet, *Red, White, and Blue: A Critical Analysis of Constitutional Law* (Cambridge: Harvard University Press, 1988), 256n31.

43. In the 1640s, for example, William Witter was presented to the County Court in Salem because of his opposition to infant baptism and his declaration that "they who stayed while a child was baptized do worship the devil." McLoughlin, *New England Dissent,* 1:18.

44. Compare Tushnet's suggestion that "religion cannot comfortably fit into our constitutional scheme because it is a form of life whose essential characteristics cannot be reduced to the rationalist premises of our legal system." Mark Tushnet, "Religion and Theories of Constitutional Interpretation," *Loyola Law Review* 33 (1987): 239-40.

45. Naomi M. Stolzenberg, "'He Drew a Circle That Shut Me Out': Assimilation, Indoctrination, and the Paradox of a Liberal Education," *Harvard Law Review* 106 (1993): 581.

46. John Clarke argued that those who objected to the infant baptism practiced by the established Congregationalist churches should "come out from among them (Oh, my people) and be ye separate from them." McLoughlin, *New England Dissent,* 1:98.

47. *Lee v. Weisman,* 505 U.S. 577 (1992).

48. Ibid., 586.

49. *Wallace v. Jaffree,* 472 U.S. 38, 70 (1985) (O'Connor, J., concurring) (quoting *Engel v. Vitale,* 370 U.S. 421, 431 (1962)): "An endorsement [of religion] infringes the religious liberty of the nonadherent, for 'when the power, prestige and financial support of government is placed behind a particular religious belief, the indirect coercive pressure upon religious minorities to conform to the prevailing officially approved religion is plain.' "

50. See, for example, Philip Gura's extended study of colonial Puritanism demonstrating the failure of the New England Puritan establishment to crush dissent. Gura, *A Glimpse of Zion's Glory.* For an account of Baptist defiance of legal sanctions levied against them in eighteenth-century Virginia, see Isaac, *The Transformation of Virginia,* 161-63, 172-77, 192-93, 200-203. Protestant dissenters were not alone, of course, in resisting government coercion in religious matters. Morton Borden has recounted the pressures, including legal pressures, exerted upon Jews to convert to Christianity during the eighteenth century but has noted that conversions were relatively rare. Borden, *Jews, Turks, and Infidels* (Chapel Hill: University of North Carolina Press, 1984), 6-7. For examples of the tendency of legal scholars to overemphasize the likely success of government coercions, see, for example, Ira C. Lupu, "Where Rights Begin: The Problem of Burdens on the Free Exercise of Religion," *Harvard Law Review* 102 (1989): 961 ("a wide range of punitive legal measures can be destructive to the free exercise of religion: the use of imprisonment, fines, and seizure of property are potent enough to

discourage all but the most ardent religious adherents"); and Neil R. Feigenson, "Political Standing and Governmental Endorsement of Religion: An Alternative to Current Establishment Clause Doctrine," *DePaul Law Review* 40 (1990): 63 ("by making religion relevant to a person's standing in the political community, government threatens to coerce or compromise that person's religious beliefs. Especially if the person is made to feel like an 'outsider,' she may be lead to change religious affiliation so as to become an 'insider,' realizing that her beliefs now 'cost' her something in terms of her standing in the secular community").

51. For accounts of the encounters between Mormons and the legal system, see Edwin B. Firmage and Richard C. Mangrum, *Zion in the Courts: A Legal History of the Church of Jesus Christ of Latter-Day Saints, 1830–1900* (Urbana: University of Illinois Press, 1988); and Orma Linford, "The Mormons, the Law, and the Territory of Utah," *American Journal of Legal History* 23 (1979): 213–35.

52. Madison, "A Memorial and Remonstrance," 12.

53. Thus, it should not have mattered in *Marsh v. Chambers* whether "the individual claiming injury by the practice [of legislative prayer] is an adult, presumably not readily susceptible to 'religious indoctrination' . . . or peer pressure." 463 U.S. 783, 792 (1983).

54. See, for example, Daniel O. Conkle, "Religious Purpose, Inerrancy, and the Establishment Clause," *Indiana Law Journal* 67 (1991): 8, which suggests that when government acts in such a way as to disapprove the religious or irreligious beliefs of some citizens, it is "likely to alienate the adversely affected individuals, thereby causing damage to the political community as well as to the individuals themselves." See also Daniel O. Conkle, "Toward a General Theory of the Establishment Clause," *Northwestern University Law Review* 82 (1988): 1167 ("we can weaken the community through actions of exclusion—actions that restrict the community's membership or that reduce the loyalty of its members"); and William Van Alstyne, "Trends in the Supreme Court: Mr. Jefferson's Crumbling Wall—A Comment on *Lynch v. Donnelly*," *Duke Law Journal* (1984): 787 (referring to the "powerful and compelling" idea of "a civil nation of free people, diverse in their thoughts, equal in their citizenship, and with none to feel alien, outcast, or stranger in relation to civil authority").

55. See Robert Cover, "The Supreme Court, 1982 Term—Foreword: *Nomos and Narrative*," *Harvard Law Review* 97 (1983): 4–68, which emphasizes the role of insular religious communities in the creation of law.

56. Conkle, "Toward a General Theory of the Establishment Clause," 1169.

57. Compare James Madison's argument that "attempts to enforce by legal sanctions, acts obnoxious to so great a proportion of Citizens, tend to enervate the laws in general, and to slacken the bands of Society." Madison, "A Memorial and Remonstrance," 12. See *Engel v. Vitale*, 370 U.S. 421 (1962): "The history of governmentally established religion, both in England and in this country, showed that whenever government had allied itself with one particular form of religion,

the inevitable result had been that it had incurred the hatred, disrespect, and even contempt of those who held contrary beliefs."

58. See Madison's argument in "The Federalist No. 10," in *The Federalist,* ed. Jacob E. Cook (Middletown: Wesleyan University Press, 1961), 64-65, that the proposed federal government would help assure that "a religious sect, may degenerate into a political faction in a part of the Confederacy, but the variety of sects dispersed over the entire face of it, must secure the national Councils against any danger from that source." Consider also his suggestion in "The Federalist No. 51": "In a free government, the security for civil rights must be the same as for religious rights. It consists in the one case in the multiplicity of interests, and in the other, in the multiplicity of sects." Ibid., 351-52. For an argument that civil religious exercise increases the potential of destructive factionalism, see Yehuda Mirsky, "Civil Religion and the Establishment Clause," *Yale Law Journal* 95 (1986): 1254.

59. The phrase comes from John Adams's legal argument in a 1769 case involving the claim of a Baptist minister for the tax exemption enjoyed by ministers of established Congregationalist churches in Massachusetts. Adams argued against the claim and observed of the minister at one point: "He separates for trifles, I can't think 'em essential." McLoughlin, *New England Dissent,* 1:519. The remark was typical of establishment supporters. Patrick Henry similarly dismissed Baptist scruples against paying taxes to support an established church. "There was nothing of conscience in the matter," he observed, "it was only a contending about paying a little money." Ibid., 560.

60. *Lee v. Weisman,* 505 U.S. 577 (1992) (Scalia, J., dissenting).

61. Ibid., 632-36.

62. Ibid., 637.

63. Ibid., 645.

64. *Marsh v. Chambers,* 463 U.S. 783, 791-92 (1983).

65. For an exhaustive survey of the ecumenical impulse, see *A History of the Ecumenical Movement, 1517-1948,* 2d ed., ed. Ruth Rouse and Stephen Charles Neill (Philadelphia: Westminster Press, 1968).

66. For a useful summary of the Virginia conflict, see Thomas Curry, *The First Freedoms: Church and State in America to the Passage of the First Amendment* (New York: Oxford University Press, 1986), 134-48. For an account of the Virginia episode that focuses on the role played by Protestant dissenters, see Rhys Isaac, " 'The Rage of the Old Serpent Devil': The Dissenters and the Making and Remaking of the Virginia Statute for Religious Freedom," in *The Virginia Statute for Religious Freedom: Its Evolution and Consequences in American History,* ed. Merrill D. Peterson and Robert C. Vaughan (New York: Cambridge University Press, 1988), 139. Madison's "Memorial and Remonstrance" was written in connection with this conflict and, although perhaps the most famous document in the American history of religious liberty, was simply one of several anonymous petitions circulated against the proposed bill for supporting Christian teachers. It was not

even the petition that garnered the most signatures. An evangelical petition, arguing that the proposed bill was against the "spirit of the gospel," mustered 4,899 signatures in contrast with the 1,552 of the "Memorial and Remonstrance." William Lee Miller, *The First Liberty: Religion and the American Republic* (New York: Alfred A. Knopf, 1985), 39. In view of the fact that the Virginia Assembly that passed Jefferson's bill establishing religious liberty also passed a statute punishing Sabbath-breaking, Miller suggests (49) that "the triumph in these events in Virginia did not belong exactly to right, reason, and civic republicanism; it belong symbolically to Baptists."

67. Isaac, *The Transformation of Virginia*, 164.

68. Michael J. Perry, *Love and Power: The Role of Religion and Morality in American Politics* (New York: Oxford University Press, 1991); Conkle, "Religious Purpose," 10-15.

69. William P. Marshall, "The Other Side of Religion," *Hastings Law Journal* 44 (1993): 854.

70. For the suggestion that "a psychology approaching inerrancy might well occur in the realm of secular thought," see Conkle, "Religious Purpose," 23.

71. Compare Steven Smith's suggestion that a policy of intolerance may be justified in the name of "democracy," "community," "civic virtue," or even "tolerance." Smith, "The Restoration of Tolerance," *California Law Review* 78 (1990): 307.

72. Erwin Griswold, "Absolute Is in the Dark: A Discussion of the Approach of the Supreme Court to Constitutional Questions," *Utah Law Review* 8 (1963): 177.

73. Griswold said as much. The children of majority religious traditions "see that there are others who do not accept [the values of those traditions], and that they are wholly tolerated in their *nonacceptance.*" Griswold, "Absolute Is in the Dark," 177 (emphasis added).

74. See Douglas Laycock, " 'Noncoercive' Support for Religion: Another False Claim about the Establishment Clause," *Valparaiso University Law Review* 26 (1991): 62-63, which describes the establishment of a religion of "mushy ecumenism" that is allegedly "more tolerant" and "more enlightened."

75. See *Engel v. Vitale,* 370 U.S. 421, 423 (1962), which quotes the observation of New York state officials who composed the Regents' Prayer as part of their "Statement on Moral and Spiritual Training in Schools," which they believed would "be subscribed to by all men and women of good will."

76. Michael McConnell describes the "great evil against which the Religion Clauses are directed" as "government-induced homogeneity—the tendency of government action to discourage or suppress the expression of differences in matters of religion." McConnell, "Religious Freedom at a Crossroads," *University of Chicago Law Review* 59 (1992): 168. I have explored the Constitution's commitment to the protection of religious difference in Timothy L. Hall, "Religion, Equality, and Difference," *Temple Law Review* 65 (1992): 1.

77. H. Richard Niebuhr, *The Social Sources of Denominationalism* (New York: Henry Holt, 1929), 17-21.

78. See, for example, Marvin E. Frankel, "Religion in Public Life—Reasons for Minimal Access," *George Washington Law Review,* 60 (1992): 633, which refers to "the frightening waves of fundamentalism roaring elsewhere in the world do not fail to lap at our own shores."

79. John Donne, *Devotions upon Emergent Occasions,* ed. Anthony Raspa (Montreal: McGill-Queen's University Press, 1975, repr. New York: Oxford University Press, 1987), 87 (emphasis in the original).

80. Roger Williams to John Winthrop, 24 Oct. 1636, in *The Correspondence of Roger Williams,* 2 vols., ed. Glen W. LaFantasie (Hanover: Brown University Press, 1988), 1:68.

81. For a contemporary challenge to "Christian America" reminiscent of Williams's arguments, see Stanley Hawerwas, "A Christian Critique of Christian America," in *Religion, Morality, and the Law,* ed. J. Roland Pennock and John W. Chapman (New York: New York University Press, 1988), 110-33.

Appendix

Because Williams's writings were typically responses to the works of others, they do not take the form of organized arguments building systematically from premises to conclusions. Such order as they possess arises more out of the logic of the arguments of Williams's opponents than his own. But because Williams was a great believer in repeating a good point, it is possible to construct from his various rebuttals of other writers certain arguments that he marshaled for each new rhetorical occasion. He did this himself at the end of *The Bloudy Tenent Yet More Bloudy.* What follows is Williams's elaboration of the various senses in which the doctrine of persecution was "a foul, a black, and a bloody tenet." It was, he said,

A tenet of high blasphemy against the God of peace, the God of order, who has of one blood, made all mankind, to dwell upon the face of the earth, now, all confounded and destroyed in their civil beings and subsistences, by mutual flames of war from their several respective religions and consciences.

A tenet warring against the Prince of Peace, Christ Jesus, denying his appearance and coming in the flesh, to put an end to, and abolish the shadows of that ceremonial and typical land of Canaan.

A tenet fighting against the sweet end of his coming, which was not to destroy men's lives, for their religions, but to save them, by the meek and peaceable invitations and persuasions of his peaceable wisdom's maidens.

A tenet foully charging his wisdom, faithfulness and love, in so poorly providing such magistrates and civil powers all the world over, as might effect so great a charge pretended to be committed to them.

A tenet lamentably guilty of his most precious blood, shed in the blood of so many hundred thousands of his poor servants by the civil powers of the world, pretending to suppress blasphemies, heresies, idolatries, superstition, etc.

A tenet fighting with the spirit of love, holiness, and meekness, by kindling fiery spirits of false zeal and fury, when yet such spirits know not of what spirit they are.

A tenet fighting with those mighty angels who stand up for the peace of the saints, against Persia, Greece, etc. and so consequently, all other nations, who, fighting for their several religions, and against the truth, leave no room for such as fear and love the Lord on the earth.

A tenet, against which the blessed souls under the altar cry loud for vengeance, this tenet having cut their throats, torn out their hearts, and poured forth their blood in all ages, as the only heretics and blasphemers in the world.

A tenet which no uncleanness, no adultery, incest, sodomy, or bestiality can equal, this ravishing and forcing (explicitly or implicitly) the very souls and consciences of all the nations and inhabitants of the world.

A tenet that puts out the very eye of all true faith, which cannot but be as free and voluntary as any virgin in the world, in refusing or embracing any spiritual offer or object.

A tenet loathsome and ugly (in the eyes of the God of heaven, and serious sons of men) I say, loathsome with the palpable filths of gross dissimulation and hypocrisy: thousands of peoples and whole nations, compelled by this tenet to put on the foul vizard of religious hypocrisy, for fear of laws, losses and punishments, and for the keeping and hoping for of favor, liberty, worldly commodity, etc.

A tenet woefully guilty of hardening all false and deluded consciences (of whatsoever sect, faction, heresy, or idolatry, though never so horrid and blasphemous) by cruelties and violences practiced against them: all false teachers and their followers (ordinarily) contracting a brawny and steely hardness from their sufferings for their consciences.

A tenet that shuts and bars out the gracious prophecies and promises and discoveries of the most glorious Sun of Righteousness, Christ Jesus, that burns up the holy Scriptures, and forbids them (upon the point) to be read in English, or that any trial or search, or (truly) free disquisition be made by them: when the most able, diligent and conscionable readers must pluck forth their own eyes, and be forced to read by the (whichsoever predominant) clergies' spectacles.

A tenet that seals up the spiritual graves of all men, Jews and Gentiles, (and consequently stands guilty of the damnation of all men) since no preachers, nor trumpets of Christ himself may call them out, but such as the several and respective nations of the world themselves allow of.

A tenet that fights against the common principles of all civility, and the very civil being and combinations of men in nations, cities, etc. by commixing (explicitly or implicitly) a spiritual and civil state together, and so confounding and overthrowing the purity and strength of both.

A tenet that kindles the devouring flames of combustions and wars in most nations of the world, and (if God were not infinitely gracious) had almost ruined the English, French, the Scottish and Irish, and many other nations, German, Polish, Hungarian, Bohemian, etc.

A tenet that bows down the backs and necks of all civil states and magistrates, kings and emperors, under the proud feet of that man and monster of sin and pride the Pope, and all popish and proud clergy-men rendering such lacks and seculars (as they call them) but slavish executioners (upon the point) of their most imperious synodical decrees and sentences.

A tenet that renders the highest civil magistrates and ministers of justice (the fathers and gods of their countries) either odious or lamentably grievous unto the very best subjects by either clapping or keeping on, the iron yokes of cruellest oppression. No yoke or bondage comparably so grievous, as that upon the soul's neck of men's religion and consciences.

A tenet, all besprinkled with the bloody murders, stabs, poisonings, pistollings, powder-plots, etc. against many famous kings, princes, and states, either actually performed or attempted, in France, England, Scotland, Low-Countries, and other nations.

A tenet all red and bloody with those most barbarous and tiger-like massacres, of so many thousand and ten thousands formerly in France, and other parts, and so lately and so horribly in Ireland: of which, what ever causes be assigned, this chiefly will be found the true, and while this continues (to wit, violence against conscience) this bloody issue, sooner or later, must break forth again (except God wonderfully stop it) in Ireland and other places too.

A tenet that stunts the growth and flourish of the most likely and hopefullest commonwealths and countries, while consciences, the best, and the best deserving subjects are forced to fly (by enforced or voluntary banishment) from their native countries; the lamentable proof whereof England has felt in the flight of so many worthy English, into the Low Countries and New England, and from New England into old again and other foreign parts.

A tenet whose gross partiality denies the principles of common justice, while men weigh out to the consciences of all others, that which they judge not fit nor right to be weighed out to their own: Since the persecutors' rule is, to take and persecute all consciences, only, himself must not be touched.

A tenet that is but Machiavellianism, and makes a religion but a cloak or stalking horse to policy and private ends of Jeroboam's crown, and the priest's benefice.

A tenet that corrupts and spoils the very civil honesty and natural conscience of a nation. Since conscience to God violated, proves (without repentance) ever after, a very jade, a drug, loose and unconscionable in all converse with men.

Lastly, a tenet in England most unseasonable, as pouring oil upon those flames which the high wisdom of the parliament, (by easing the yokes on men's consciences) had begun to quench.[1]

Note

1. Roger Williams, *The Bloudy Tenent Yet More Bloudy,* in *The Complete Writings of Roger Williams,* 7 vols. (New York: Russell and Russell, 1963), 4:493-99.

Bibliography

Primary Sources

Adams, Dickinson W., ed. *Jefferson's Extracts from the Gospels*. Princeton: Princeton University Press, 1983.
Backus, Isaac. "An Appeal to the Public for Religious Liberty." In *Isaac Backus on Church, State, and Calvinism*. Edited by William McLouglin. Cambridge: Harvard University Press, 1968.
————. *A History of New England with Particular Reference to the Denomination of Christians Called Baptists*. Providence: Providence Press, 1871. Reprint. New York: Arno Press, 1969.
Bradford, William. *Of Plymouth Plantation*. Edited by Samuel Eliot Morison. New York: Alfred A. Knopf, 1952.
Browne, Robert. *A Treatise of Reformation without Tarrying for Anie, and of the Wickednesse of Those Preachers which will not Reforme till the Magistrate Commande or Compelle Them*. 1582.
Calvin, John. *Institutes of the Christian Religion*. 2 volumes. Translated by Ford L. Battles. Edited by John T. McNeill. Philadelphia: Westminster Press, 1960.
Clarke, John. *Ill News from New-England*. London: Henry Hills, 1652.
Cobbet, Thomas. *The Civil Magistrates Power in Matters of Religion*. London: W. Wilson, 1653. Reprint. New York: Arno Press, 1972.
Cook, Jacob E., ed. *The Federalist*. Middletown: Wesleyan University Press, 1961.
Cotton, John. "An Abstract of the Lawes of New England." In *Tracts and Other Papers Relating to the Origin, Settlement, and Progress of the Colonies in North America, from the Discovery of the Country to the Year 1776*, edited by Peter Force. New York: P. Smith, 1947.
————. *The Bloudy Tenent, Washed, and Made White in the Bloud of the Lambe*. London: Matthew Symmons, 1647. Reprint. New York: Arno Press, 1972.
————. *An Exposition upon the Thirteenth Chapter of the Revelation*. London, 1656. Reprinted in *The Puritans: A Sourcebook of Their Writings*. 2 volumes. Revised

edition. Edited by Perry Miller and Thomas H. Johnson. New York: Harper
and Row, 1963.

———. *A Reply to Mr. Williams, His Examination.* In *The Complete Writings of
Roger Williams.* 7 volumes. New York: Russell and Russell, 1963.

———. *The Way of the Congregational Churches Cleared.* London: Matthew Symmons, 1648. Reprinted in *John Cotton on the Churches of New England*, edited
by Lazer Ziff. Cambridge: Harvard University Press, 1968.

Donne, John. *Devotions upon Emergent Occasions.* Edited by Anthony Raspa. Montreal: McGill-Queen's University Press, 1975. Reprint. New York: Oxford
University Press, 1987.

Hooker, Thomas. *A Survey of the Summe of Church-Discipline.* London: Printed by
A. M. for John Bellamy, 1648. Reprint. New York: Arno Press, 1972.

Hutchinson, William T. et al., eds. *The Papers of James Madison.* 17 volumes.
Chicago: University of Chicago Press, 1962-69.

Jefferson, Thomas. "Notes on Locke and Shaftesbury." In *The Papers of Thomas
Jefferson.* 20 volumes. Volume 1, edited by Julian P. Boyd. Princeton: Princeton University Press, 1950-95.

———. *Notes on the State of Virginia.* In *Thomas Jefferson: Writings.* Edited by Merrill D. Peterson. New York: Library of America, 1984.

Johnson, Edward. *Wonder-Working Providence of Sion's Saviour in New-
England.* London, 1654. Reprint. Delmar: Scholars' Facsimiles and Reprints,
1974.

LaFantasie, Glen W., ed. *The Correspondence of Roger Williams.* 2 volumes. Hanover:
Brown University Press, 1988.

The Laws and Liberties of Massachusetts. Cambridge, 1648.

Lechford, Thomas. "Plain Dealing, or Newes from New-England." London, 1641.

Leland, John. "A Plea for Liberty of Conscience." In *The Writings of the Late Elder John Leland*, edited by L. F. Greene. New York: G. W. Wood, 1845.
Reprint. New York: Arno Press, 1969.

———. "The Rights of Conscience Inalienable." In *The Writings of the Late Elder John Leland*, edited by L. F. Greene. New York: G. W. Wood, 1845.
Reprint. New York: Arno Press, 1969.

Locke, John. *A Letter Concerning Toleration.* Edited by James H. Tully. Indianapolis: Hackett Publishing, 1983.

Madison, James. "Detached Memoranda." In *James Madison on Religious Liberty*,
edited by Robert S. Alley. Buffalo: Prometheus Books, 1985.

———. "Memorial and Remonstrance." In *The Mind of the Founder: Sources of the
Political Thought of James Madison.* Revised edition. Hanover: University Press
of New England for Brandeis University Press, 1981.

Mather, Cotton. *Magnalia Christi Americana.* London: Printed for T. Parkhurst,
1702. Reprint. New York: Arno Press, 1972.

McLoughlin, William, ed. *Isaac Backus on Church, State, and Calvinism.* Cambridge: Harvard University Press, 1968.

Mill, John Stuart. *On Liberty.* Edited by Elizabeth Rapaport. Indianapolis: Hackett Publishing, 1978.

Miller, Perry, and Thomas H. Johnson, eds. *The Puritans: A Sourcebook of Their Writings.* 2 volumes. Revised edition. New York: Harper and Row, 1963.

Myers, Marvin, ed. *The Mind of the Founder: Sources of the Political Thought of James Madison.* Revised edition. Hanover: University Press of New England, 1981.

Penn, William. *The Great Case for Liberty of Conscience.* In *A Collection of the Works of William Penn.* 2 volumes. London: Printed by the Assigns of J. Sowle, 1726. Reprint. New York: AMS Press, 1974.

Penniman, Howard R., ed. *John Locke: On Politics and Education.* Toronto: D. Van Nostrand, 1947.

Rutland, Robert A., ed. *The Papers of George Mason.* 3 volumes. Chapel Hill: University of North Carolina Press, 1970.

Shurtleff, Nathaniel B., ed. *Records of the Governor and Company of the Massachusetts Bay in New England (1628–86).* 5 volumes. Boston: William White, 1853–54.

Smith, Joseph H., ed. *Colonial Justice in Western Massachusetts (1639–1702):* The Pynchon Court Record. Cambridge: Harvard University Press, 1961.

Walker, Williston, ed. *The Creeds and Platforms of Congregationalism.* New York: Scribner's, 1892. Reprint. Philadelphia: Pilgrim Press, 1960.

Ward, Nathaniel. *The Simple Cobler of Aggawam in America.* Edited by P. M. Zall. Lincoln: University of Nebraska Press, 1969.

Whitmore, W. H., ed. *The Colonial Laws of Massachusetts.* Boston: Rockwell and Churchill, 1889.

Williams, Roger. *The Bloudy Tenent, of Persecution.* In *The Complete Writings of Roger Williams.* 7 volumes. New York: Russell and Russell, 1963.

———. *The Bloudy Tenent Yet More Bloudy.* In *The Complete Writings of Roger Williams.* 7 volumes. New York: Russell and Russell, 1963.

———. *Christenings Make Not Christians.* In *The Complete Writings of Roger Williams.* 7 volumes. New York: Russell and Russell, 1963.

———. *The Examiner Defended.* In *The Complete Writings of Roger Williams.* 7 volumes. New York: Russell and Russell, 1963.

———. *The Fourth Paper, Presented by Major Butler.* In *The Complete Writings of Roger Williams.* 7 volumes. New York: Russell and Russell, 1963.

———. *George Fox Digg'd out of His Burrowes.* In *The Complete Writings of Roger Williams.* 7 volumes. New York: Russell and Russell, 1963.

———. *The Hireling Ministry None of Christs.* In *The Complete Writings of Roger Williams.* 7 volumes. New York: Russell and Russell, 1963.

———. *A Key to the Language of America.* In *The Complete Writings of Roger Williams.* 7 volumes. New York: Russell and Russell, 1963.

———. *Mr. Cottons Letter Lately Printed, Examined and Answered.* In *The Complete Writings of Roger Williams.* 7 volumes. New York: Russell and Russell, 1963.

———. *Queries of Highest Consideration.* In *The Complete Writings of Roger Williams.* 7 volumes. New York: Russell and Russell, 1963.

Winthrop, John. *The History of New England from* 1630 to 1649. 2 volumes. Edited by James Savage. Boston: Phelps and Farnham, 1825. Reprint. New York: Arno Press, 1972.

———. "A Modell of Christian Charity." In *The Puritans: A Sourcebook of Their Writings.* 2 volumes. Revised edition. Edited by Perry Miller and Thomas H. Johnson. New York: Harper and Row, 1963.

———. *Winthrop Papers.* 6 volumes. Edited by Allyn Bailey Forbes and Malcolm Freiberg. Boston: Massachusetts Historical Society, 1929-92.

Secondary Sources

Aaron, Richard I. *John Locke.* 3d ed. New York: Oxford University Press, 1971.

Ackerman, Bruce A. *Social Justice in the Liberal State.* New Haven: Yale University Press, 1980.

Adair, John. *Founding Fathers: The Puritans in England and America.* London: J. M. Dent and Sons, 1982.

Adams, Arlin M., and Charles Emmerich. *A Nation Dedicated to Religious Liberty: The Constitutional Heritage of the Religion Clauses.* Philadelphia: University of Pennsylvania Press, 1990.

Adams, Arlin M., and Sarah Barringer Gordon, "The Doctrine of Accommodation in the Jurisprudence of the Religion Clauses." *DePaul Law Review* 37 (1988): 317-45.

Ahlstrom, Sidney. *A Religious History of the American People.* New Haven: Yale University Press, 1972.

Allen, David Grayson. *In English Ways: The Movement of Societies and the Transferal of English Local Law and Custom to Massachusetts Bay in the Seventeenth Century.* Chapel Hill: University of North Carolina Press, 1981.

Anderson, Virginia DeJohn. *New England's Generation: The Great Migration and the Formation of Society and Culture in the Seventeenth Century.* New York: Cambridge University Press, 1991.

Audi, Robert. "The Separation of Church and State and the Obligations of Citizenship." *Philosophy and Public Affairs* 18 (1989): 269-96.

Aylmer, G. E. "Unbelief in Seventeenth-Century England." In *Puritans and Revolutionaries: Essays in Seventeenth-Century History Presented to Christopher Hill,* edited by Donald Pennington and Keith Thomas. New York: Oxford University Press, 1982.

Banning, Lance. "Madison, the Statute, and Republican Convictions." In *The Virginia Statute for Religious Freedom: Its Evolution and Consequences in American History,* edited by Merrill D. Peterson and Robert C. Vaughan. New York: Cambridge University Press, 1988.

Baritz, Loren. *City on a Hill: A History of Ideas and Myths in America.* New York: John Wiley and Sons, 1964.

Barnes, Thomas G. "Law and Liberty (and Order) in Early Massachusetts." In *The English Legal System: Carryover to the Colonies.* Los Angeles: William Andrews Clark Memorial Library, University of California, 1975.

Bartlett, John R., ed. *Records of the Colony of Rhode Island and Providence Plantations, in New England.* Providence: A. Crawford Greene and Brother, 1856.

Bercovitch, Sacvan. *The Puritan Origins of the American Self.* New Haven: Yale University Press, 1975.

————. "Typology in Puritan New England: The Williams-Cotton Controversy Reassessed." *American Quarterly* 19 (1967): 166-191.

Berman, Harold J. "Law and Belief in Three Revolutions." *Valparaiso University Law Review* 18 (1984): 569-629.

————. "Religion and the Law: The First Amendment in Historical Perspective." *Emory Law Journal* 35 (1986): 777-93.

Berman, Harold, and John Witte. "The Transformation of Western Legal Philosophy in Lutheran Germany." *Southern California Law Review* 62 (1989): 1573-660.

Berns, Walter. *The First Amendment and the Future of American Democracy.* New York: Basic Books, 1976.

Billias, George Athan, ed. *Law and Authority in Colonial America.* Barre, Mass.: Barre Publishers, 1965.

Bonomi, Patricia U. *Under the Cope of Heaven: Religion, Society, and Politics in Colonial America.* New York: Oxford University Press, 1986.

Boorstin, Daniel. *The Lost World of Thomas Jefferson.* Boston: Beacon Press, 1948.

Borden, Morton. *Jews, Turks, and Infidels.* Chapel Hill: University of North Carolina Press, 1984.

Bozeman, Dwight. *To Live Ancient Lives: The Primitivist Dimension in Puritanism.* Chapel Hill: University of North Carolina Press, 1988.

————. "Religious Liberty and the Problem of Order in Early Rhode Island." *New England Quarterly* 45 (1972): 44-64.

Brachlow, Stephen. *The Communion of Saints: Radical Puritan and Separtist Ecclesiology 1570-1625.* New York: Oxford University Press, 1988.

Bradley, Gerard V. "Beguiled: Free Exercise Exemptions and the Siren Song of Liberalism." *Hofstra Law Review* 20 (1991): 245-319.

————. "Imagining the Past and Remembering the Future: The Supreme Court's History of the Establishment Clause." *Connecticut Law Review* 18 (1986): 827-43.

————. "The No Religious Test Clause and the Constitution of Religious Liberty: A Machine That Has Gone of Itself." *Case Western Reserve Law Review* 37 (1987): 674-747.

Breen, T. H. *The Character of the Good Ruler: A Study of Puritan Political Ideas in New England, 1630-1730.* New Haven: Yale University Press, 1970.

————. "Persistent Localism: English Social Change and the Shaping of New England Institutions." In *Puritans and Adventurers: Change and Persistence in Early America.* New York: Oxford University Press, 1980.

Breen, T. H., and Stephen Foster. "Moving to the New World: The Character of Early Massachusetts Immigration." *William and Mary Quarterly*, 3d. ser., 30 (1973): 189-222.

———. "The Puritans' Greatest Achievement: A Study of Social Cohesion in Seventeenth-Century Massachusetts." In *Puritan New England: Essays on Religion, Society, and Culture*, edited by Alden T. Vaughan and Francis J. Bremer. New York: St. Martin's Press, 1977.

Bremer, Francis J. *The Puritan Experiment: New England Society from Bradford to Edwards.* New York: St. Martin's Press, 1976.

———. *Puritan Crisis: New England and the English Civil Wars, 1630-1670.* New York: Garland Publishing, 1989.

Bridenbaugh, Carl. *Fat Mutton and Liberty of Conscience: Society in Rhode Island, 1636-1690.* Providence: Brown University Press, 1974.

Brockunier, Samuel Hugh. *The Irrepressible Democrat: Roger Williams.* New York: Ronald Press, 1940.

Brownstein, Alan E. "Harmonizing the Heavenly and Earthly Spheres: The Fragmentation and Synthesis of Religion, Equality, and Speech in the Constitution." *Ohio State Law Journal* 51 (1990): 89-174.

Brumm, Ursula. *American Thought and Religious Typology.* Translated by John Hoaglund. New Brunswick: Rutgers University Press, 1970.

Brunkow, Robert D. "Love and Order in Roger Williams' Writings." *Rhode Island History* 35 (1976): 115-26.

Buckley, Thomas. "The Political Theology of Thomas Jefferson." In *The Virginia Statute for Religious Freedom: Its Evolution and Consequences in American History*, edited by Merrill D. Peterson and Robert C. Vaughan. New York: Cambridge University Press, 1988.

Bush, Sargent, Jr. "'Revising What we have done amisse': John Cotton and John Wheelwright, 1640." *William and Mary Quarterly*, 3d ser., 45 (1988): 733-750.

Butler, Jon. *Awash in a Sea of Faith: Christianizing the American People.* Cambridge: Harvard University Press, 1990.

Cahn, Mark D. "Punishment, Discretion, and the Codification of Prescribed Penalties in Colonial Massachusetts." *American Journal of Legal History* 33 (1989): 107-36.

Canty-Letsone, Rosezella. "John Winthrop's Concept of Law in Seventeenth-Century New England, One Notion of Puritan Thinking." *Duquesne Law Review* 16 (1977): 331-57.

Canup, John. *Out of the Wilderness: The Emergence of an American Identity in Colonial New England.* Middletown: Wesleyan University Press, 1990.

Carroll, Peter N. *Puritanism and the Wilderness: The Intellectual Significance of the New England Frontier 1629-1700.* New York: Columbia University Press, 1969.

Carter, Stephen L. *The Culture of Disbelief: How American Law and Politics Trivialize Religious Devotion.* New York: Basic Books, 1993.

Chapin, Bradley. *Criminal Justice in Colonial America, 1606–1660.* Athens: University of Georgia Press, 1983.

Choper, Jesse. "Defining 'Religion' in the First Amendment." *University of Illinois Law Review* (1982): 579-613.

Chu, Jonathan M. *Neighbors, Friends, or Madmen: The Puritan Adjustment to Quakerism in Seventeenth-Century Massachusetts Bay.* Westport: Greenwood Press, 1985.

Clarke, John. *Ill newes from New-England, or, A nar[r]ative of New-Englands persecution.* London: Henry Hills, 1652.

Cockburn, James S., ed. *Crime in England, 1550–1800.* Princeton: Princeton University Press, 1977.

Cohen, Charles Lloyd. *God's Caress: The Psychology of Puritan Religious Experience.* New York: Oxford University Press, 1986.

Collison, Patrick. *The Elizabethan Puritan Movement.* Berkeley: University of California Press, 1967.

———. *The Religion of Protestants: The Church in English Society, 1559–1625.* New York: Oxford University Press, 1982.

Conkle, Daniel O. "Religious Purpose, Inerrancy, and the Establishment Clause." *Indiana Law Journal* 67 (1991): 1-24.

———. "Toward a General Theory of the Establishment Clause." *Northwestern University Law Review* 82 (1988): 1113-14.

Conley, Patrick T. *Democracy in Decline: Rhode Island's Constitutional Development 1776–1841.* Providence: Rhode Island Historical Society, 1977.

Coquilette, Daniel R., ed. *Law in Colonial Massachusetts, 1630–1800.* Charlottesville: University Press of Virginia, 1985.

Cord, Robert. *Separation of Church and State: Historical Fact and Current Fiction.* New York: Lambeth Press, 1982.

Corwin, E. T., ed. *Ecclesiastical Records of the State of New York.* 7 volumes. Albany: J. B. Lyon, 1901-16.

Cover, Robert. "The Supreme Court, 1982 Term—Foreword: *Nomos* and Narrative." *Harvard Law Review* 97 (1983): 4-68.

Covey, Cyclone. *The Gentle Radical: A Biography of Roger Williams.* New York: Macmillan, 1966.

Cressy, David. *Coming Over: Migration and Communication between England and New England in the Seventeenth Century.* New York: Cambridge University Press, 1987.

Curry, Thomas. *The First Freedoms: Church and State in America to the Passage of the First Amendment.* New York: Oxford University Press, 1986.

Dane, Perry. "Religious Exemptions under the Free Exercise Clause: A Mode of Competing Authorities." Student note. *Yale Law Journal* 90 (1980): 350-76.

Daniels, Bruce C. *Dissent and Conformity on Narragansett Bay: The Colonial Rhode Island Town.* Middletown: Wesleyan University Press, 1983.

———. "Dissent and Disorder: The Radical Impulse and Early Government in the Founding of Rhode Island." *Journal of Church and State* 24 (1982): 357-78.

Davis, Jack L. "Roger Williams among the Narragansett Indians." *New England Quarterly* 43 (1970): 593-604.

Davis, Thomas M. "The Traditions of Puritan Typology." In *Typology and Early American Literature*, edited by Sacvan Bercovitch. Amherst: University of Massachusetts Press, 1972.

Delbanco, Andrew. *The Puritan Ordeal*. Cambridge: Harvard University Press, 1989.

Demos, John Putnam. *Entertaining Satan: Witchcraft and the Culture of Early New England*. New York: Oxford University Press, 1982.

Drakeman, Donald L. "Religion and the Republic: James Madison and the First Amendment." *Journal of Church and State* 25 (1983): 427-445.

Dreisbach, Daniel L. "Thomas Jefferson and Bills Number 82-86 of the Revision of the Laws of Virginia, 1776-1786: New Light on The Jeffersonian Model of Church-State Relations." *North Carolina Law Review* 69 (1990): 159-211.

Dunn, Richard S. *Puritans and Yankees: The Winthrop Dynasty of New England, 1630-1717*. Princeton: Princeton University Press, 1962.

Easton, Emily. *Roger Williams: Prophet and Pioneer*. Boston: Houghton Mifflin, 1930.

Eisgruber, Christopher L., and Lawrence G. Sager. "The Vulnerability of Conscience: The Constitutional Basis for Protecting Religious Conduct." *University of Chicago Law Review* 61 (1994): 1245-315.

Epstein, Richard A. "Religious Liberty in a Welfare State." *William and Mary Law Review* 31 (1990): 375-408.

Erikson, Kai T. *Wayward Puritans: A Study in the Sociology of Deviance*. New York: John Wiley, 1966.

Ernst, James. *The Political Thought of Roger Williams*. Seattle: University of Washington Press, 1929.

————. *Roger Williams: New England Firebrand*. New York: Macmillan, 1932.

Emerson, Everett. *John Cotton*. Revised edition. Boston: Twayne Publishers, 1990.

Eusden, John D. "Natural Law and Covenant Theology in New England, 1620-1670." *Natural Law Forum* 6 (1960): 1-30.

Farrell, John T. "The Early History of Rhode Island's Court System." *Rhode Island History* 9 (1950): 65-71, 103-17; 10 (1951): 1425.

Feigenson, Neil R. "Political Standing and Governmental Endorsement of Religion: An Alternative to Current Establishment Clause Doctrine." *DePaul Law Review* 40 (1990): 53-114.

Felker, Christopher D. "Roger Williams Use of Legal Discourse: Testing Authority in Early New England." *New England Quarterly* 63 (1990): 624-48.

Firmage, Edwin B., and Richard C. Mangrum. *Zion in the Courts: A Legal History of the Church of Jesus Christ of Latter-Day Saints, 1830-1900*. Urbana: University of Illinois Press, 1988.

Fischer, David Hackett. *Albion's Seed: Four British Folkways in America*. New York: Oxford University Press, 1989.

Flaherty, David H. "Law and the Enforcement of Morals in Early America." In *Law in American History,* edited by Donald Fleming and Bernard Bailyn. Boston: Little, Brown, 1971.

Foster, Stephen. *The Long Argument: English Puritanism and the Shaping of New England Culture, 1570–1700.* Chapel Hill: University of North Carolina Press, 1991.

———. *Their Solitary Way: The Puritan Social Ethic in the First Century of Settlement in New England.* New Haven: Yale University Press, 1971.

Frankel, Marvin E. "Religion in Public Life: Reasons for Minimal Access." *George Washington Law Review* 60 (1992): 633–44.

Freund, Paul. *The Supreme Court of the United States: Its Business, Purposes and Performance.* Cleveland: World Publishing, 1961.

Frost, J. William. *A Perfect Freedom: Religious Liberty in Pennsylvania.* New York: Cambridge University Press, 1990.

Fuller, Lon. "The Case of the Speluncean Explorers." *Harvard Law Review* 62 (1949): 616.

Gardner, E. Clinton. "John Locke: Justice and the Social Compact." *Journal of Law and Religion* 9 (1992): 347–71.

Garrett, John. *Roger Williams: Witness beyond Christendom, 1603–1683.* New York: Macmillan, 1970.

Garvey, John. "Free Exercise and the Values of Religious Liberty." *Connecticut Law Review* 18 (1986): 779–802.

Gaustad, Edwin Scott. *Dissent in American Religion.* Chicago: University of Chicago Press, 1973.

———. *Liberty of Conscience: Roger Williams in America.* Grand Rapids: Eerdmans, 1991.

———. "Religion and Ratification." In *The First Freedom: Religion and the Bill of Rights,* edited by James E. Wood, Jr. Waco: J. M. Dawson Institute of Church-State Studies, 1990.

Gedicks, Frederick Mark. "Public Life and Histility to Religion." *Virginia Law Review* 78 (1992): 671–96.

George, Timothy. "Between Pacifism and Coercion: The English Baptist Doctrine of Religious Toleration." *Mennonite Quarterly Review* 58 (1984): 30–49.

Giannella, Donald. "Religious Liberty, Nonestablishment, and Doctrinal Development. Part 1: The Religious Liberty Guarantee." *Harvard Law Review* 80 (1967): 1381–431.

Gilpin, W. Clark. *The Millenarian Piety of Roger Williams.* Chicago: University of Chicago Press, 1979.

Goen, C. C. *Revivalism and Separatism in New England.* New Haven: Yale University Press, 1962.

Goffman, Erving. *Stigma: Notes on the Management of Spoiled Identity.* Englewood Cliffs: Prentice-Hall, 1963.

Goldie, Mark. "The Theory of Religious Intolerance in Restoration England." In *From Persecution to Toleration: The Glorious Revolution and Religion in England,* edited by Ole Peter Grell, Jonathan I. Israel, and Nicholas Tyacke. New York: Oxford University Press, 1991.

Greenawalt, Kent. *Religious Convictions and Political Choice.* New York: Oxford University Press, 1988.

Greenberg, Douglas. "Crime, Law Enforcement, and Social Control in Colonial America." *American Journal of Legal History* 26 (1982): 293-325.

Greene, Abner S. "The Political Balance of the Religion Clauses." *Yale Law Journal* 102 (1993): 1611-44.

Greene, Jack P. "Interpretive Frameworks: The Quest for Intellectual Order in Early American History." *William and Mary Quarterly,* 3d ser., 48 (1991): 515-30.

Griswold, Erwin. "Absolute Is in the Dark: A Discussion of the Approach of the Supreme Court to Constitutional Questions." *Utah Law Review* 8 (1963): 167-82.

Gura, Philip F. *A Glimpse of Sion's Glory: Puritan Radicalism in New England, 1620-1660.* Middletown: Wesleyan University Press, 1984.

Hall, David D. *The Faithful Shepherd: A History of the New England Ministry in the Seventeenth Century.* Chapel Hill: University of North Carolina Press, 1972.

———. *Worlds of Wonder, Days of Judgment: Popular Religious Belief in Early New England.* New York: Alfred A. Knopf, 1989.

Hall, David D., John M. Murrin, and Thad W. Tate. *Saints and Revolutionaries: Essays on Early American History.* New York: W. W. Norton, 1984.

Hall, Kermit L. *The Magic Mirror: Law in American History.* New York: Oxford University Press, 1989.

Hall, Timothy L. "Religion and Civic Virtue: A Justification of Free Exercise." *Tulane Law Review* 67 (1992): 87-134.

———. "Religion, Equality, and Difference." *Temple Law Review* 65 (1992): 1-89.

———. "The Sacred and the Profane: A First Amendment Definition of Religion." *Texas Law Review* 61 (1982): 139-73.

Hamburger, Philip A. "A Constitutional Right of Religious Exemption: An Historical Perspective." *George Washington Law Review* 60 (1992): 915-48.

Hamilton, Marci A. "The Belief/Conduct Paradigm in the Supreme Court's Free Exercise Jurisprudence: A Theological Account of the Failure to Protect Religious Conduct." *Ohio State Law Journal* 54 (1993): 713-96.

———. "The First Amendment's Challenge Function and the Confusion in the Supreme Court's Contemporary Free Exercise Jurisprudence." *Georgia Law Review* 29 (1994): 81-135.

Hancock, Ralph C. *Calvin and the Foundations of Modern Politics.* Ithaca: Cornell University Press, 1989.

Haskins, George Lee. "Codification of Law in Colonial Massachusetts: A Study in Comparative Law." *Indiana Law Review* 30 (1954): 1-17.

———. *Law and Authority in Early Massachusetts: A Study in Tradition and Design.* New York: Macmillan, 1960.

————. "Precedents in English Ecclesiastical Practices for Criminal Punishments in Early Massachusetts." In *Essays in Legal History in Honor of Felix Frankfurter,* edited by Morris D. Forkosch. Indianapolis: Bobbs-Merrill, 1966.

Hatch, Nathan O. *The Sacred Cause of Liberty: Republican Thought and the Millenium in Revolutionary New England.* New Haven: Yale University Press, 1977.

Hawerwas, Stanley. "A Christian Critique of Christian America." In *Religion, Morality, and the Law,* edited by J. Roland Pennock and John W. Chapman. New York: New York University Press, 1988.

Heyrman, Christine L. *Commerce and Culture: The Maritime Communities of Colonial Massachusetts, 1630-1750.* New York: W. W. Norton, 1983.

Hirsh, Adam J. "From Pillory to Penitentiary: The Rise of Criminal Incarceration in Early Massachusetts." *Michigan Law Review* 80 (1982): 1179-1269.

Hoffer, Peter Charles. *Law and People in Colonial America.* Baltimore: Johns Hopkins University Press, 1992.

Holifield, E. Brooks. *Era of Persuasion: American Thought and Culture, 1521-1680.* Boston: Twayne Publishers, 1989.

Holstun, James. *A Rational Millenuim: Puritan Utopias of Seventeenth-Century England and America.* New York: Oxford University Press, 1987.

Horton, John, and Susan Medus, eds. *John Locke: A Letter Concerning Toleration in Focus.* London: Routledge, 1991.

Howe, Mark DeWolfe. *The Garden and the Wilderness: Religion and Government in American Constitutional History.* Chicago: University of Chicago Press, 1965.

————. "The Sources and Nature of Law in Colonial Massachusetts." In *Law and Authority in Colonial America,* edited by George Athan Billias. Barre: Barre Publishers, 1965.

Hudson, Winthrop S. "Locke: Heir of Puritan Political Theorists." In *Calvinism and Political Order,* edited by George L. Hunt. Philadelphia: Westminister Press, 1965.

Huntley, William B. "Jefferson's Public and Private Religion." *South Atlantic Quarterly* 79 (1980): 286-301.

Ingber, Stanley. "Religion or Ideology: A Needed Clarification of the Religion Clauses." *Stanford Law Review* 41 (1989): 233-333.

Isaac, Rhys. " 'The Rage of the Old Serpent Devil': The Dissenters and the Making and Remaking of the Virginia Statute for Religious Freedom." In *The Virginia Statute for Religious Freedom: Its Evolution and Consequences in American History,* edited by Merrill D. Peterson and Robert C. Vaughan. New York: Cambridge University Press, 1988.

————. *The Transformation of Virginia, 1740-1790.* New York: W. W. Norton, 1982.

James, Sydney V. *Colonial Rhode Island: A History.* New York: Charles Scribners Sons, 1975.

————. "Ecclesiastical Authority in the Land of Roger Williams." *New England Quarterly* 57 (1984): 323-46.

————. "The Worlds of Roger Williams." *Rhode Island History* 37 (1978): 99-109.

Jennings, Francis. *The Invasion of America: Indians, Colonialism, and the Cant of Conquest.* New York: W. W. Norton, 1976.

Johnson, Edward. *Wonder-Working Providence of Sions Saviour in New-England.* London, 1654. Reprint. Delmar: Scholars' Facsimiles and Reprints, 1974.

Karst, Kenneth L. "The First Amendment, the Politics of Religion, and the Symbols of Government." *Harvard Civil Rights-Civil Liberties Law Review* 27 (1992): 505-30.

———. "Why Equality Matters." *Georgia Law Review* 17 (1983): 245-89.

Kawashima, Yasuhide. *Puritan Justice and the Indian: White Man's Law in Massachusetts, 1630-1763.* Middletown: Wesleyan University Press, 1986.

Kelly, P. J. "John Locke: Authority, Conscience and Religious Toleration." In *John Locke: A Letter Concerning Toleration in Focus,* edited by John Horton and Susan Medus. London: Routledge, 1991.

Kent, Joan R. "Attitudes of Members of the House of Commons to the Regulation of Personal Conduct in Late Elizabethan and Early Stuart England." *Bulletin of the Institute of Historical Research* 46 (1973): 39-71.

Kessler, Sanford. "Locke's Influence on Jefferson's 'Bill for Establishing Religious Freedom.'" *Journal of Church and State* 24 (1983): 231-52.

Konig, David Thomas. *Law and Society in Puritan Massachusetts: Essex County, 1629-1692.* Chapel Hill: University of North Carolina Press, 1979.

Konvitz, Milton. *Religious Liberty and Conscience.* New York: Viking Press, 1968.

Kramnick, Isaac, and R. Lawrence Moore. *The Godless Constitution.* New York: W. W. Norton, 1996.

Kurland, Philip. "Of Church and State and the Supreme Court." *University of Chicago Law Review* 29 (1961): 1-96.

———. "The Irrelevance of the Constitution: The Religion Clauses of the First Amendment and the Supreme Court." *Villanova Law Review* 24 (1978): 3-27.

———. "The Origins of the Religion Clauses of the Constitution. *William and Mary Law Review* 27 (1986): 839-61.

———. "The Religion Clauses and the Burger Court." *Catholic University Law Review* 34 (1984): 1-18.

———. "The Supreme Court, Compulsory Education, and the First Amendment's Religion Clauses." *West Virginia Law Review* 75 (1973): 213-45.

Kurland, Philip, and Ralph Lerner, eds. *The Founders' Constitution.* 5 volumes. Chicago: University of Chicago Press, 1987.

LaFantasie, Glen W. "A Day in the Life of Roger Williams." *Rhode Island History* 46 (1987): 95-111.

———. "Roger Williams: The Inner and Outer Man." *Canadian Review of American Studies* 16 (1985): 375-94.

———. "Roger Williams and John Winthrop: The Rise and Fall of an Extraordinary Friendship." *Rhode Island History* 47 (1989): 85-95.

Lang, Amy Schrager. *Prophetic Woman: Anne Hutchinson and the Problem of Dissent in the Literature of New England.* Berkeley: University of California Press, 1987.

Laycock, Douglas. "Formal, Substantive, and Disaggregated Neutrality Toward Religion." *DePaul Law Review* 39 (1990): 993-1018.

———. " 'Noncoercive' Support for Religion: Another False Claim about the Establishment Clause." *Valparaiso University Law Review* 26 (1991): 37-67.

———. "Nonpreferential Aid to Religion: A False Claim About Original Intent." *William and Mary Law Review* 27 (1986): 875-923.

Laycock, Douglas, and Oliver S. Thomas. "Interpreting the Religious Freedom Restoration Act." *Texas Law Review* 73 (1994): 209-45.

Lee, C. "Discretionary Justice in Early Massachusetts." *Massachusetts Institute Historical Collection* 112 (1976): 120.

Levinson, Sanford. *Constitutional Faith.* Princeton: Princeton University Press, 1988.

Levy, Leonard W. *The Establishment Clause: Religion and the First Amendment.* New York: Macmillan, 1986.

———. *Jefferson and Civil Liberties: The Darker Side.* Cambridge: Harvard University Press, 1963. Reprint. Chicago: Ivan R. Dee, 1989.

Linford, Orma. "The Mormons, the Law, and the Territory of Utah." *American Journal of Legal History* 23 (1979): 213-35.

Little, David. "Thomas Jefferson's Religious Views and Their Influence on the Supreme Court's Interpretation of the First Amendment." *Catholic University Law Review* 26 (1976): 57-72.

———. *Religion, Order, and Law: A Study in Pre-Revolutionary England.* New York: Harper and Row, 1969.

———. "Roger Williams and the Separation of Church and State." In *Religion and the State: Essays in Honor of Leo Pfeffer,* edited by James E. Wood, Jr. Waco: Baylor University Press, 1985.

Lockridge, Kenneth A. *A New England Town: The First Hundred Years.* New York: W. W. Norton, 1970.

Lovejoy, David S. "Roger Williams and George Fox: The Arrogance of Self-Righteousness." *William and Mary Quarterly,* 3d ser., 62 (1993): 199-225.

Lucas, Paul R. *Valley of Discord: Church and Society along the Connecticut River, 1636-1725.* Hanover: University Press of New England, 1976.

Lupu, Ira. "Keeping the Faith: Religion, Equality and Speech in the U.S. Constitution." *Connecticut Law Review* 18 (1986): 739-78.

———. "Where Rights Begin: The Problem of Burdens on the Free Exercise of Religion." *Harvard Law Review* 102 (1989): 933-90.

Malbin, Michael. *Religion and Politics: The Intentions of the Authors of the First Amendment.* Washington, D.C.: American Enterprise Institute, 1978.

Mangrum, Richard C. *Zion in the Courts: A Legal History of the Church of Jesus Christ of Latter-Day Saints, 1830-1900.* Urbana: University of Illinois Press, 1988.

Manwaring, David Roger. *Render unto Caesar: The Flag-Salute Controversy.* Chicago: University of Chicago Press, 1962.

March, Kathleen Davidson. "Uncommon Civility: The Narragansett Indians and Roger Williams." Ph.D. diss., University of Iowa, 1985.

Marini, Stephen A. *Radical Sects of Revolutionary New England.* Cambridge: Harvard University Press, 1982.

Marshall, William P. "The Case against the Constitutionally Compelled Free Exercise Exemption." *Case Western Reserve Law Review* 40 (1989-90): 357-412.

———. "The Concept of Offensiveness in Establishment and Free Exercise Jurisprudence." *Indiana Law Journal* 66 (1991): 351-77.

———. "The Other Side of Religion." *Hastings Law Journal* 44 (1993): 843-63.

———. "Solving the Free Exercise Dilemma: Free Exercise as Expression." *Minnesota Law Review* 67 (1983): 545-94.

Marty, Martin. "On Medial Moraine: Religious Dimensions of American Constitutionalism." *Emory Law Journal* 39 (1990): 9-20.

———. *Pilgrims in Their Own Land: Five Hundred Years of Religion in America.* Boston: Little, Brown, 1984.

McConnell, Michael. "Accommodation of Religion." *Supreme Court Review* (1987): 17-18.

———. "The Origins and Historical Understanding of Free Exercise of Religion." *Harvard Law Review* 103 (1990): 1409-517.

———. "Religious Freedom at a Crossroads." *University of Chicago Law Review* 59 (1992): 115-94.

McLoughlin, William G. *Isaac Backus and the American Pietistic Tradition.* Edited by Oscar Handlin. Boston: Little, Brown, 1967.

———. *New England Dissent, 1630-1883.* 2 volumes. Cambridge: Harvard University Press, 1971.

McManus, Edgar J. *Law and Liberty in Early New England: Criminal Justice and Due Process, 1620-1692.* Amherst: University of Massachusetts Press, 1993.

Mendus, Susan. "Locke: Toleration, Morality and Rationality." In *John Locke: A Letter Concerning Toleration in Focus,* edited by John Horton and Susan Medus. London: Routledge, 1991.

Merel, Gail. "The Protection of Individual Choice: A Consistent Understanding of Religion Under the First Amendment." *University of Chicago Law Review* 45 (1978): 805-43.

Meyers, Diana T. *Inalienable Rights: A Defense.* New York: Columbia University Press, 1985.

Miller, Perry. *The New England Mind: The Seventeenth Century.* Cambridge: Harvard University Press, 1939.

———. *Orthodoxy in Massachusetts, 1630-1650.* Cambridge: Harvard University Press, 1933.

———. *Roger Williams: His Contribution to the American Tradition.* Indianapolis: Bobbs-Merrill, 1953.

Miller, Perry, and Thomas H. Johnson, eds. *The Puritans: A Sourcebook of Their Writings.* 2 volumes. Revised edition. New York: Harper and Row, 1963.

Miller, William Lee. *The First Liberty: Religion and the American Republic.* New York: Alfred A. Knopf, 1985.

Mirsky, Yehuda. "Civil Religion and the Establishment Clause." *Yale Law Journal* 95 (1986): 1237-57.

Moore, LeRoy. "Religious Liberty, Roger Williams, and the Revolutionary Era." *Church History* 34 (1965): 57-76.

———. "Roger Williams and the Historians." *Church History* 32 (1976): 432-51.

Moore, R. Lawrence. *Religious Outsiders and the Making of Americans.* New York: Oxford University Press, 1986.

Morgan, Edmund S. *The Puritan Dilemma: The Story of John Winthrop.* Boston: Little, Brown, 1958.

———. *Roger Williams: The Church and the State.* New York: W. W. Norton, 1967.

———. *Visible Saints: The History of a Puritan Idea.* Ithaca: Cornell University Press, 1963.

Morrison, Samuel Eliot. *The Oxford History of the American People.* New York: Oxford University Press, 1965.

Mosely, James G. *John Winthrop's World: History as a Story; the Story as History.* Madison: University of Wisconsin Press, 1992.

Nicholson, Peter. "John Locke's Later Letters on Toleration." In *John Locke: A Letter Concerning Toleration in Focus,* edited by John Horton and Susan Medus. London: Routledge, 1991.

Niebuhr, H. Richard. *The Social Sources of Denominationalism.* New York: Henry Holt, 1929.

Parks, Henry Bamford. "Morals and Law Enforcement in Colonial New England." *New England Quarterly* 5 (1932): 441-47.

Parrington, Vernon Louis. *Main Currents in American Thought.* 2 volumes. New York: Harcourt, Brace, 1927.

Peace, Nancy E. "Roger Williams: A Historigraphical Essay." *Rhode Island History* 35 (1976): 103-13.

Pestana, Carla Gardina. *Quakers and Baptists in Colonial Massachusetts.* New York: Cambridge University Press, 1991.

Penniman, Howard R., ed. *John Locke: On Politics and Education.* Toronto: D. Van Nostrand, 1947.

Pennington, Donald, and Keith Thomas, eds. *Puritans and Revolutionaries: Essays in Seventeenth-Century History Presented to Christopher Hill.* New York: Oxford University Press, 1978.

Pepper, Stephen. "The Case of Human Sacrifice." *Arizona Law Review* 23 (1981): 897-934.

———. "Reynolds, Yoder, and Beyond: Alternatives for the Free Exercise Clause." *Utah Law Review* (1981): 309-78.

———. "Taking the Free Exercise Clause Seriously." *Brigham Young University Law Review* (1989): 299-336.

Perry, Michael J. *Love and Power: The Role of Religion and Morality in American Politics.* New York: Oxford University Press, 1991.

Perry, Richard L., and John C. Cooper, eds. *Sources of Our Liberties: Documentary Origins of Individual Liberties in the United States Constitution and Bill of Rights.* Revised edition. Chicago: American Bar Foundation, 1978.

Pestana, Carla Gardina. *Quakers and Baptists in Colonial Massachusetts.* New York: Cambridge University Press, 1991.

Peterson, Merrill D., and Robert C. Vaughan, eds. *The Virginia Statute for Religious Freedom: Its Evolution and Consequences in American History.* New York: Cambridge University Press, 1988.

Pettit, Norman. *The Heart Prepared: Grace and Conversion in Puritan Spiritual Life.* New Haven: Yale University Press, 1966.

Pfeffer, Leo. "Madison's 'Detached Memoranda': Then and Now." In *The Virginia Statute for Religious Freedom: Its Evolution and Consequences in American History,* edited by Merrill D. Peterson and Robert C. Vaughan. New York: Cambridge University Press, 1988.

Powers, Edwin. *Crime and Punishment in Early Massachusetts, 1620-1692.* Boston: Beacon Press, 1966.

Preyer, Kathryn. "Penal Measures in the American Colonies: An Overview." *American Journal of Legal History* 26 (1982): 326-53.

Reinitz, Richard. "The Separatist Background of Roger Williams' Argument for Religious Tolerations." In *Typology and Early American Literature,* edited by Sacvan Bercovitch. Amherst: University of Massachusetts Press, 1972.

Richards, David A. J. *Toleration and the Constitution.* New York: Oxford University Press, 1986.

Ricoeur, Paul. *The Symbolism of Evil.* Boston: Beacon Press, 1967.

Roetger, Robert W. "The Transformation of Sexual Morality in 'Puritan' New England: Evidence from the New Haven Court Records, 1639-1968." *Canadian Review of American Studies* 15 (1984): 243-57.

Rosenmeier, Jesper. "The Teacher and the Witness: John Cotton and Roger Williams." *William and Mary Quarterly,* 3d ser., 25 (1968): 408-31.

Rossiter, Clinton. "Roger Williams on the Anvil of Experience." *American Quarterly* 3 (1951): 14-21.

Rouse, Ruth, and Stephen Charles Neill, eds. *A History of the Ecumenical Movement, 1517-1948.* 2d ed. Philadelphia: Westminster Press, 1968.

Rutman, Darrett B. *Winthrop's Boston: Portrait of a Puritan Town, 1630-1649.* Chapel Hill: University of North Carolina Press, 1965.

Salisbury, Neal. *Manitou and Providence: Indians, Europeans, and the Making of New England, 1500-1643.* New York: Oxford University Press, 1982.

Sandel, Michael. "Freedom of Conscience or Freedom of Choice?" In *Articles of Faith, Articles of Peace: The Religious Liberty Clauses and the American Public Philosphy,* edited by James Davison Hunter and Os Guinness. Washington, D.C.: Brookings Institution, 1990.

Sandler, S. Gerald. "Lockean Ideas in Thomas Jefferson's 'Bill for Establishing Religious Freedom.'" *Journal of the History of Ideas* 21 (1960): 110-16.

Sanford, Charles B. *The Religious Life of Thomas Jefferson.* Charlottesville: University Press of Virginia, 1984.

Schweninger, Lee. *John Winthrop.* Boston: Twain Publishers, 1990.

Shamas, Carole. "English Inheritance Law and Its Transfer to the Colonies." *American Journal of Legal History* 31 (1987): 145-63.

Simpson, Alan. "How Democratic Was Roger Williams?" *William and Mary Quarterly Review,* 3d ser., 13 (1956): 53-67.

Slotkin, Richard. *Regeneration through Violence: The Mythology of the American Frontier, 1600-1860.* Middletown: Wesleyan University Press, 1973.

Smith, Elwyn A. *Religious Liberty in the United States.* Philadelphia: Fortress Press, 1972.

Smith, James W., and Jamison A. Leland, eds. *The Shaping of American Religion.* Princeton: Princeton University Press, 1961.

Smith, Joseph H., and Thomas G. Barnes. *The English Legal System: Carryover to the Colonies.* Los Angeles: William Andrews Clark Memorial Library, University of California, 1975.

Smith, Michael. "The Special Place of Religion in the Constitution." *Supreme Court Review* (1983): 83-123.

Smith, Steven D. *Foreordained Failure: The Quest for a Constitutional Principle of Religious Freedom.* New York: Oxford University Press, 1995.

———. "The Restoration of Tolerance." *California Law Review* 78 (1990): 305-56.

———. "The Rise and Fall of Religious Freedom in Constitutional Discourse." *University of Pennsylvania Law Review* 140 (1991): 149-240.

———. "Separation and the 'Secular': Reconstructing the Disestablishment Decision." *Texas Law Review* 67 (1989): 955-1031.

Smolinski, Reiner. "*Israel Redivivus:* The Eschatological Limits of Puritan Typology in New England." *New England Quarterly* 63 (1990): 357-95.

Snyder, David C. "John Locke and the Freedom of Belief." *Journal of Church and State* 30 (1988): 227-43.

Spurgin, Hugh. *Roger Williams and the Puritan Radicalism in the English Separatist Tradition.* Lewiston: Edwin Mellen Press, 1989.

Stavely, Keith W. F. *Puritan Legacies: Paradise Lost and the New England Tradition, 1630-1890.* Ithaca: Cornell University Press, 1987.

Stoever, Williams K. B. *"A Faire and Easie Way to Heaven": Covenant Theology and Antinomianism in Early Massachusetts.* Middletown: Wesleyan University Press, 1978.

Stokes, Anson Phelps, and Leo Pfeffer. *Church and State in the United States.* Revised edition. New York: Harper and Row, 1964.

Stolzenberg, Naomi M. " 'He Drew a Circle That Shut Me Out': Assimilation, Indoctrination, and the Paradox of a Liberal Education." *Harvard Law Review* 106 (1993): 581-667.

Stone, Suzanne Last. "In Pursuit of the Counter-Text: The Turn to the Jewish Legal Model in Contemporary American Legal Theory." *Harvard Law Review* 106 (1993): 813-94.

Storing, Herbert J., ed. *The Complete Anti-Federalist.* 7 volumes. Chicago: University of Chicago Press, 1981.

Stout, Harry S. *The New England Soul: Preaching and Religious Culture in Colonial New England.* New York: Oxford University Press, 1986.

———. "Word and Order in Colonial New England." In *The Bible in America: Essays in Cultural History,* edited by Nathan O. Hatch and Mark A. Noll. New York: Oxford University Press, 1982.

Strout, Cushing. "Jeffersonian Religious Liberty and American Pluralism." In *The Virginia Statute for Religious Freedom: Its Evolution and Consequences in American History,* edited by Merrill D. Peterson and Robert C. Vaughan. New York: Cambridge University Press, 1988.

Sweet, William Warren. *Religion in the Development of American Culture, 1765-1840.* New York: Charles Scribner's Sons, 1952.

Taylor, Charles. "Religion in a Free Society." In *Articles of Faith, Articles of Peace: The Religious Liberty Clauses and the American Public Philosophy,* edited by James Davison Hunter and Os Guinness. Washington, D.C.: Brookings Institution, 1990.

Thomas, Keith. "The Puritans and Adultery: The Act of 1650 Reconsidered." In *Puritans and Revolutionaries: Essays in Seventeenth-Century History Presented to Christopher Hill,* edited by Donald Pennington and Keith Thomas. New York: Oxford University Press, 1978.

Thompson, Roger. " 'Holy Watchfulness' and Communal Conformism: The Function of Defamation in Early New England Communities." *New England Quarterly* 56 (1983): 504-22.

Todd, Margo. *Christian Humanism and the Puritan Social Order.* New York: Cambridge University Press, 1987.

"Toward a Constitutional Definition of Religion." *Harvard Law Review* 91 (1978): 1056-89.

Tribe, Lawrence. *American Constitutional Law.* 2d ed. Mineola: Foundation Press, 1988.

Turner, James. *Without God, without Creed: The Origins of Unbelief in America.* Baltimore: Johns Hopkins University Press, 1985.

Tushnet, Mark. "The Emerging Principle of Accommodation of Religion (Dubitante)." *Georgetown Law Journal* 76 (1988): 1691-714.

———. " 'Of Church and State and the Supreme Court': Kurland Revisited." *Supreme Court Review* (1989): 373-402.

———. *Red, White, and Blue: A Critical Analysis of Constitutional Law.* Cambridge: Harvard University Press, 1988.

———. "Religion and Theories of Constitutional Interpretation." *Loyola Law Review* 33 (1987): 239-40.

Van Alstyne, William. "Trends in the Supreme Court: Mr. Jefferson's Crumbling Wall—A Comment on *Lynch v. Donnelly.*" *Duke Law Journal* (1984): 770-87.

Vaughan, Alden T., ed. *The Puritan Tradition in America, 1620-1730.* Columbia: University of South Carolina Press, 1972.

Von Frank, Albert J. *The Sacred Game: Provincialism and Frontier Consciousness in American Literature, 1630-1860.* New York: Cambridge University Press, 1985.

Waldron, Jeremy. "Locke: Toleration and the Rationality of Persecution." In *Justifying Toleration: Conceptual and Historical Perspectives,* edited by Susan Mendus. New York: Cambridge University Press, 1988.

Walker, Williston, ed. *The Creeds and Platforms of Congregationalism.* New York: Scribner's, 1892. Philadelphia: Pilgrim Press, 1960.

Wall, Robert E., Jr. *Massachusetts Bay: The Crucial Decade, 1640-1650.* New Haven: Yale University Press, 1972.

Walters, "New England Society and the Laws and Liberties of Massachusetts, 1648." *Essex Institute Historical Collection* 106 (1970): 145.

Walzer, Michael. "Puritanism as a Revolutionary Ideology." In *Puritan New England: Essays on Religion, Society, and Culture,* edited by Alden T. Vaughan and Francis J. Bremer. New York: St. Martin's Press, 1977.

———. *The Revolution of the Saints: A Study in the Origins of Radical Politics.* Cambridge: Harvard University Press, 1976.

West, Elias. "The Case against a Right to Religion-Based Exemptions." *Notre Dame Journal of Law, Ethics and Public Policy* 4 (1990): 591-638.

Westbrook, Perry D. *The New England Town in Fact and Fiction.* Rutherford: Fairleigh Dickinson University Press, 1982.

White, B. R. *The English Separatist Tradition: From the Marian Martyrs to the Pilgrim Fathers.* New York: Oxford University Press, 1971.

Wills, Gary. *Under God: Religion and American Politics.* New York: Simon and Schuster, 1990.

Winship, Michael P. "Encountering Providence in the Seventeenth Century: The Experiences of a Yeoman and a Minister." *Essex Institute Historical Collections* 126 (1990): 27-36.

Winslow, Ola Elizabeth. *Master Roger Williams.* New York: Macmillan, 1957.

Witte, John, Jr. "Blest Be the Ties That Bind: Covenant and Community in Puritan Thought." *Emory Law Journal* 36 (1987): 579-601.

———. "The Essential Rights and Liberties of Religion in the American Constitutional Experiment." *Notre Dame Law Review* 71 (1996): 371-445.

———. "How to Govern a City on a Hill: The Early Puritan Contribution to American Constitutionalism." *Emory Law Journal* 39 (1990): 41-64.

Wolford, Thorp L. "The Laws and Liberties of 1648: The First Code of Laws Enacted and Printed in English America." *Boston University Law Review* 28 (1948): 426-63.

Wright, Thomas Goddard. *Literary Culture in Early New England, 1620-1730.* New York: Russell and Russell, 1966.

Zakai, Avihu. *Exile and Kingdom: History and Apocalypse in the Puritan Migration to America.* New York: Cambridge University Press, 1992.

Zaller, Robert. "The Debate on Capital Punishment during the English Revolution." *American Journal of Legal History* 31 (1987): 126-44.

Zanger, Jules. "Crime and Punishment in Early Massachusetts." *William and Mary Quarterly,* 3d ser., 22 (1965): 471-77.

Ziff, Larzer. *Puritanism in America: New Culture in a New World.* New York: Viking Press, 1973.

Index

and forced worship, 87-88, 119; and religious minorities, 110, 113n29, 121, 139n39, 160-61; and religious pluralism, 89; and Sabbath observance, 77, 87; and secularism, 82-83, 166; and the limits of religious liberty, 103-11; and the prevalence of unbelief, 32-33; approval of magistrates encouraging true religion, 91; attitude toward the Bible, 73-77, 88-89; banishment from Massachusetts Bay, 38-39, 48; biographical information, 17-18, 39n1, 116; *Bloudy Tenent, of Persecution,* 10, 72; *Bloudy Tenent Yet More Bloudy,* 73, 179-82; concern for order, 109-10; confidence in ability to discern spiritual truth, 28, 43n64, 88; debate with John Cotton, 72-73; denial that civil magistrate had authority over religion, 78-79, 85-86, 103, 128, 129, 150; denial that religious error had public consequences, 84, 85, 96n71; dogmatism of, 10, 18; duties owed by citizens to government, 107-9; historical assessments, 15n29; influence upon framers of the Constitution, 3, 116-17; objections to persecution, 81, 86, 87, 88, 90; on "Christian" nations, 76; on "civility" and barbarism, 79, 82, 106-7, 120; on common moral principles, 82, 110; on exemptions for religious believers from general laws, 103-4, 109, 114nn44,53, 119-20, 129; on

the church and the city, 80-81; on the necessity and authority of civil government, 77, 79, 103-4, 108, 118; on the two tables, 77; opposition to the civil magistrate's authority over religion, 33, 36-37; opposition to the idea of "Christendom," 33; persecution as having some beneficial consequences for the godly, 98n115; persecution as spiritual rape, 86-87, 124, 128, 133, 151; positions that contributed to his banishment from the Massachusetts Bay Colony, 33-37; religiously grounded arguments for religious liberty, 147-49; role in the founding of Providence Colony, 99-103; separatism of, 5-6, 18-33, 88, 152-53; tolerance of atheists and typology, 75-76, 92n10; writing style, 9, 15n32

Wills, Gary, 62

Winthrop, John: and the Providence Colony, 100, 101; and Williams's banishment, 163; as a source for understanding church-state relations in Massachusetts, 50-51; migration to New World to avoid God's judgment on England, 60; on accusations that magistrates administered justice arbitrarily, 54-55; on God's covenant with the Massachusetts Bay Colony, 53, 76; on Providence's treatment of Joshua Verin, 104; response to Williams's criticisms of the Massachusetts Bay Colony, 34

TIMOTHY L. HALL was a judicial clerk for Judge Will Garwood of the U. S. Fifth Circuit Court of Appeals and practiced law in Austin, Texas, before joining the faculty of the University of Mississippi Law School. An associate professor, he teaches constitutional law and legal ethics and has published extensively on law and religion and on legal ethics. He holds a J. D. from the University of Texas and a bachelor of arts degreee from the University of Houston.

Printed by Printforce, United Kingdom